Leaders, Believers
and Expert Deceivers

An antidote to one-size-fits-all organisational models

STEPHEN E. MORRIS

THE CHOIR PRESS

Illustrations by: Nick Gowman Cartoons & Illustration

First published in the United Kingdom in 2024 by
The Choir Press

ISBN: 978-1-78963-487-7

For Juliet and Chris

Contents

Preface

Our protagonist stands isolated in front of the troops, brow furrowed, breathing deeply. Their gaze traces the horizon, accompanied only by the rip of their crimson cape behind them. This is it. This is the moment when a leader's legacy is forged. When a champion of the people, defender of the land and rightful heir claims their immortal destiny.

No matter how compelling this heroic image of a leader might be, it is a long way from reality when Monday morning arrives. In our offices, there are no scripts or Hollywood special effects, no perfect leaders and no guarantees that the movie is going to end with a win for the good guys. Instead, those seeking to lead teams and organisations face a task that can stretch their cognitive, emotional and physical limits to the extreme.

The edge-of-seat fear of collapse and inability to pay salaries in new businesses. The toll from long and stressful service incidents. The isolation standing in front of a room full of disappointed customers. The sad days when great colleagues leave, projects dissolve and contracts cease. The transformations that send morale plunging through the floor. The gut-wrenching feeling when you make someone redundant – someone you *know* needs that job. Realising that you will not see your children or a loved one *again* tonight. To cap it all, the detail – the legislation, compliance, vendors, supply chain, targets, budgets, reports, pay reviews – and somehow, being expected to deliver a winning strategy through it all.

Yet there's also the joy of seeing products, projects and services evolve into remarkable achievements. The privilege of accompanying people through their development. Witnessing colleagues reach heights beyond our own. The pride in solving the unsolvable. Receiving that coveted award. Always, always learning.

Every leader can tell stories like these – and more.

When I talk to leaders about *how* they lead, I observe two basic responses. With the first, leaders pay limited attention to the mechanics of leading and organising, choosing to 'get on with it' rather than thinking too much about the how. This can come from a self-deprecating stance – 'I'm not really a leader, I'm doing what I can' – presumably until the real leader turns up. More commonly, however, it's the opposite – a keen sense of self-belief and perhaps even a faith in the idea that leaders are born, not created. Leaders like this often struggle with the relevance of self-development and don't care much for labels or opinions. One leader I knew, receiving encouragement from a colleague to invest in leadership training declined to take any himself: 'I don't need a coach. I've never needed a coach.'

The second response is an endeavour to become the *right kind* of leader. This type of leader will source leadership techniques and frameworks to get the best from their teams and relationships, track down delivery methods to drive productivity, and study other leaders, mentors and pioneers. This search naturally picks up ideas and values that are in vogue, and the results remind me of the shipping forecast.*

Leadership Forecast

Agile good, waterfall poor.
Command poor, servant leadership moderate, authentic leadership good.
Collaboration and sharing good, silos very poor.
Transparency and openness good.
Segregated service management poor becoming DevOps later.
Strategies that AI and ML, good.
Home working occasionally good, back to office poor.
And finally for the Spiral Dynamics forecast.
Red and Blue poor, Orange occasionally moderate.
Green and Yellow rising rapidly, Teal good.

Such a list prompts a few questions. When a training provider, consultancy or framework author advocates a particular strategy, what do they know about our particular organisation? Even if we produce the same product as another company, do our companies operate in the same way? When we hear that, say, 'every leader should be a servant leader', how do they imagine that will apply in our office, let alone across cultures in our global organisation? The answers must either be so broad or watered down that they encompass any eventuality.

---

* The shipping forecast is provided by the Maritime & Coastguard Agency, broadcasting weather and safety information to ships at sea around the UK. The BBC provides a lyrical readout of the forecast four times each day.

And here's the thing. The detail of your organisation is *not* known, and nor are practices suitable across all reaches of one company, let alone many. That being true, to pay consultants multiple millions to recommended global changes and then, when they fail, to pay them again for the next option seems counter-intuitive at best.

> *You will be best served by conscious, contextual action.*

That is why I wrote this book. In the first part, I will argue that to thrive in the current paradigm and to meet the spectrum of challenges that leaders face, you will be best served by conscious, contextual action. As you look at your customers' needs and at the environments and systems that you are working within, you can formulate an approach through the lens of your unique situation, your unique people and your unique goals. I will show you that if you choose to apply default tools and frameworks by rote, or apply them universally, you are fundamentally risking your potential. Building on that, in the second part of the book I will take us through several aspects of leadership and organisational practice, from strategy to delivery, teams to change. The ideas and techniques that I describe will not be presented as answers, rather as building blocks and insights to help you navigate your own route.

If you are a leader, project manager, coach or anyone else trying to be the *right kind* of something, this is for you. If you have noticed that off-the-shelf frameworks, approaches and methods continue to come up short, this is for you. If you are sceptical about the imposition of another mandatory framework, this is for you. And if, by writing this book, I prevent someone investing in the next snake-oil programme that swings by, it will have all been worthwhile. Thank you for trying it.

PART I

The obsession with organisational formulas

CHAPTER 1

All hail the right way!

'This – is my way – where is yours?' I answered unto those who asked me 'for the way'. 'For the way – existeth not!'[1]
— FRIEDRICH NIETZSCHE

The quest for optimal leadership

During my career, I have spent time seeking the best and, more specifically, the *correct* way to lead teams. I believed that someone out there knew how to do it, and that by following those practices and processes, my teams and I would be more successful. I attended events, training and workshops on leadership. I read large numbers of books, academic papers and articles. I learned and shared discoveries with those who were seeking answers too. As I researched, I was confronted with a market full of terms and ideas, all professing to give me something I should have. To illustrate, we are faced with a dizzying range of leadership styles to choose from:

- Servant leader
- Supportive leader
- Enabling leader
- Authentic leader
- Autocratic leader
- Directive leader
- Authoritative leader
- Visionary leader
- Transformational leader
- Strategic leader
- Charismatic leader
- Pace-setting leader
- Distributed leader
- Ethical leader
- Coaching leader
- Laissez-faire leader
- Relationship-oriented leader
- Participative leader
- Democratic leader
- Task-oriented leader

One paper, reviewing the link between leadership style and personality (Hassan et al), lists defining characteristics for 39 distinct types of leader.[2] I was also told that being a creative leader is better than being a reactive one – and neither of those is my list or in Hassan's paper.

There are, however, predominant themes. The narrative direction is that bureaucratic, commanding, micro-managing and autocratic approaches are bad and should be outgrown. We should abandon boss-knows-best, 'waterfall' and monitoring of timesheets. We should empower, consult and support. We should be authentic, visionary, and Agile (with a capital 'a').

Leadership courses pushed these concepts on me and promised that, with the right application, I too could stop being a manager and become a *leader*. In no time, I would be creating phenomenal results, backed by a team that loved, admired and respected me. With thunderous applause, I would take a bow and the curtain would drop.

Unfortunately, the reality was not quite like that. More prosaically, I do not think I knew what it meant for me. Did I have the skills and experience necessary to use that approach? Did I know what to do on Monday morning now that I was an *authentic* leader and no longer a *directive* one? No-one really talked about what would happen if my authentic behaviour was to dismiss my team's well-being and castigate them for every minor indiscretion. When things went wrong, was I to assume that I had not been *servant-y* enough?

> ## When things went wrong, was I to assume that I had not been servant-y enough?

More importantly, none of these ideas scratched the itch of situation – a battlefield needs a different leader to a colouring competition. When we are working with the belief that autocratic leadership styles are bad, what should we do when the fire alarm sounds? Bring people around the table to discuss and consider the relative priority of the event before deciding action? Begin the meeting with an ice-breaking exercise to find out how everyone is feeling today? How about launching a new product line to a virgin market segment? Would we be best served by blindly following the opinions and decisions of a single leader? Would we stick rigidly to a plan of action written months in advance? None of those responses is sensible but consider those situations on a spectrum for a moment (Figure 1-1).

All hail the right way!

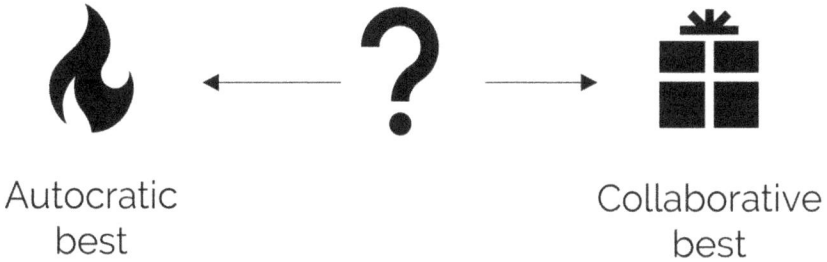

Autocratic
best

Collaborative
best

Figure 1-1. Spectrum of leadership from autocratic to collaborative

The fire alarm is better suited to more autocratic decision making, on the left, while a new product is more suited to a collaborative approach, on the right. But what do we do about everything in between? The range that contains the myriad situations where a customer raises a complaint, an employee leaves, a project commences, a server crashes, a large client on-boards or a deer gets into the data centre.* If it does not ring true that autocratic, commanding and bureaucratic methods are always 'wrong' nor that collaborative, open and visionary ones are 'right', what then is optimal leadership?

---

* This happened in a US data centre in 2019: https://www.datacenterdynamics.com/en/news/deer-broke-data-center (accessed 26.1.24)

'At least he's being authentic.'

The greats of leadership

Perhaps we can find an answer if we look to history. Much of what we perceive to make a great leader comes from the people before us – and the pedestals we put them on. Accepting the bias created by victors writing their own histories (with vainglorious recall), many famous leaders are inextricably linked to military campaigns and battles. We could think of Leonidas, king of the Spartans, who led his 300 Spartans (plus or minus 7,000 Greeks) at the battle of Thermopylae. Maybe Rommel, who is remembered as a 'chivalrous, humane and professional officer' by his troops and enemies.[3] How about Churchill, Napoleon, Sun Tzu, Hannibal or more recent generals like Petraeus or Powell? I will stick with three: Alexander the Great, Genghis Khan and Lord Horatio Nelson.

Alexander the Great (356–323 BC)

Alexander was born in 356 BC to the reigning king of Macedon, Philip II, and was one of seven children. He was widely educated, learning philosophy, music, art and morals alongside the virtuous physical skills of riding and fighting. Among his retinue of teachers was none other than Aristotle, the Greek polymath and philosopher, who tutored him until he was 16 years old.[4] Following the assassination of his father four years later in 336 BC, Alexander ascended to the throne. From there, he focused his energy on military campaigns until his death in 323 BC. In that 13-year reign he conquered large parts of Asia, spreading Hellenistic culture across one of the largest empires in history. Astonishingly, the record of his battles is unblemished by loss – this is often attributed to his excellent strategic skills and the experience of the soldiers fighting alongside him. There are various explanations as to his cause of death, but all put his last moments far away from the battlefield. It is easy to see why authors praise his military successes. Peter Green's biography of Alexander notes that 'Alexander's true genius was as a field commander: perhaps taken in all, the most incomparable general the world has ever seen.'[5]

However, we also know that Alexander could be ruthless and quick-tempered, with a belief that he was of divine birth. Even before he was born, there were supposed omens of his future prominence, including his mother Olympias dreaming 'that there was a peal of thunder and that a thunder-bolt fell upon her womb'.[6] Alexander's own confidence in his lineage was concentrated following consultation with the Oracle of Zeus-Ammon at Siwah in Egypt. Greeted by a priest as 'Son of Ammon', Alexander 'confirmed his sense of his own uniqueness' and developed an 'unshakeable belief in his connection to his divine father Ammon' becoming the 'linchpin of his personality'.[7] Naming many of the cities he founded as 'Alexandria' seems to support this notion too.

We also know from contemporary accounts that Alexander was violent-tempered, rash and impulsive. He lacked self-control with alcohol and murdered one of his officers.[8] Cleitus the Black (375–328 BC) served closely with Alexander and was celebrated for saving the king's life at the Battle of Granicus in 334 BC. However, in a drunken quarrel six years later Alexander 'snatched a spear from one of his guards, ran at his foster-brother and thrust him through the body. Cleitus fell to the ground and expired with a groan'.[9] In a martial society, that is perhaps less surprising, but it is interesting that our reverence for and shorthand description of Alexander as 'one of the greatest leaders in world history' still holds. That is true – but clearly he could get a bit touchy in an argument.

Figure 1-2. The quarrel between Alexander and Cleitus[10]

Genghis Khan (1162–1227)

From the death of his father and abandonment from the tribe at age eight, Genghis Khan established one of the largest empires in history and a vast legacy. At its peak in 1270, the Mongol Empire controlled nearly 18% of the world.[11] At 24 million km², that ranks second only to the later British Empire, which peaked at 35 million km², and 4.6 times larger than Alexander's Macedonian Empire.[12]

The manner of that expansion needs little introduction, however, with Kahn noted for his cruel, brutal and bloodthirsty practices. In 1221, an infamous massacre saw the total annihilation of the city of Nishapur, part of modern-day Iran. Once captured, survivors of the onslaught, residents and even domestic animals were summarily executed, with heads allegedly piled in ever-increasing pyramids. Estimates of population before the assault were over 1.7 million and the overwhelming destruction has led to the myth that all were killed in one day. The exact details are disputed and likely the attack lasted several days, but development of such stories served to strengthen Khan's repute. Khan certainly appreciated this, and customs like 'driving prisoners in front of the main army as arrow-fodder' and ruthlessly slaughtering inhabitants of non-surrendering 'bad cities' caused many to capitulate before conflict.[13] In all it is estimated that anywhere from 30 to 60 million people were killed under Khan's rule[14] – a vast headcount equating to the death of 10% of the world's population and noted as the only example of a war or epidemic having a noticeable impact on climate.[15]

Despite that undeniable brutality, the Mongol Empire created a clear imperial identity and enjoyed many freedoms and advancements under Khan. Skilled artisans, philosophers and scientists were highly valued, rewarded on merit and encouraged to better the empire. Trade routes were developed and protected, including the vital Silk Road between China and Europe. Laws were established to declare tolerance and freedom for all religions, and 'even granted tax exemptions for places of worship'.[16]

As with Alexander, we might admire Genghis Khan's accomplishments – unification of an empire and the progress it brought with it, or we might see him as tyrannical and destructive. Indeed, *Time* magazine listed Khan as one of the millenium's 'worst villains', while the Washington Post made him the 'Sunday Style Man of the Millennium'.[17] Either way, he left a permanent mark on the pages of world history and continues to be revered by some. The shining 40-metre-high stainless-steel statue of Genghis, close to the Mongolian capital of Ulaanbaatar, suggests this will continue for many years to come.

Lord Horatio Nelson, 1st Viscount Nelson (1758–1805)

We could also consider Lord Horatio Nelson, the officer responsible for multiple British naval victories during the Napoleonic Wars. Joining the navy in 1771 at the grand age of 12, Nelson went on to serve and command his first ship only six years later in 1777. Across his career, his achievements in the Mediterranean, the Baltics and the East and West Indies secured Nelson a timeless reputation as a strategic genius. His success at the Battle of the Nile is described by many as the most absolute victory in naval history.[18] While the Battle of Trafalgar in 1805 saw his death, it represented the culmination of the Napoleonic Wars and a period of dominance for British naval power.

Despite what we might imagine of the late 1700s, Nelson is said to have been an engaging and inspirational leader, with a considerate awareness of the needs of his men. From David Davies' *A Brief History of Fighting Ships,* we learn that: 'Nelson's heartfelt conviction, and his flair for imparting communal purpose, gave each captain two invaluable gifts, first, a clear knowledge of his duty in any situation, and, second, the esprit de corps that comes from being part of an efficient organisation, whose members are also friends'.[19] Imagining the literal fog of war and confusion during a sea battle, having captains waiting for orders from a commander would have been devastating. Instead, the captains were equipped with knowledge and autonomy in their actions, bestowing an advantage that was, in Davies' words, 'sublime'. He continues to describe Nelson as having a 'gift which is beyond competence, beyond even brilliance, which creates confidence and esprit de corps'. Davies is evidently a fan.

There is another side to Nelson, as you might expect. The admiralty held some concerns over Nelson's behaviour away from the navy and in deployment to Copenhagen he was placed as deputy to a more guarded commander, Admiral Parker.[20] This particularly related to his public and scandalous relationship with Emma Hamilton, the wife of his friend Sir William Hamilton. Nelson, who was already married to Frances, had reportedly at least one other lover before Emma, and despite those that might like to protect his image, he was clearly not without fault.

His marriage with Frances broke down, for which she was seemingly blamed, and in 1801 Emma gave birth to Nelson's daughter, Horatia.* Before the Battle of Trafalgar that would take his life, Nelson wrote an amendment to his will calling for Emma and Horatia to be given the necessary means to live in the manner to which they were accustomed.[21] However, after his death, those requests were ignored, with Emma herself later dying in poverty.

Outside of his love life, we might also remember his conservatism and pro-slavery support. Nelson, undoubtedly shaped by eighteenth-century society and experiences in the East and West Indies, was keen to see a continuation of the status quo. In letters between him and one of the richest plantation owners in Jamaica, Simon Taylor, Nelson notably puts his own shoulder against the efforts of the abolitionist campaigner William Wilberforce. His missive, published around two years after his death in the *Cobbett's Weekly Political Register* (and we now understand with amendments made), included: '*I have ever been, and shall die, a firm friend to our present Colonial system. I was bred, as you know, in the good old school, and taught to appreciate the value of our West India possessions.*'[22]

Yeah, yeah, I get it, Stephen

Every leader has their difficulties, good days and bad. Just like everyone else on the planet. That is true, and the idea that 'nobody's perfect' stands strong, especially when we attempt to judge historical figures through a modern lens. However, for each of these past leaders, it is worth noting that their legacies come overwhelmingly from what they have achieved, not how they behaved. How their followers saw them, and even their trans-gressions, are often merely postscripts. In fact, it seems the only time we start with any moral assessment of character before discussing results is in the cases of the *notorious* leaders. Vlad the Impaler, for example, was famed for his cruel and barbarous leadership but is celebrated in Romania as one of their greatest leaders due to his fight for the independence of Romanian soil.[23]

---

* I see what they did there.

And so, we are still trying to understand what *good* leadership is. Something like 'the best results and damn the consequences' does not sit right – but nor does the idea of indulging every desire and whim of our team members at the expense of those same results. Perhaps we are limited to thinking about all leaders, whether Alexander, Nelson or otherwise, as great leaders in context. We can choose to learn from elements of their behaviour or legacy, but none are a recipe for end-to-end success.

Indeed, the historic discussion brings up the two fundamental sides of leadership: results and environment. The mark of a great leader, from the perspective of those who want results and who will be in a position to bask in the reflected glory, is that they *deliver*, no matter the cost. Conversely, from the viewpoint of those under the boot or with mountains to climb and rivers to cross, a great leader makes those labours bearable.

The narrative in organisations and training suggests that we want our leaders to deliver results *and* make the process bearable, but we know which tends to carry more weight. The example of a commercially successful sales director found with a large, catalogued collection of sadomasochistic pornography on their laptop and simply told to 'be more careful' speaks for itself.* And most of us will know a leader who emphasised well-being and created a close team with high degrees of trust and collaboration, yet was removed from the organisation because the results just were not there.

Even leaders who fail on both counts – failing to deliver and making everyone miserable – can hold firm in post. One recent example is Elon Musk's egotistical pantomime in the purchase of Twitter. The culture at Twitter, now 'X', was ripped up in the first weeks of Musk's ownership, with changes to home working, staff culls, expectations of long hours, exhaustive code reviews, product policy changes and approaches to decision-making all radically different.[24] Moreover, less than a year later in May 2023, Twitter was reportedly worth one-third of what Musk paid for it.[25] Despite that, and the pundits calling the 'end of Twitter', X and Musk are still here, if poorer. I could also look to the prospect of at least 64 global elections in 2024.[26] The field includes flagrantly corrupt and narcissistic politicians and parties, also responsible for

---

* Actually, he was told to make sure that the laptop did not have anything incriminating on it next time it came into technical support. IT were told not to make such a big deal if it happened again.

devastating economic decisions and archaic foreign policies, still commanding public opinion.

The day-to-day of leadership

As Friedrich Hegel, the eighteenth-century German philosopher so wisely noted, 'The only thing we learn from history is that we learn nothing from history' – so let us try something else. How about the raw, practical side of leadership? What are the activities a leader undertakes? What does a leader do in that meeting when they are leading? What are all of those appointments in the diary for anyway? I have looked back over my own leadership roles, and this is a list of the typical tasks I would carry out in any given week:

- Budgeting, reporting and other financial administration
- Consulting, collaborating, creating plans and strategies
- Supplier engagement, and occasionally escalation
- Documentation and process reviews, assessment preparation and audits
- Signing off team holiday, absence and overtime
- Client meetings, service reporting, listening (and apologising) to customers
- Reviewing candidate CVs and attending interviews
- Networking and making connections between individuals and teams
- Executive and management meetings
- Attending reviews and demonstrations of work done and goals reached
- Coaching and encouraging progress
- Fostering understanding of goals
- Listening to and supporting individual and team concerns

The list can, and did, go on. What is immediately noticeable is that most of my time was spent managing. Managing people, budgets, schedules and suppliers. Administering process, procedure and adherence to policy. There are elements of everyday management that are more aligned to our general impression of leadership – such as creating strategies or fostering understanding – but they are few. I am sorry to say that the reality of day-to-day leadership is pretty dull.*

> *What is immediately noticeable is that most of my time was spent managing. Managing people, budgets, schedules and suppliers.*

In Sveningsson and Alvesson's book *Managerial Lives*, this subject is examined more scientifically.[27] The book summarises interviews with leaders to portray 'managerial work as it is experienced and understood by managers'[28] and it both demonstrates the diversity of the work and the dichotomy at the heart of many views of leadership. Of those interviewed: 'What they say with one voice is that as a manager you should avoid the traditional administrative and bureaucratic type of excessive micromanagement.'[29] Yet, like myself, much of the actual work 'involves administrative matters and establishing practical conditions for the organization to work … recruitment, premises, budgets, form-filling, labour laws and IT.'[30]

Moreover, as managers seek to become authentic and personalise their efforts to 'make a difference' (encouraged by training and current trends), this sets up a frustrating and worrying contradiction. How can you express your personal leadership style on such operational tasks, and if you cannot, what is your role? If all you do is administration, does your role have any longevity and are you a leader at all? In the spectrum between choreographed desires in PowerPoint and the visceral reality of a Monday morning, there is every chance your expectations for leadership will jar, and that is going to hurt. Sadly then, this perspective does not shed any light on what optimal leadership might be.

---

* I thought of this recently when reading Stephen Mangan's excellent children's book *The Fart that Changed the World* (Scholastic, 2022) with my son. In one scene, a kitchen boy, imagining the high-purposed conversations that royalty must have, instead overhears the king in conversation about his niggling foot condition. Never meet your heroes.

Frameworks for leadership

While there is a very long list of leadership frameworks we might try, is it reasonable to assume that over their long evolution, crowd-based wisdom has uncovered some reliable practices? That, for example, what was state-of-the-art in 1920 – even 1420 – has developed and sharpened into what we now discuss in 2024?* Let us find out.

Great Man theory of leadership

I will start with the 'Great Man theory of leadership' which, as the name suggests, is rooted in the idea that some people hold the innate skills necessary to lead. In a series of lectures in 1840 and later a book, *On Heroes, Hero-Worship, and the Heroic in History*, Thomas Carlyle popularised this thinking and it is to him that the theory is attributed.[31] In the work, Carlyle urges us to understand heroes and their importance across roles, from prophets and priests to poets and men of letters. It is for kings that he reserves a particular admiration, having translated king as 'Konning, which means Can-ning, Able-man', he writes:

> *Find in any country the Ablest Man that exists there; raise him to the supreme place, and loyally reverence him: you have a perfect government for that country; no ballot-box, parliamentary eloquence, voting, constitution-building, or other machinery whatsoever can improve it a whit. It is in the perfect state; an ideal country. The Ablest Man; he means also the truest-hearted, justest, the Noblest Man: what he tells us to do must be precisely the wisest, fittest, that we could anywhere or anyhow learn; – the thing which it will in all ways behoove us, with right loyal thankfulness and nothing doubting, to do!*

Carlyle does acknowledge that the search for the ideal is fraught with difficulty – 'No bricklayer builds a wall perfectly perpendicular' – but presses the need for us to find our Able-man:

---

* If you want to read more about the evolution of leadership, I recommend John Antonakis and David V. Day (eds.), *The Nature of Leadership* (Sage Publications, 2017), by which I have often been inspired.

May I say here, that the finding of your Ableman and getting him invested with the symbols of ability, with dignity, worship (worth-ship), royalty, king-hood, or whatever we call it … is the business, well or ill accomplished, of all social procedure whatsoever in this world!

These ideas taken to their conclusion imply that only some people – some men – are born leaders, and they cannot be made. We are not able to teach leadership skills to those without and must seek out the few who already have what it takes. Moving forward to the first half of the twentieth century, trait-based leadership attempted to codify ideas of Great Man theory into identifiable behaviours and skills. Trait theory proposed that if successful leaders tend to have self-confidence and insight, we can discover ways to test them and therefore find our Able-man.

One hundred years later, Charles Bird, a British psychologist and professor of psychology at the University of Minnesota, sought to discover and codify desirable leadership traits. Bird surveyed 20 companies and recorded a total of 79 traits in his 1940 book, *Social Psychology*.[32] The traits ranged from things that are familiar today, like 'adaptable' and 'courageous', through to those more in tune with their time, like 'dignified' and 'poised'.

Bird reflects that from the lists he received, '51 of these traits, or 65 per cent, are mentioned once [and] 16 or 20 per cent are common to two lists.' The two traits that occurred most frequently were 'initiative', appearing on six lists (about 30%), and 'high intelligence', on ten (about 50%).*

What does this tell us? One might conclude that these repeating skills are always relevant in leaders. However, even the most cited trait – intelligence – only appeared in half of the surveys. Should we assume that the other companies excluded it because it is so obviously important? Or, like twentieth-century scholars, might we surmise that the wide variety of traits demonstrates an important gap: situation? The wide distribution of traits suggests we need leaders tuned to cope with *their* specific context. Indeed, a leader forged from Bird's list being 'cultured', 'talkative' and having 'high motor ability' has limited application unless they are leading say, a team of jugglers in a theatre company. *Unless.* I think we have heard that before.

---

* That 'humor (sense of)' was present in a quarter of the surveys warmed my heart. I do worry that only three of the enquiries included the simultaneously important 'tactful', however.

'I can feel him moving.'
'Yes, he's finishing his first organisational transformation.'

Context-based leadership

The conclusion that effective traits are inseparable from situation led to a decline in trait-based leadership, replaced by a number of other theories. *Behavioural leadership* continued a focus on leaders themselves, looking to identify how they led, rather than who they were, but it was *context-based leadership* that gained the most popularity.

Context is an extremely broad term, covering every aspect of a leader themselves and the environment that they operate within. A leader's mood, skill and style are context, members of the team and their relationships are context, an organisation's culture and expectations, market conditions and reputation are context, and so on. Indeed, one offshoot of context-based leadership – *contingency-based leadership* – extended the principle to whether leaders are needed at all. Contingent leadership suggests that there are situations where leaders are necessary and must be engaged, for example when the team, organisational practices and norms cannot continue alone, but there is no automatic need for their presence – that leaders are required in certain contexts only, invited in by the teams who need their involvement.

The significance of context is intuitive, and I suggested as much in the introduction to this chapter: the manager overseeing a product launch needs to operate very differently to the one charged with responding to a fire. That leaves us with a question, however. What context are we in, and what kind of leader is a good fit for that? The answer for many organisations – at least those willing to sidestep the one-size-fits-all recipes – is to observe, discover and understand context *before* hiring or placing roles.

Two examples illustrate this well. The first, from 1982, relates to a government exercise testing the response in the aftermath of a potential nuclear attack on Britain. A serving scientific officer, Jane Hogg, considered an potential unusual response to the difficult and urgent decisions that would be necessary: using psychopaths, because 'they have no feelings for others, nor moral code and tend to be very intelligent and logical'.[33] It makes sense. Like a trolley-problem* with vastly higher consequences, could you make the call to close a door to keep thousands alive, simultaneously condemning many hundreds to death?

---

* The thought experiment with application in the development of autonomous systems, like self-driving cars. A trolley (or tram car) is out of control and is going to kill a group of people. If you pull the lever, the trolley will divert and kill one person. Do you pull it?

In less extreme circumstances, Google provides a second example. In their hiring and ongoing (and scientific) evaluation of managers, they have discovered the capabilities that work well for them. One particularly relates to skill – that a manager must be able to understand, if not do, the work of the team. Here's a question from Google's manager feedback survey: 'My manager has the technical expertise (e.g., coding in Tech, selling in Global Business, accounting in Finance) required to effectively manage me.'[34] Whether you agree or disagree with the hiring of psychopaths or baulk at the idea of an 'artisan manager' overseeing a team does not matter. In both cases, an assessment of the situation and a response to it have been decided.

And like a great closed loop, we have arrived back where we started. Perhaps not quite to a belief in a Great Man, but absolutely to trait theory. Google is looking for traits, the science officer was looking for traits, and just about everyone else is too. How about the five-factor model of personality (Big 5 Personality Traits), Myers-Briggs Type Indicator (MBTI) or the Sixteen Personality Factor Questionnaire (16PF)? All looking for traits. Or we pick up a more overtly commercial list from a consultant, like in John C. Maxwell's 1998 book *The 21 Irrefutable Laws of Leadership*.[35] The subtitle even boldly suggests 'Follow them and people will follow you.' Some claim.

A deeper look at servant leadership

Hold on. If we have been researching and following frameworks for well over a century, they must add some value, right? Yes and no. Let us hold that thought up against a key tenet of many training courses – that the right kind of leader amplifies the environment around a team and thus drives results. To explore this, let's take a deeper look at servant leadership, a collection of ideas that are commonly discussed in organisations and seemingly dominate posts on LinkedIn.

Starting with the basics and a definition of servant leadership, as the name implies, the motivation of a servant leader is to serve the people around them: those that work for them, their customers and stakeholders. Servant leadership sets out its philosophical stall on this point, no better illustrated than by a quote from Robert K. Greenleaf, the originator of the modern ideas being discussed:

The servant-leader is servant first... It begins with the natural feeling that one wants to serve, to serve first. Then conscious choice brings one to aspire to lead. That person is sharply different from one who is leader first, perhaps because of the need to assuage an unusual power drive or to acquire material possessions.[36]

So, a servant leader is a specific kind of leader – not driven by gain, but by service. Therefore, the best qualified are those who were never leaders in the first place. That is not very practical, but it does imply traits, and one such set comes from the *Seven Pillars of Servant Leadership*.[37] Those pillars are: a person of character, who puts people first, who is a skilled communicator, a compassionate collaborator, has foresight, is a systems thinker, and leads with moral authority.

My reading of the pillars splits them into two themes. First, moral authority, person of character and puts people first talk about who the leader is as a person. Beyond the basics of being a good guy or gal who prefers to serve, the ideal candidate follows some kind of higher and *moral* purpose in their actions. If you think this already sounds a little religious in tone, you are right. Chapter 26 of *Servant Leadership In Action* spends several pages under the title 'Jesus: The Greatest Example of a Servant Leader'.[38] This includes a number of passages from the Bible and a quote from Reverend Robert Schuller concluding that 'Jesus was the greatest One Minute Manager of all time.'*

The second theme of the pillars approach is more practical. Systems thinker relates to understanding of environment, and foresight suggests an ability to make enough sense of all of that complexity to then communicate (with skill) and to collaborate (with compassion).

To confirm that this is not an isolated case, we can refer to other authors on servant leadership. The focus continues on ethics and virtues, emphasising even a therapeutic role for a leader. Shann Ferch and Larry Spears in *The Spirit of Servant-Leadership* titles the preface: 'Servant-Leadership: Healing the Person, Healing the World'.[39] It seems we are to use our position to 'help make whole' anyone with whom we interact. Not only that, we also might assume

---

* For researching this book, it seems much of the literature on servant leadership is published through Paulist Press, whose mission is to publish materials that 'foster religious values and wholeness in society.'

that we have a duty to succeed. Patrick Lencioni, of *Five Dysfunctions of a Team* fame, also writes in *Servant Leadership In Action*, 'With enough time, patience, and attention from a good manager, almost anyone can learn to become a team player. I believe that. I feel the same way about servant leaders.'[40]

Back to the hypothesis at hand, however. Does it work? A priori, servant leadership does not hold dominion over being nice to others. Phrases like collaboration and empathy appear in many other frameworks and I have never found any approach that advocates self-serving choices which create difficulty for others. However, there does seem to be some correlation, evidenced in research under the title of 'Impact of Servant Leadership on Performance: The Mediating Role of Affective and Cognitive Trust'.[41] Specifically, the researchers found 'strong evidence of trust as a key construct in the underlying mechanism influencing servant leadership and individual performance'. More, that 'Servant leadership has no direct effect on task performance, although it has a significant direct impact on the OCB of subordinates.'

All of that needs some unpacking, but it is important. First, the research distinguishes between two types of trust: affective trust, based on feelings of concern and care, and cognitive trust, based on a belief in a leader's ability. Affective trust has a positive impact on individual performance and organisational citizenship behaviour (OCB), while cognitive trust has a positive impact on task performance. Second, and using those definitions, the research concludes that servant leadership boosts affective, emotional trust, but has little or no impact on the cognitive, competence-based trust. In other words, the actions of a servant leader have a direct influence on the way followers behave in and around the organisation, but limited or no influence on task performance. Third, the study describes a crucial dependency, that teams will develop affective trust – necessary for those organisational behaviours – only after cognitive trust is established.

Thus, if we want a team with high OCB and driven individuals, servant leadership is a good choice, but without a base of cognitive trust, those advantages may be unattainable. The good news – especially for those people pushing for more servant leadership in organisations – is that our hierarchies can also affect trust. For instance, a direct manager who is highly competent can foster strong cognitive trust, facilitating affective trust built by other leaders within the organisation.

As we have seen multiple times, context is king. In the right circumstance, sure – but you would be ill advised to put money on servant leadership or any other as a universal model. To underscore that point, many famous theories in psychology and economics still lack definitive scientific validation or proof. Take a recent exchange of views on authentic leadership in *The Leadership Quarterly*: 'We have yet to see proof for (or refutations of) Cohen, March and Olsen's garbage can model, Maslow's hierarchy of needs, Freud's structure of the mind or Smith's invisible hand.'[42]

> *How often has a leadership course introduced Abraham Maslow's hierarchy of needs by saying: 'Remember, none of this is proven and it might not be relevant.'*

Take a moment. How often has a leadership course introduced Abraham Maslow's hierarchy of needs by saying: 'Remember, none of this is proven and it might not be relevant.' We are entitled to know and make choices based on those facts. And we should rightly be even more sceptical of the ones that rhyme. Forming-Storming-Norming-Performing, anyone? Many people know the words, but are less aware of the original research. The study was completed between 1963 and 1965 by psychologist Bruce Tuckman on a small group at the US Naval Medical Research Institute in Bethesda.[43] The study's participants were individuals in similar roles working together at the institute, where their group behaviours and development could be observed. It is absurd to assume that those same patterns would occur with all other groups, and even less so when people are working online, remotely distributed around the planet.

Leadership and optimal followers

In all of the discussions so far, I have focused on one thing. Whether a fabled hero, an acolyte of a particular framework or just that person who signs off your overtime, the focus has always been the leader. Within an organisation, however, there are many more stakeholders and conditions for performance. Our suppliers, customers and competition, our country of operation, our financial position and tools.

There is also a sizeable omission: our followers. As Freud noted, 'Individual psychology must … be just as old as group psychology, for from the first there were two kinds of psychologies, that of the individual members of the group and that of the father, chief, or leader.'[44]

I am going to try to address that imbalance here by first, paradoxically, talking about CEOs. Consider your organisation's CEO, or any other with which you are familiar. As figureheads of the company, they have the opportunity to represent, market and convince others to work with you. They also have the power to make choices that have far reaching consequences internally. So, what impact do you think that they, personally, have on the performance of the company?

One perspective is the Hollywood ideal, the heroes of leadership I looked at earlier – people like Steve Jobs.* It is possible that those reputations are deserved and one individual does make all the difference, but when the 'CEO effect' (or leadership effect) has been studied, the evidence does not quite stack up. Accounting for confounding factors of company, industry, year and performance lag between action and result, the most favourable study I found – by Lieberson and O'Connor in 1972 – puts the CEO effect at between 6.5% and 14.5%.[45] They conclude by stating: 'These results suggest that in emphasizing the effect of leadership, we may be overlooking far more powerful environmental influences.'

More recent research entitled 'How large must the CEO effect be to rule out chance?' attempts to address the variability involved more satisfactorily.[46] Taking the effect of chance into account, Fitza concludes that 'the effect CEOs have on company performance that can clearly be distinguished from the effect of chance is between 3.9 and 5.0 percent'. Compared to the company effect of 27.1% in the same study, that is pretty poor. Moreover, Fitza suggests that due to the randomness of so many other factors, 'even if two CEOs are exactly equal in their ability to lead a firm, the performance of that firm will vary between their tenures'.

---

* Evidently people wish to catch something from his apparent greatness, with biographies and chapters dedicated to Jobs across the spectrum. Amazon offered me 441 options in the 'Biographies & Memoirs' section for Steve Jobs, but only 75 for Nelson and a paltry 26 for Gandhi.

> ## *If leaders and CEOs have less measurable impact than we think, it begs the question of why we choose to follow at all.*

If leaders and CEOs have less measurable impact than we think – less even than pure luck – it begs the question of why we choose to follow at all. As we saw, Carlyle's view was that we follow a 'Great Man' because we *should*. Freud subsequently replaced that *should* with a *want*, noting: 'All the members must be equal to one another, but they all want to be ruled by one person.'[47] Neither offers a particularly satisfactory explanation, but we do know that organising ourselves into hierarchical groups is deep in our evolutionary psyche. From a hunt in humanity's earliest days to planning a mission to Mars, we naturally act to coordinate our roles. Together we can accomplish more than we would alone, and some of us will lead, others follow.

Looking beyond coordination, Bastardoz and Van Vugt outline three more reasons we choose to follow:[48]

1. There is more success in numbers. Being alone – by choice or forced social exclusion – is less favourable than being a lowly member of a group, even if that means that we forfeit authority and receive smaller shares of rewards and opportunity. Isolation from a community that provides food and shelter could even mean death.
2. Leadership is expensive. As Shakespeare noted in *Henry IV*, 'Uneasy is the head that wears a crown'[49] – and that bears out. The medieval king may sleep in the best tent on the battlefield, but their shiny armour is an obvious target for arrows. The director of the multinational receives the best bonuses but can be hauled to jail for company conduct about which they had no knowledge. If the balance of risk to love, life and liberty is too high, followership is a good option.
3. We are not a good or popular leader. A person's ability to lead or attract followers may be poor, or they hold limited experience. Followership provides both a role and an opportunity to learn.

'You're right, Miriam. This motif wasn't a good choice.'

In general, that makes intuitive sense, but there is some nuance to explore. At one extreme, would a group of people who follow simply to avoid repercussions – for example, because they do not fancy being shot – attract success? And at the other, why would a group of extremely capable leaders choose to defer and follow someone else? Bastardoz and Van Vugt offer an insight, describing followership as 'part of an adaptive psychological system to coordinate actions with others'.[50]

The key word here is *adaptive*. Firstly, a group will use its available resources to organise and achieve its objectives. For instance, someone who is proficient in project management is better placed to lead delivery efforts compared with someone whose expertise lies in software development. However, when the conversation shifts to application architecture, this reverses. Secondly, as Bastardoz and Van Vugt go on to note, 'To ensure smooth and efficient group coordination, followership styles should match … different leadership styles.'[51] That makes sense. It is not enough just to follow or have the skills to take on a task; it's crucial for followers – or leaders – to adapt their behaviour to each other. For example, a group of soldiers who all insist on discussing their personal opinion on strategy are not ideal followers – just as unquestioning agreement would not be ideal in devising a new marketing campaign. If this all seems to relate back to context, you're correct. But now, we are also considering the styles and attitudes of both followers *and* leaders.

Ideal teams therefore will need not only 'great' leaders and 'great' followers – but also, crucially, those people working well together. Inefficient or conflicting relationships between followers and leaders will clearly have detrimental effects on performance. Even if we intentionally hire context-appropriate people into our particular group, conflict about task handling, relationships and process can spiral.[52] Groups will fall in and out of love with one another. They will argue, pressure and change shape. Therefore, working on good relationships becomes key. According to Baird and Benson, 'Effective followers help to support others' decisions, put team goals ahead of self-interests, and carry out the tasks needed to accomplish team goals.'[53] If this is true, then sending a leader on another training course to improve their delegation skills will be less helpful than investment in team dynamics. To put it bluntly, it does not matter how authentic a leader you are if the followers in your team are distrustful of you and each other.

Taking the decision to follow someone inherently describes an assessment of the situation. As Bastardoz and Van Vugt suggest, we will consider if we could have more success in a group, whether the protection of the leader is worth the compromise on rewards, and if the leader is better placed than us. For instance, if we are about to go out on a hunt with several members of the tribe, does it make sense to follow the person wishing to lead? Assuming that they represent our strongest and most capable hunter, probably so. Importantly, that assessment of whether to follow and if the trade-offs are worth it happens continuously. Should we see our own situation and abilities out of step, we seek change. That leader will therefore be replaced, in time, by a more suitable candidate, or we will find an alternative for ourselves.

Bringing that up to date, consider the addition of an egalitarian leader to a hierarchical task- and process-driven team. The new leader's natural disposition to expect equality and wide engagement in practice development will jar with those followers used to something else, and we cannot foresee individual responses. A broader example I have been part of is the global roll-out of agile practice. While it is not universally true, more meritocratic European teams have tended to find shared ownership and flattened structure easier to adopt than some Asian cultures where deference to a knowing leader is more socially commonplace.

The situation gets more complex still in large organisations. Away from the intimacy of the hunting party or our local team, how can we possibly assess whether we should follow the CEO sitting ten-plus levels away from our position? We are unlikely to even meet them, let alone have the opportunity to see how they operate, allowing us to determine whether we should sacrifice our opportunities and benefits. Worse still, do the followers who get a new leader imposed upon them get the chance to engage and evaluate their capabilities?

Back to Bastardoz and Van Vugt: 'modern organizations have structures in place that de facto reduce followers' engagement with their leaders'.[54] And, more scathingly, 'Because would-be leaders are not tested over years of personal interactions, narcissistic or over-confident individuals have extant opportunities to make good first impressions without being checked'.[55]

Finally, none of this is to say that we must immediately do away with every leader. Google is at least one company that attempted to remove managers and, in doing so, discovered their value.[56] However, it is time that we gave up on archaic images of leaders being special and wildly influential beings. It is time to stop searching for the ultimate way to lead teams and organisations, and it is time to cease blind observance of in-vogue methods of leadership. As Haslam, Alvesson and Reicher put it, 'Zombie leadership: Dead ideas that still walk among us' are doing us no favours at all.[57]

The quest for optimal practice

Let us park leadership for the moment and turn to the partner challenge of practice: the organisation, planning and administration of the day-to-day. Exactly like the leadership world, countless individuals and companies will offer you their 'award-winning' model or practice to adopt, often targeting a particular situation. Looking for a way to manage incidents? No problem. Wanting to carry out meaningful root cause analysis or improve user requirements gathering? Of course. Looking for project delivery methods, release management techniques or frameworks for defining strategy? Sure. Want to organise objectives through your organisation and get everyone working on something meaningful? We have just the thing. To illustrate, here is a list of the various frameworks and methods I have used in organisations so far:

Delivery: Managing Successful Programmes (MSP), PRINCE2, Project Management Book of Knowledge (PMBOK), Scrum, Large Scale Scrum (LeSS), Scaled Agile Framework (SAFe), Kanban, Dynamic Systems Development Method (DSDM), Extreme programming (XP) and the Microsoft Solutions Framework (MSF).

Operations: IT Infrastructure Library (ITIL), Lean, Control Objectives for Information and Related Technologies (COBIT), Kepner-Tregoe, compliance standards (ISO, SOx, GDPR, NIST, HIPAA), Microsoft Operations Framework (MOF), DevOps / DevSecOps and Site Reliability Engineering (SRE).

Discovery and organisation: Management by objectives (MBO), Objectives and Key Results (OKRs), Wardley Maps and other value chain mapping ideas, sense-making (Snowden, Kurtz, Stacey, etc), Spiral Dynamics, Balanced Score Cards and Plan-Do-Study-Act.

Change: Prosci's ADKAR Model, Lewin's Change Management Model, Kotter's 8-Step Process, McKinsey's 7-S Framework, nudge theory and Kübler-Ross' Change Curve.

That is a healthy list, and while I am obviously no expert in even half of them, the variety gives us an excellent choice dependent on our context. Unfortunately, it also demonstrates another overwhelming set of options with plenty of opportunity to use tools in poorly-fitting situations. Once again, we might wonder how on earth we pick the right combination of tools for us. Thus, in the coming pages I will attempt to answer that by looking at the origins and propagation of such solutions.

Organisation and practice through history

Let us start with a simplified description of how work gets done: with required input (A), actions are taken (B) that lead to an output (C). This flow could represent anything from a farmer growing crops to an author writing a book or a soldier capturing a position. Figure 1-3 illustrates the process for producing a loaf of bread.

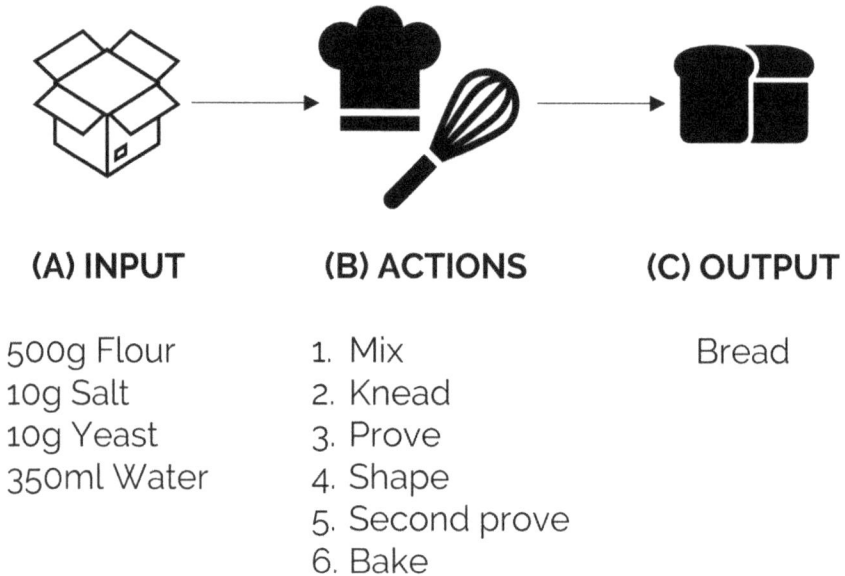

(A) INPUT	(B) ACTIONS	(C) OUTPUT
500g Flour	1. Mix	Bread
10g Salt	2. Knead	
10g Yeast	3. Prove	
350ml Water	4. Shape	
	5. Second prove	
	6. Bake	

Figure 1-3. Simple workflow for bread

With this information it is easy to see the steps taken once the inputs and tools are with the baker. Reality, of course, is not so simple, and even in small endeavours, there will be many chains and branches of supply to achieve those outputs. If we inspect the immediate supply chain for the baker, we quickly develop a more complicated set of steps (see Figure 1-4), but this is by no means complete. If we included earlier and later steps or the various intangibles, like the management of competition, human interactions and wider social order, the diagram would expand exponentially. The adage that 'It takes a village to raise a child' seems to apply to business too.

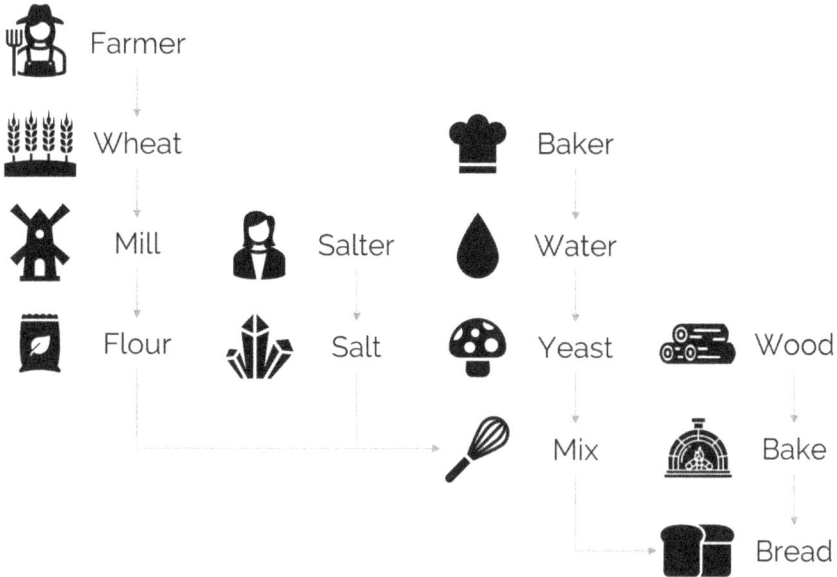

Figure 1-4. Expanded workflow map for bread

Even if we could visualise it all, what we describe will be significantly less complicated than many of the challenges we face each day, and doubly so for large endeavours. Creating such a map for the production of a battleship, landing a probe on Mars, or erecting a castle is unlikely to be possible. Further, with so many diverse, interconnected things in the flow, our picture would be out of date before we had even put our pen down. Unsurprisingly, a perpetual human question has been how to organise the people, skills and knowledge we need.

The Middle Ages

To examine that, let us first consider an artisan blacksmith in the Middle Ages, operating the only forge in a small village. Customers for the forge would have been other workers needing tools in the village, from farriers to farmers, from individuals to small-holdings. For resources unavailable locally, like iron and coal, the forge would have imported goods from merchants outside the area. On a small scale this setup would have been relatively stable and would have been found in many villages and towns. However, as the number of people and the need for goods increased, a pressing need for more organisation was created. By the nature of artisans and workshops being independent, buying a similar product in different areas could yield major differences in quality and cost. Considering a large order – for example, a military request for thousands of standardised, reliable weapons – the choice of waiting for production or working with multiple, independent artisans was far from ideal. For the artisans themselves, how could they know that the price they were paying for resources was fair? How could buyers be confident that they were getting a good deal from an experienced supplier?

From the 1300s in Europe, one answer was the establishment and membership of guilds.[58] Artisan guilds provided a natural home and official organisation around the smaller workshops and individuals within each of the many trades. Guilds created recognisable hierarchies of experience, with apprentices learning from master craftsmen before applying those skills to their own orders and contracts. They provided central and dominant places to set prices and negotiate on the cost and delivery of goods, offered protection from racketeers, and created a reliable standard for purchasers. Individuals remained able to set up their own workshops and negotiate their own terms, but did so despite guild disapproval, pressure and competition, making it increasingly hard to do.

The result of these structures was twofold. First, the system provided an effective way to organise disparate groups, leading to increases in quality and reliability of labour. For large undertakings, such as the erection of a cathedral, guilds could be used to identify and recruit the many hundreds of artisans necessary. Simultaneously, their adoption of standards and early industrial techniques led to less variable outputs in everything from tools to shoes and clocks to artwork. That combination also had significant applications for the military – for example, 'Vast quantities of standardized muskets, uniforms and boots were turned out of countless artisan shops across Europe.'[59]

Secondly, for social order, the guilds helped reinforce existing hierarchical and patriarchal structures, providing a strong and influential link between government and the people. These controls thus defined who and what was deemed important.

One leading voice in the late 1600s, Johann Joachim Becher, echoed the enforcement of social order. Becher, a German physician, alchemist and scholar, experimented with a hierarchical system for laboratories that would ensure knowledge and labour remained separate.[60] At the top, he placed a knowledgeable counsellor, a *Consilarius Laboratorii* responsible for overall production. Beneath them worked a *Dispensator Laboratorii* who distributed the various tasks to a final level of labourers below. All instructions were to be created by the counsellor, shared verbatim by dispensators, and then followed unquestioningly by those receiving them. In summary, the guilds:

> *sought, in the name of rationalisation of the work process, to replace the inefficient, inarticulate, mysterious, and indisciplined art of the craftsman with a public, open, and widely available mechanical practice that was built upon a strict, mindless, and hierarchically ordered division of labor.*[61]

The Industrial Revolution and beyond

Bringing us forward to the second industrial and scientific revolution of the nineteenth century, a call for efficiency and control of output intensified. Many new names built on previous advances, and we could consider Edmund Cartwright's power loom, George Stephenson's steam engines or Sir Henry Bessemer's process for the mass production of steel as examples. However, in the world of management practice and organisation, one name appears often: Frederick Winslow Taylor (1856–1915). Taylor was an American mechanical engineer who, through his research and experimentation in factories and workshops, developed his own theory of scientific management. The theory, in essence, applied his knowledge of scientific and engineering principles to analyse tasks, people and process in pursuit of best practices. So successful was this approach that Taylorism has become a noun, and an example comes with the design of the shovel. Taylor observed that while small, lightweight shovels were easy to wield, they were not efficient or durable, whereas large, heavy shovels were strong but difficult to use with some materials. From his analysis, Taylor asserted that the optimum weight for a full shovel should be 21 pounds, regardless of the material being moved. In effect, therefore, smaller shovels would be used for heavier materials like iron, and larger ones for coal.*

By equipping workers with these scientifically specified tools, variability and waste could be reduced and thus predictability, productivity and yield increased.

Approaching the twentieth century, we come to another colossus of industry with Alfred P. Sloan Jr. (1875–1966), the CEO, president and chairman of General Motors. Sloan conveyed similar Taylorist ideas in his view of production, and being interviewed in 1954 by NBC on running a successful business, said:

I've learned that no problem, no matter how complicated it appears to be, is really complicated when you divide it into its component parts. If you look at an intricate machine you'll marvel in its complexity and you say, 'whoever could build such a machine.' But the mechanic who has to build the machine doesn't look at it as a complete machine, he looks at it as component parts, and when you take it down into the component parts, it's simplified, and you can understand it. It's the same way with a business problem. If your organisation has the ability to break down a complex problem in its simplest parts, in that way you can make the most constructive decision.[62]

Sloan, then, considered business and management from a reductionist perspective. If we break down the process we are studying into simple constituents, then identify better methods for each, we end up improving the whole.

The two philosophies of practice

As we move into the latter half of the twentieth century, new philosophies for organising work and increasing quality led to a fork in the road. In one direction, we continue with an intent to control task and process – the *management of outputs* – and in the other, we relinquish control with more egalitarian methods – *systems and enablement*. Following are brief examples to illustrate each school of thought.

---

* This is why snow shovels are so large and light, while you can still buy a standard No. 1 or No. 10 shovel and everything in between depending on your load.

Philosophy 1: Management of outputs

ISO 9000, the International Organization for Standardization's set of quality management systems, is well-known. Many readers will have experience of working to or being audited against these standards, which seem to emanate from a good place: a desire for quality. The standard that we know has something of a history, covered in detail in John Seddon's *The Case Against ISO 9000*.[63] In the spirit of Taylorism, ISO 9000's life began during the Second World War in UK munitions factories. In an environment where bombs are being manufactured, it is vital that everyone is handling things in a safe and standard way, so strict procedures were created to control output. Seddon goes on to describe the expansion of output control beyond the military, the publication of BS 5179 'Guidelines for Quality Assurance' by the British Standards Institute (BSI) in 1974 and the beginnings of third-party inspection for quality. By 1979, the UK government, which by now employed over 15,000 inspectors, put its weight behind BSI and a new standard, BS 5750, that provided common controls for production across industries. BS 5750, which states that management must be responsible for defining and documenting quality policy, seems to link directly back to Becher's experiments and roles 300 years before. As noted in an article by D. J. Pratt, 'The main tenet of BS 5750 is that by writing down, and adhering to, set procedures a high-quality product or service will be produced. This unfortunately does not ensure quality, only repeatability and conformity to a standard.'[64]

Despite challenges to its efficacy and ethos, BS 5750 became ISO 9000, and a standard concerning the way work is designed and managed spread around the world. In the UK, the then government made compliance to ISO 9000 conditional for contracts,* with some 60,000 companies registered by 1998.

---

* Seddon includes the infamous example of a troop of morris men – traditional folk dancers – being forced to apply to ISO 9000 in order to dance at a local government event. It is worth noting too that the requirement for registration encourages some adverse behaviour. I have seen many examples of compliance managers seeking 'soft' assessors for an easy ride, or one collecting an inspector then driving to get petrol in order to limit actual assessment time.

Philosophy 2: Systems and enablement

Active throughout the time BS 7570 became ISO 9000, William Edwards Deming (1900–1993) in his work describes a second philosophy. Deming was an American engineer, statistician, author, lecturer, musician and management consultant – something of a polymath – and is famous for his influence on industry in Japan and the US. His work with the Ford Motor Company following its significant losses at the start of the 1980s led to it becoming America's most profitable motor company in 1986. Deming did not subscribe to task-control like Taylor, nor reductionist principles from Sloan. Instead, his approach was to consider the whole – the system – and how work flowed through it to achieve its levels of quality and variability. This point is worth emphasising. A systems view implies that the results we get, good or bad, are because of the system they were created within. In that way, your products are not necessarily bad, and nor did your customers complain because of one employee's actions. The situation was caused by the whole: the services, customer expectations, staff training, working conditions, organisational structures, processes and everything else besides. As such, rather than a task-based approach where we insist process adherence equates to quality, a product perspective seeks actual evidence of quality and encourages everyone to engage in its improvement. Overall responsibility still remains with an organisation's leaders, but their role is now one of enablement, not enforcement.

Deming summarised his thinking as 14 points in his best-selling book, *Out of the Crisis*.[65] Two examples already help to demonstrate the difference between his philosophy and the hierarchical and control-based alternatives:

- Cease dependence on inspection to achieve quality: As Deming wrote, 'Quality can not be inspected into a product or service; it must be built into it.'[66] That is, inspection can identify flaws, but the responsibility should not exist only at the end of the process.
- Drive out fear: If you want people to engage, it makes no sense to penalise and threaten them when things go wrong. That only encourages backside-covering behaviours that contribute nothing to overall quality.

Contemporary practices

Bringing us up to date, we can see the two philosophies – management of outputs and systems and enablement – in many of today's practices. For control of outputs, we could look at:

- Predictive project management, such as a simple PRINCE2 project, where we consider everything that needs to happen in advance.
- Management by objectives (MBO), where we hierarchically set objectives across an organisation and test their completion after a set period, typically a year.
- The IT Infrastructure Library (ITIL) approach to capacity management where the aim is to 'ensure that services achieve the agreed and expected levels of performance'.[67]
- The hierarchical nature of some scaled agile frameworks, like SAFe.[68] While some versions of agile tools are embedded, they are encased in layers of control, with delivery teams at the bottom of the pile.*
- Other frameworks that state if we 'do it this way' we will automatically succeed.

For systems and enablement we could look at:

- Lean manufacturing, which focuses on end-to-end flow of value and the removal of waste to make a whole system improve.
- Motorola's Six Sigma emphasis on defect and variation reduction in production.
- An agile framework, like Scrum, when operated by an autonomous team, possibly cross-functional, with a focus on achieving value together.
- DevOps, which collapses the boundaries between development and operations (hence the name) and tasks the teams with achieving valuable product outcomes.
- Other frameworks or philosophies with limited governance that offer a starting point from which to adapt.

---

* Like the directors in their smart office on the top floor, teams sit at the bottom of the SAFe diagrams.

You may disagree with my categorisations, and indeed, later iterations of ITIL and ISO 9001 have introduced more systems-based thinking into their structure. The fourth edition of ISO 9001 (2015) includes acknowledgement that we must adapt to the situation we find ourselves in, and ITIL now includes its own take on organisational change management. It is important to note therefore that this is not a binary choice, rather a continuum based on a desired level of control, as illustrated in Figure 1-5.

As we shall see in the next chapter, however, none of this makes the practices themselves right or wrong. As the saying goes, 'All roads lead to Rome', but what we do not know is if the road leads to Rome in Tennessee, Queensland, or Lazio, and that is something we will only find out when we arrive.

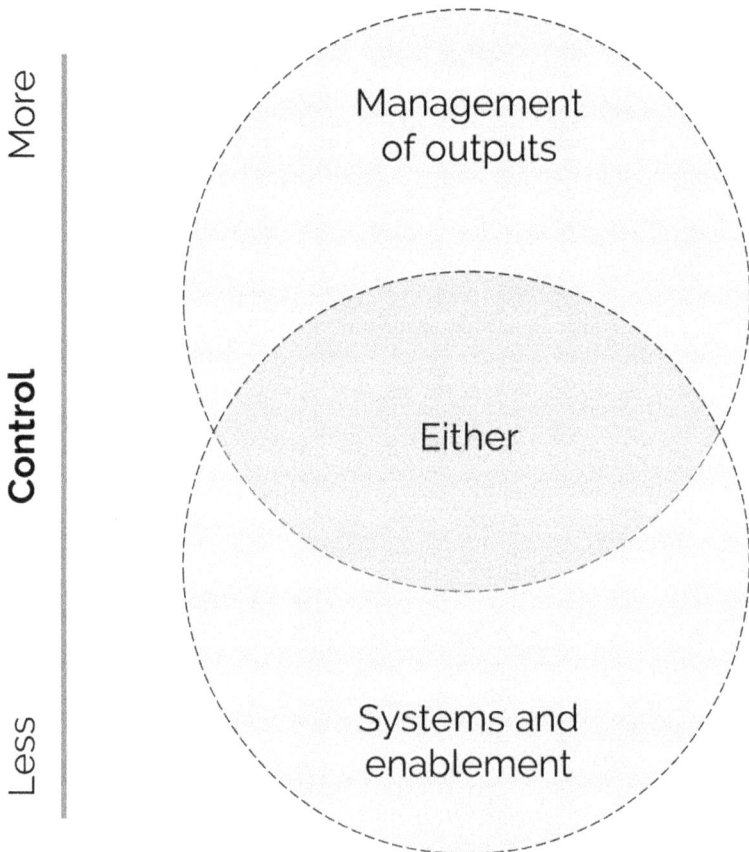

Figure 1-5. Level of desired task and practice control

CHAPTER 2

Systems and context

*'Earlier on today apparently, a woman rang the BBC and said she had heard that there was a hurricane on the way. Well, if you are watching, don't worry there isn't.'**

— MICHAEL FISH, BBC WEATHER FORECASTER, 1987[69]

An unpredictable story

Many years ago, in a village in ancient rural China, lived a farmer. On his land, the farmer was assisted only by his son and a single horse.

One morning, the farmer woke to find that his horse had escaped. Later that morning, his neighbours in the village found out and came to commiserate with the farmer on his poor luck.

'What misfortune!' they cried.

The farmer simply replied, 'Maybe'.

A few days later, the farmer awoke to the sight of his runaway horse having returned, but more, it was accompanied by four other wild horses. His neighbours again visited him, and this time applauded his great fortune.

'What wonderful luck!' they exclaimed.

And the farmer replied, 'Maybe'.

---

* Except that there was, and the worst since 1707. Fish denies this version of events, saying that the edited clip does not include his reference to Florida, not the UK.

The next week, the farmer's son was thrown off one of the wild horses that he was trying to tame and broke his leg badly. The neighbours sympathised with the farmer and the impact this latest tragedy would have.

'Your only son injured! What terrible, awful luck!' they lamented.

And the farmer again replied, 'Maybe'.

The very next day, the army came through the village looking for conscripts. They arrived at the farm and, seeing the old farmer and his son with the broken leg, passed through and left them be. The neighbours, whose sons were conscripted, rushed to tell the farmer how blessed he was. 'What chance that your son was injured!' they declared.

And the farmer simply replied, 'Maybe'.

This is my version of the Taoist parable of the Chinese farmer, and the principle that an event is neither good nor bad out of context. As we progress in the story, it is clear how one thing leads to another to cause the farmer's son to be spared conscription. Had the horse not escaped, the new horses arrived, or the boy had not broken his leg, the outcome could have been very different. However, despite this link between cause and effect, what we cannot say is that the horse escaping would yield the same result again. Indeed, if I had told you that the story was about a boy avoiding conscription because his horse escaped, it is unlikely you would have imagined this chain of events.

In business, we will all have comparable stories of events leading to other events that are obvious looking back, regardless of their opacity to begin with. Here are some examples to illustrate.

Adoption of a leadership framework

In step with the constant discussion about what a leader should or should not be, a consultant* wrote a blog post about the top-level behaviours a leader should exhibit. The post was not scientific, rather an opinion piece, using general ideas. A few weeks later, a senior leader that the consultant was

---

* Not your author, dear reader-someone at one of the Big Four consulting companies.

working with noticed the concepts in general conversation. The leader took that concept and forwarded it to his team as advice. Within three months, the behaviours were acknowledged as what people should be doing and became part of the company's leadership expectations and training. To facilitate this move, the consultant was invited back into the organisation to create the materials and train those behaviours to leaders. Six months on, the ideas were everywhere (even with a catchy acronym), notably becoming part of a competency framework used to determine fit for existing and new-hire project managers. It is said that, to this day, the dollar signs have not faded from the consultant's eyes.

Loss of critical staff

After a strong year of business performance by my then employer, 100% of employee bonuses were confirmed in full. Yet within a week, we received several resignations from members of technical teams. Why? Earlier that year, a new policy had been introduced whereby annual bonuses were no longer paid if a person was working their notice period. Instead of a normal turnover of technical staff spread out over the year, people chose to hold on and receive their bonuses, resulting in a considerable number quitting at once.

The successful launch of Threads

Following the purchase and associated shake-up of Twitter by Elon Musk, a large number of engineers resigned, or were asked to leave the company. Naturally, those people went searching for jobs, and thankfully for them, Silicon Valley in San Francisco is a hotbed of technology companies. Included among them is Meta, Facebook's parent company, and clearly it saw an opportunity to snap up some quality engineering staff. Fair enough. Things became more controversial not long after, when Meta launched its own Twitter-like application, Threads. Twitter's response was to launch a legal challenge citing that 'Meta has hired dozens of former Twitter employees' and that Meta 'deliberately assigned these employees to develop, in a matter of months, Meta's copycat "Threads" app.'[70]

Like the farmer story, all three of these cases show a clear set of steps to the outcome *in hindsight*. None of the results was obvious or predictable in advance and similar event relationships can be found in every corner of our lives. This is an important observation and serves as an excellent introduction to contexts and systems.

Systems, contexts and environments

A system or context* refers to the idea that wherever an action is being taken, there are characteristics of the environment that influence how predictable the results might be. At a high level, we have two main systems, those that are predictable and those that are not.

Predictable or ordered systems

A predictable system, with limited components arranged in relatively simple relationships, allows us to accurately foresee the results of our actions. For example, were I to make a paper plane or open a known application on my computer, I can be confident of the results. Even for something with more components, like a mechanical clock, I can – with appropriate skill – dismantle and reassemble it without affecting its operation. This predictability also means that I can record my actions and provide dependable instructions for others to follow.

Unpredictable or disordered systems

An unpredictable system has many independent and interoperating components such that we cannot, with any accuracy, predict what will happen when we take action. We might anticipate a result – even a range of results – but like the examples from the farmer to Twitter, things may not happen as we expect. It can be helpful to think of such systems as more than the sum of their parts. Unlike our predictable system where we could indefinitely dismantle and rebuild the clock, even with its multiple components, the same cannot be said for an owl!

---

* You may also hear systems being labelled as 'domains' or 'environments'. For the purposes of this book, these mean the same thing.

In our daily lives and workplace, there will be a mixture of systems at play. Predictable things might include core facilities (the lift arrives when I call it), familiar and common procedures or the behaviour of tools we use. Far less predictable might be how a marketplace evolves, how recent technology will impact the organisation or the impact of a new CIO kicking off a digital transformation. Being conscious that the work we are doing exists on a spectrum, we begin to see how our approaches might also need to flex.

Thus, imagining that everything can be predicted can lead to failed plans when we meet anything unforeseen. Similarly, assuming nothing can be predicted will prevent us gaining efficiency from repetition.

The concept of systems or contexts clearly is not new, and there are plenty of idioms in the English language to prove the point. We 'test the water' when something is uncertain, we suggest that people do not 'use a sledgehammer to crack a nut' and should never 'bring a knife to a gun fight'. For our purposes, the one to remember is 'horses for courses', being a reference to achieving the best performance by picking the animal and rider most suited to the conditions. Similarly, in our offices and organisations, if we can make sense of which systems are at play, our strategies, plans and actions can be tuned to fit.

Cynefin

To make practical use of this insight, and to get more scientific than discussing colloquial phrases, let us briefly examine one of the popular sense-making tools, Cynefin – pronounced 'ku-nev-in' (in Welsh meaning 'haunt' or 'habitat').[71] Cynefin is a free, open-source framework developed by Professor David Snowden (Figure 2-1).* There is a good deal of information in the diagram, which can seem overwhelming, but I promise with some guidance it is both easy to understand and powerful. For the moment, all we need to do however is focus on the main headings: Clear, Complicated, Complex, Chaotic and the overlapping A and C in the centre. These terms break down predictable and unpredictable systems based on some specific ideas.

---

* Reference and usage information is available freely at cynefin.io. I will provide an example of Cynefin in practice in Chapter 4.

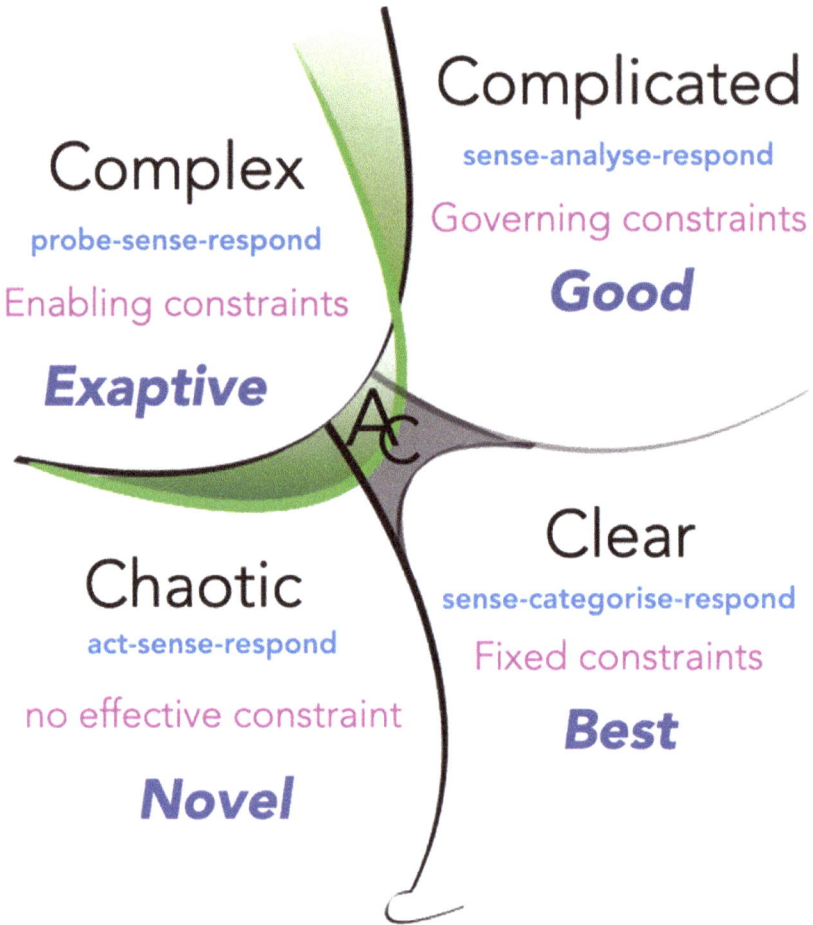

Figure 2-1. The Cynefin Framework as at February 2021[72]

Predictable systems (right-hand side)

Clear: The domain of recipes. There is a knowable and stable relationship between cause and effect, often simple enough to be obvious. With the same inputs and process, we will reliably achieve the same output each time. For example, if I begin with a sheet of A4 paper and follow instructions to make a paper aeroplane, that is what I will achieve.

Complicated: The domain of experts. We still have a predictable relationship between cause and effect, however that link is not evident to everyone. To decide how to act here we will require expert knowledge to examine and decide on the best course. We might consider fitting out a new data centre, or even launching a satellite to orbit around Mars. In both cases there are multiple calculations, considerations and technical options, but with the right expertise a plan can be created and executed confidently.

Unpredictable systems (left-hand side)

Complex: The domain of unintended consequences. In complexity, there is a dynamic network of interactions from multiple independent components at play. That motion means that we can no longer calculate or predict cause-and-effect relationships with any accuracy, and like our farmer, can only know those relationships in hindsight. We may have a sense of what could happen based on past experience. However, even with the same inputs and process, millions of variations may occur. Complex systems are frequent in nature, from your garden to a coral reef, and as a rule of thumb almost anything involving humans. Think about the impact of new species on an ecosystem, the emergence of dangerous political movements or the forgotten petri dish from which Fleming discovered penicillin. Their causes seem obvious now, but the results were not certain before they happened. In such systems, even with the greatest expertise, we cannot assume our plans are accurate and therefore we must experiment, explore and learn to make progress.

Chaotic: The domain of randomness, volatility and crisis. In the chaotic domain, there is no knowable relationship between cause and effect, even in hindsight. This is the emergency, the collapse of a government or, more positively, the unconstrained and spontaneous celebration. With such immediate situations, we have no time to plan or experiment and our only option is to act. Hopefully, through that action, we achieve something that moves the situation to another domain.

Not sure which system (centre)

Confusion and Aporia: The domain of not knowing. Here, we are not certain which domain applies without further review and this is typically a bad place to be. It may prevent us from taking action – at least in context – but ignorance can also lead to innovation. To represent this tension the domain is split into 'Confusion' – unintentionally or unknowingly confused – and Aporia – deliberately confused so as to elicit new thinking.*

Catastrophic fold (bottom)

While not a domain, the final component to understand is the 'hook' or fold at the base of the diagram. This represents a common situation in our lives and work: we are operating in Clear and everything is going well, then suddenly, disaster! Our predictable practices and processes are thrown into disarray – into Chaotic, actually – and we are faced with urgent choices. We are walking along, and our ankle gives way. Our computer system goes down and no-one remembers how to do the task on paper. Or a recent example, where I could not get into an escape room party because the host had forgotten their keys!

The oversimplification of categories

Before we move on, it is worth repeating the key insight and the reason I am starting with an explanation of these systems. It is easy and often tempting to assign a label or category to an environment that we might be working with – for example, saying that 'we work in a complex space'. I find, however, that people do not really know what that means. Indeed, an organisation is probably complex at a combined layer: we have multiple, independent actors, interacting and adapting in ways that we cannot predict. Simultaneously, however, many component parts within the organisation will be ordered, predictable and known. A more useful assumption is that our organisations are made up of all domains, to a lesser or greater degree, all of the time.

---

* Aporia is a term from philosophy meaning to be puzzled or stumped. For example, a theory with unresolved contradicting arguments cannot sustain both at the same time and would be in a state of aporia. Incidentally, many of Plato's works are labelled as aporetic due to presented contradictions remaining open.

Assuming everything is complex – or ordered – invites broad categorisation and the application of thinking and methods that are not appropriate. Work will still get done, but with the penalty of otherwise avoidable waste, errors and other unintended results. One of my favourite examples of this is VUCA. You are likely familiar with this acronym, describing a collection of terms: volatile, uncertain, complex and ambiguous. VUCA has been around since the late 1980s, initially used by the US Army War College before more mainstream adoption.[73]

Each of the terms, by intention, invites critical thinking and sense-making about a situation or strategy, where:

- Volatility = the propensity of a situation or environment to change
- Uncertainty = levels of unpredictability
- Complexity = numerous moving parts, no cause-effect chain
- Ambiguity = lack of specific definition, blurred meanings, risk of misunderstanding

Great. Anything that encourages people to think about their context, I wholeheartedly support. Unfortunately, however, I find that VUCA is used as both a noun and an adjective. It is also used as a threat. It has become a convenient soundbite to invoke in consultant sales patter:

Scrum/SAFe/OKRs are your answer to VUCA.
You need to implement Agile HR because we're in a VUCA world.

And so on. One such consultant I met professed that to deal with VUCA, you 'should learn lessons to apply in future situations'. I cannot help feeling that the irony was lost on them.*

In line with our Cynefin discussion, whether it is VUCA or a model from Kurtz, Stacey or Dervin, the *differences* between the nature of the domains is where the power and insight comes from. If we are facing significantly more uncertainty than ambiguity, we can organise ourselves to meet that challenge. More simply, if we are travelling from a warm country to a cold one, we know to pack a coat.

---

* The toolkit for consultants continues to expand, and alongside VUCA we can now harass our clients with BANI, RUPT and TUNA too. I will leave you to look those up yourself.

If, however, we simply say the world is 'complex' or 'VUCA', we throw away all of the nuance that could have helped us. A second point is the increasingly common call to simplify things, perhaps a natural response to being told that things are complex. To quote two recent phrases I have been party to, leaders have wanted to 'eradicate complexity' and 'embrace radical simplicity.' Again, I can see the temptation, but both of their organisations were simultaneously promoting flatter structures with more agility. Can you see what the problem might be here? Consider with me the scale and potential of human systems in organisations, which I am sorry to say will involve some ham-fisted mathematics.

Starting with a company with only two people, person A and person B, there is one relationship between them. If we increase that to a five-person company, each could have a relationship with four others. For example, person A could now interact with persons B, C, D and E. Adding that up, that gives a potential of ten relationships (Figure 2-2).

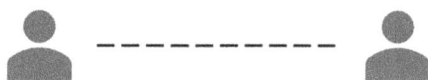

Two-person company: 1 relationship

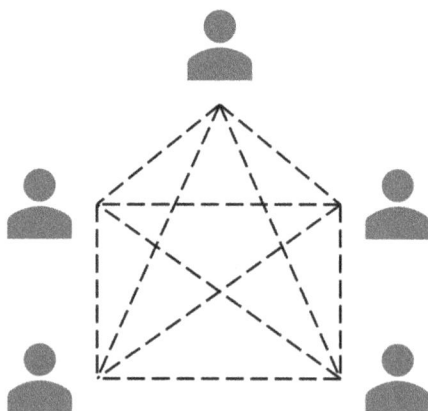

Five-person company: 10 relationships

Figure 2-2. Number of potential relationships in two-person and five-person companies

That all seems quite manageable, but the possible relationships ramp up quickly as the number of people increases (Figure 2-3 and Figure 2-4):*

10-person company = 45 potential relationships
20-person company = 190 potential relationships
50-person company = 1,225 potential relationships
75-person company = 2,775 potential relationships
150-person company = 11,175 potential relationships
5,000-person company = 12,497,500 potential relationships

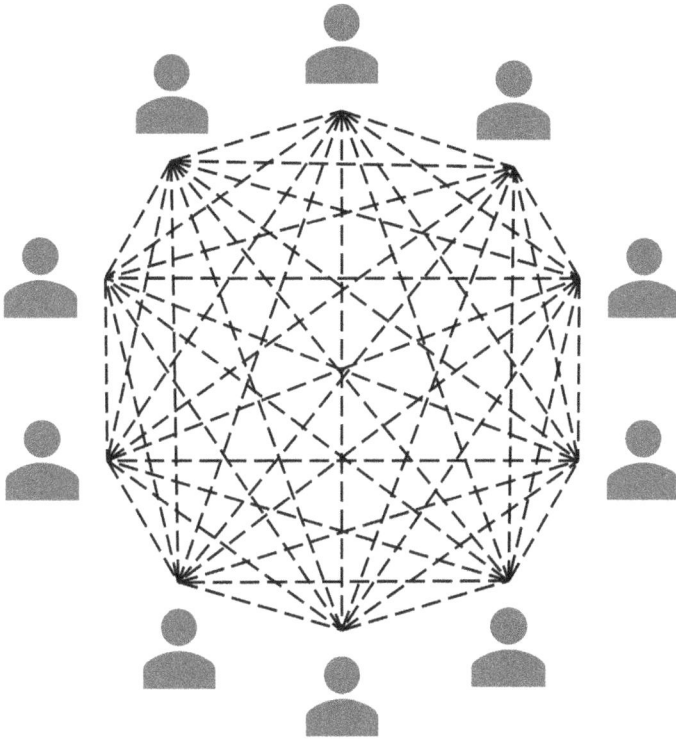

Ten-person company: 45 relationships

Figure 2-3. Number of potential relationships in a ten-person company

---

* If you want to work out the total for your company, use the formula $(N*(N-1))/2$, where N is the number of people.

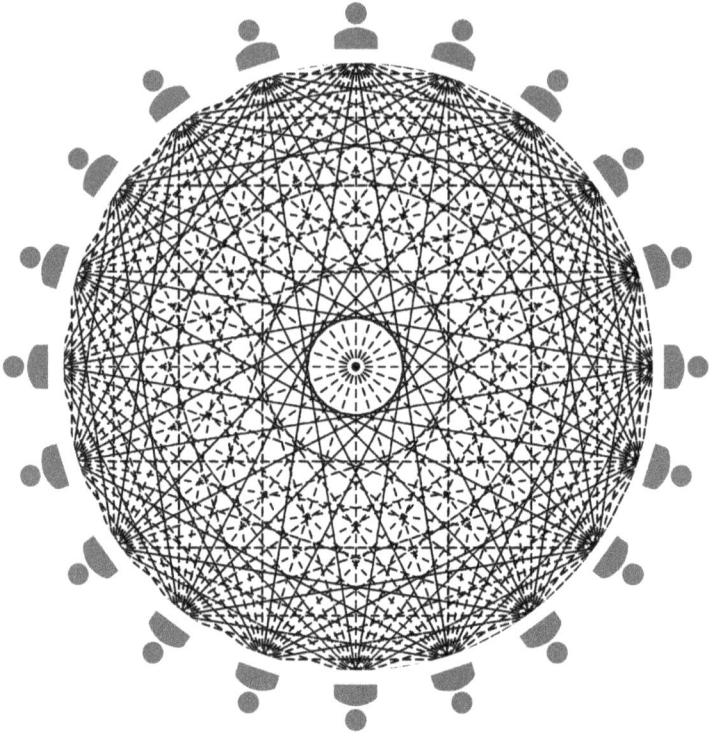

Twenty-person company: 190 relationships
Figure 2-4. Number of potential relationships in a twenty-person company

I realise of course that this is simplistic. If we imagine that 5,000-person company, not every individual will interact equally, or at all, with 4,999 others. What if instead, we use Robin Dunbar's famous number of 150 maximum relationships in primates.[74] Given that we have relationships outside our work, let us assume for our calculations that 50% of our relationships are inside the organisation. Thus, each of us can know 75 other people within the company. It is tempting to conclude that this means 5,000 people x 75 relationships = 375,000, but that does not account for the variance of who we might engage with. To calculate that, we now need to look at the number of combinations of 75 people that each person could make. In other words, how many ways can we group 75 people in 5,000?

The answer is a tremendously large number: 6.108 x 10^{167}, but it doesn't stop there. Each group of 75 people has 2,775 potential relationships, so we need to multiply the two together, giving us 1.695 x 10^{171}. In case that is not clear enough, here is the actual number!

*1,694,970,014,776,335,754,384,402,670,096,635,573,114,798,717,5
81,339,180,811,056,460,393,914,218,424,559,231,760,440,950,359,
437,956,173,951,231,530,431,639,371,376,276,322,297,400,440,56
7,857,645,262,134,075,610,509,316,560,000*

Oh, but that is still not accurate. We are not accounting for the value of relationships, the movement of people and changing of relationships over time, the formal and informal structures that govern how people interact, the opinions, knowledge and experiences of those people, and our myriad relationships with suppliers, customers, families and wider society. We have good evidence that if a judge is hungry, they are likely to hand out harsher sentences, so you would be forgiven if this all feels a bit overwhelming.[75]

> *We have good evidence that if a judge is hungry, they are likely to hand out harsher sentences.*

To quote Professor Brenda Dervin, an influential and substantial voice in the world of sense-making (who we sadly lost in 2022), we must not overlook the individual, their experiences and agency:

> *Each person is a person who has past struggles, a body, mind, heart, and spirit moving through time and space, with a past history, a present reality and future dreams and ambitions.[76]*

With this context, no matter how simple we make our processes, how clear we make our statements about vision and direction, or how much we train people in the latest leadership framework, we are operating with an immeasurable layer of uncertainty. No matter how much conviction we put into our voice when we announce that our organisation is going to 'become agile!', 'simplify!' or 'be customer-centric!', we ultimately have no control whatsoever over the picture that will emerge. No matter how clean and beautiful we make our presentations, diagrams and models, the reality will be fuzzy, even ugly.

Directors who seek 'radical simplicity' may only achieve it when there are two people in a secure, clean room, carrying out a repetitive task. Even then, one may be suffering a migraine or have just found out that the other is sleeping with their spouse. Context does not just matter: it is absolutely fundamental to everything else we do.

CHAPTER 3

Our compulsion to follow

*'Great things are not accomplished by those who yield to
trends and fads and popular opinion.'*

– CHARLES KURALT[77]

Why do we follow the trends?

As a summary so far, we have discussed the fact that our organisations and teams occupy multiple systems or contexts. Some parts of our organisations' activities will be predictable and allow mechanical and repeatable processes. Others will need detailed analysis by specialists, require sensitive adaptation to changing events or demand immediate action.

Against that background, we can use any number of leadership styles and deploy a variety of practices and techniques for discovery, delivery and operation. The choice is vast, from autocratic to absent, labour-intensive to lightweight, and task-oriented to transformative. In short, we have a wide spectrum of approaches to meet a similarly wide spectrum of situations. On paper, this is superb and, like a well-equipped kitchen, we can adapt to meet the needs of a wildly diverse range of customer tastes.

Despite that reality, my experience is that few organisations think in this way. Rather, as we have seen, many teams align to a limited doctrine in leadership or practice that is perceived as correct. Regarding practices, agility is an obvious example. In a number of companies I have worked with, the core narrative is that 'We must be agile to succeed' – and all else is subordinated to that idea. If a team is not agile, it is old-fashioned, change-averse and wrong. If an agile team is failing to deliver, it can still claim a win for agility and its ambassadorship of the 'New Way'.* For leadership, we have a similar story. We must be visionary! We must inspire! We must be authentic! Publicly

---

* This was actually a term used by one company I was with. George Orwell would be proud.

supporting other techniques (or, worse, using them) will get challenged regardless of the reality.

To move us forward, a critical question to ask is *why*. *Why* might people subscribe to the idea of a single correct solution? *Why* might people actively implement ideas and practice, even knowing they could be detrimental to productivity? *Why* do people continue to use frameworks and ideas once there is evidence of their poor fit? In no fixed order, I offer eight reasons.

1. 'I got told to'

This is the most straightforward of explanations, since if an organisation insists on or is forced to work in a certain way, hands are tied. For example:

- Legal or regulatory requirements: With significant penalties for non-compliance, laws and regulations like the Sarbanes–Oxley Act (SOx), Health and Safety at Work Act and GDPR require strict adherence.
- Customer demand for a particular approach, standard or method: Customers insisting on practices and processes, like we saw with the UK government's supplier requirement for ISO 9000.
- A senior executive or shareholder exercising their influence: The Google investor, John Doerr, who encouraged the company to use objectives and key results (OKRs), also did so across several other companies he invested in.[78]

In all these cases it is going to be difficult, if not illegal, for a team to make different choices about how they work.

2. 'I got sold to'

A common response when asking why a particular practice is in use is that a consultant or provider recommended it. Often that is born of a genuine desire to help, sharing hard-won knowledge to give you a head start. It can also be far less magnanimous and may represent a snake-oil seller attempting to find a snake-oil buyer at all costs. Either way, a consultant with rapport has immense power to influence and direct choices, even if the decisions are unnecessary, unqualified or simply wrong.

As a brief parallel, consider a dental surgeon discussing a painful tooth. If they recommend an expensive surgery, do we assume the choice is in our best interests or theirs? Since we know less than the dentist, and their actions are governed by ethical standards, it would be rational to trust their opinion. Scale this to a situation where we need brain or heart surgery and the power the surgeon holds to affect our choice is colossal.[79]

A selling strategy that exploits this trust, and that goes some way to explain the proliferation of models, is to present ideas in a sharp, smart-looking process. As part of a business development course, I was told that a simplified procedure was one of *the* most important and key assets I could have. It did not particularly matter if my process made sense, was logical or if it even worked – the magic happened with clients just by having *something*. People like a process, and to prove the point, here is my model for a leadership programme (Figure 3-1). Introducing The Open Leader Method, a framework comprising five core themes, each with three sub-areas.

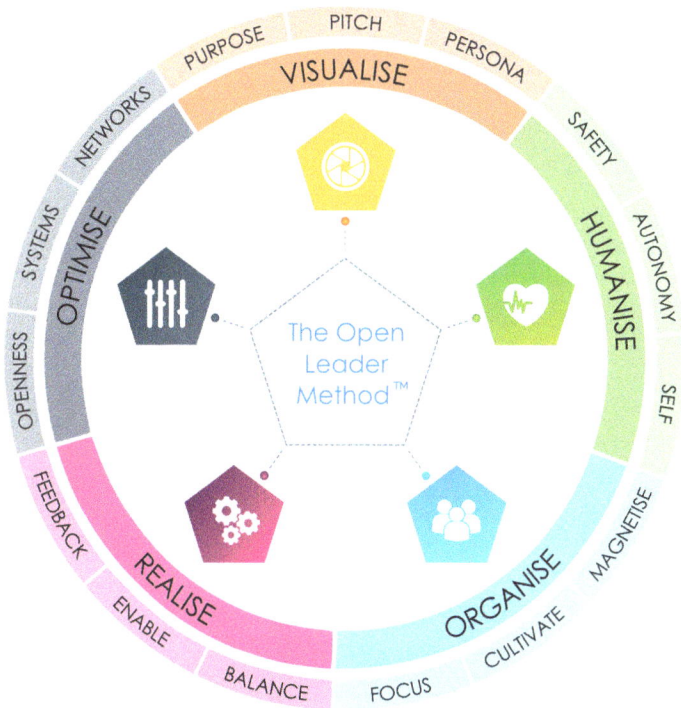

Figure 3-1. The Open Leader Method

The narrative, basically, is that we should give direction (Visualise), give space (Humanise), grow skills and relationships (Organise), deliver and measure (Realise) and then improve (Optimise). It took me a while to make them rhyme, but with a documented process for delivery and follow up, I was set. Did the model give people a sense of confidence that I knew what I was talking about? Definitely. Did the content have depth and value? Yes. Did the content suggest that this was the right thing to do? Yes. Crucially though, was the content suitable in all circumstances? Absolutely not.

Once you recognise this practice, you can see it everywhere. It is absolutely pervasive in leadership methods and delivery processes and terrifyingly easy to do. Mats Alvesson's excellent paper 'Upbeat Leadership: A recipe for – or against – "successful" leadership studies' even provides some step-by-step instructions for people wanting to create their own universal leadership framework.[80] Naturally, that our creation cannot be applied in all circumstances, from soldiers to scientists, surgeons to salespeople, must be quietly ignored.

3. 'I'm doing what everyone else is doing'

> *Most people are other people. Their thoughts are someone else's opinions, their lives a mimicry, their passions a quotation.*
> — OSCAR WILDE, DE PROFUNDIS, 1905

A common observation in organisations and a general principle of adoption is that successful ideas gain dominance. That does not necessarily mean that the ideas are good, rather that they gain a foothold and before you know it, everyone is onboard. A well-known model for this is Everett Rogers' Diffusion of Innovations, described in a book of the same title.[81] Rogers' research defines five stages of adoption, beginning with 'innovators' – those who are willing to experiment and take the most risks – running through 'early adopters', and early and late 'majority', before finally reaching 'laggards' – those who typically join because they must.*

---

* The web serves as a quick example, where, within a year of its 1991 public launch, around ten websites were available. At the millennium, approximately 7.5 million websites were active, raising to 83 million by 2010. At the start of 2024, the number of sites was approaching 1.1 billion. With an active website for every eight humans on the planet, the web is practically inescapable. January 2024 Web Server Survey, Netcraft, https://www.netcraft.com/blog/january-2024-web-server-survey.

Imagine other teams in your organisation or your industry using a particular approach, buying new technology or positioning themselves differently to clients. If they appear to be successful – at least according to their media output – what might you do? Do you stick with your current methods and risk missing out? Can you explain that choice when the boss wants to know why you are not doing something on the list of 'Top-10 Things That *All* Successful Companies Must Do'? It is going to be tough.

Thus, pressure mounts to fit in and be part of the group, to follow the crowd, and to 'steal with pride'. I find it wonderfully hypocritical that we tell our children not to copy, yet as adults we actively take that choice. At what point does, 'If Harry jumped off a bridge, would you do that too?' give way to 'They have adopted Agile, why haven't we done that yet?'

4. 'I believe it works'

Witnesses of accidents and those giving evidence in criminal cases often recall different details of an event. With the help of suggestion, they can wholly believe that they saw something that was not there. One study at Cornell University told a story to two groups about someone leaving a restaurant without paying.[82] The first group were told it was due to an emergency, but the second, that the customer skipped out on their bill for fun. A week after the story, those in the 'for fun' group remembered the bill higher than it really was, while the 'emergency' group picked a lower number. Scale that to a more complex situation, like a project running over many months and our memory of detail and the role that we played in events will not be accurate. Correlation will get confused with cause, false memories will merge with facts and, more simply, we will forget. Imagine this scenario:

Interviewer: What made you successful in this project?

Leader: Good question! I think it was because I remained self-aware and authentic to my values throughout. I had a gut feeling for the strategy and I went with that, and of course deciding to use Agile was a great decision.

Interviewer: What would you do differently next time?

Leader: I'll trust my intuition sooner and make sure that we spend time teaching everyone Agile principles at the start of every project.

For this person, simplifying and drawing out favourable details and their role in them will confirm their beliefs and conviction. Were those actions the cause of the project's success? We can say that a version of these practices was being used when the success happened, but we cannot know if the practices were the cause, no matter how much we believe. What would have happened if they had not done those things?

Coming back to John Doerr, his book about OKRs, *Measure What Matters,* has the subtitle 'How Google, Bono, and the Gates Foundation Rock the World with OKRs.'[83] I will admit, there is some value in objectives and key results used the right way (context dependent, of course) but to 'rock the world'? Are we to believe that Google would *not* have rocked the world without OKRs? We know that there is a correlation – they used OKRs – but without a control in the experiment, we can never know if this was the cause. We do not have the multiverse version of Google without OKRs, and nor do we have a perfect copy of the project where our leader did not think they were authentic.

As a final thought, I find that it is easier to confuse cause and correlation when the action and result are closely related. The use of objectives to coordinate work is commonplace, so saying that Google got a benefit from OKRs is at the very least plausible. Where links are more tenuous it is harder to support their impact, as Tyler Vigen's list of spurious and often ridiculous correlations illustrate. Quoting correlation #1,522: 'The distance between Saturn and the Sun correlates with Google searches for "how to make a baby".'[84]

5. 'I trust the process'

Another reason that people stick with frameworks and ideas – even if they might be a poor fit – is because a written process has power. Rather like the assumption that a person must know what they are talking about if they have written a book (be kind, dear reader). That can, of course, be true: when we see a well-researched and tested thesis, the extensive treatment trials or the general benefits of a diet, they provide an opportunity to sidestep risk and prevent the cognitive load of researching our own answers. Where there is a problem, however, is when we assume that all such materials are equally valid. I am not trying to suggest that we trust nothing and no-one – that would be a depressing state of mind – rather that we should be cautious when we are operating in an uncertain context. When someone else drives your car, it is safe to assume that the method they have used everywhere else will work fine – but that rule does not apply to running your 3,000-person organisation.

6. 'I don't understand (any better)'

In our journey towards value for our stakeholders, we cannot be more than our existing knowledge and experience. Even if we include our customers, our peers and suppliers, there will be limits and we must act, decide and operate with those constraints. As Donald Rumsfeld so famously described in his 2002 briefing to the US Department of Defense, these limits affect us all:

> *There are known knowns; there are things we know we know. We also know there are known unknowns; that is to say we know there are some things we do not know. But there are also unknown unknowns – the ones we don't know we don't know. And if one looks throughout the history of our country and other free countries, it is the latter category that tends to be the difficult ones.*[85]

If we do not know that there is a different way of thinking or a possibility that there might be, we are ourselves like Hans Christian Andersen's emperor without clothes. Until someone shines a light on what we are missing, or we realise our own predicament, there is no situation to interpret or problem to solve. Drowning in the river, we are going to grab what floats past – whether it is a branch or a crocodile. That is further exacerbated by non-specific, broad descriptions of terms and concepts in leadership and practice. For example, working on being a better leader or becoming 'big-A' Agile are general ideas that allow just about any action to apply.

7. 'I want to be X'

On an individual level, to be successful in our current organisation – and especially to claim an opportunity elsewhere – we must keep our skills and experience relevant. This can create a tension between what is in the best interest of an organisation and of an employee. Consider the new CIO launching a strategic transformation, the sales launch into a new country or the inspired marketing campaign. All *could* be of high value to the organisation, but all *will* be of value to the respective leaders and those that can claim association to them on their CVs.

Making use of this demand as an effective sales tool, suppliers link their methods to certifications and prestige. We can look at almost any supplier for this option: Microsoft, VMware, Salesforce, Scaled Agile Inc (the company behind SAFe), SAP, Amazon Web Services and some that link to prestigious universities. For the supplier, this is a brilliant move. As people adopt technologies – say, Microsoft for desktop computing – certifications prove competence in the engineers. In turn, when companies are hiring, they look to those certifications as screening for candidates, encouraging even more people to take them up.

When our engineering manager with Microsoft certifications is choosing technologies, hiring or training, what are they going to recommend we use? Suddenly, we have an ecosystem full of desire to gain achievements and to benefit from those that *we* hold.

It is important to highlight that this is massive business for the suppliers, regardless of its use to you. In the UK alone, in 2022, reported training expenditure across organisations broke £53 billion.[86] For context, UK manufacturing revenue for the year 2021 was £200 billion.[87] And note that the training costs are before licence fees, direct consulting, materials and so on.

8. 'I don't see the problem'

Looking out of the window in my office last summer, I saw that our neighbour had just mowed their lawn. It was only Thursday and yet this was the third time that he had cut regimental stripes into his tiny lawn, cleaning and storing the mower in his impeccable garage. No doubt the house that he returned to was also perfected and military in its conduct.

Our neighbour on the other side is not like this. Their garden is one of wilderness, occasional barbecues and neglect. Racks outside accumulate objects that have been ejected from the garage to make way for a teenage rock band. Then, we are in-between. When the meticulous neighbour looks into our garden, our mix of order and wildness falls short of their impeccable standard. Hedges are irregular, leaves remain unconstrained and birds are welcomed. They might judge that our house is similar, with patches of neatness juxtaposed with a well-lived-in look. By contrast, when our easy-going neighbour looks over our fence, they see us more like we see the meticulous neighbour. We seem to be forever fiddling with plants and trees, tidying up and controlling the space.

Why the story? In our organisations and between our employees, the same applies. One person's agile is another's command and control, one person's command and control is another's servant leadership. For others, the distinctions do not matter. Indeed, between the organisation's people and relationships, things will get done in a way that could be more efficient, but exist within tolerance. In line with that sentiment, other priorities are the focus. If sales are strong, customers are happy and shareholders are satisfied, who cares if leadership means being visionary or not?

'That's Mars – and if you look over there, that's Agile.'

Why don't we stop?

If you assume that we discover (or otherwise admit to ourselves) that what we are doing is, at best, inefficient, why do we carry on? Consider a recent client that had spent millions adopting new ideas, going so far as to mandate the change. Despite new ways of working being less effective and teams needing to work around a variety of problems, the leadership response was to double down, to do more of the thing that was not working.

The answer could be lazily summed up as 'human nature' – but that is a very large suitcase indeed. Rather than attempt to unpack it all, I will cover three repeating themes and return with more about humans in the later Teams and Change chapters.

Theme 1: 'Phew! It's not my fault'

> *[Most people] prefer to be coaxed or wheedled, or even driven. That way they never make a mistake: if there is one, it's anyways due to something or somebody else.*
>
> — JOHN WYNDHAM, *DAY OF THE TRIFFIDS*, 1951

Consciously chosen or not, many of the reasons above provide an opportunity to transfer responsibility in the event of failure. That is an attractive prospect when put up against our embarrassment, dented ego and risk to reputation. Take the famous phrase in the IT industry that 'Nobody ever got fired for buying IBM' as illustration. Being able to say, 'I chose IBM because of their reputation, pedigree, etc' is a safe, risk-averse and defensible position. The alternative is to accept the vulnerability that, even if the choice is a better fit, it will still be questioned. Sure, you can choose Linux for your desktops, but why did you decide to move away from Microsoft? This certainly is not limited to IT providers either, and we could replace IBM and Microsoft with many others: McKinsey, Deloitte, PwC, Ernst & Young, Bain & Company, so on.

Similar to the supplier benefit of certifications, providers enjoy the dependable status that this deference bestows. What is more, deploying a little FUD (fear, uncertainty and doubt) can quickly nudge a wavering customer back to your arms: 'Yes, you could use the other provider, and they're much cheaper. I really don't know what they compromise on to reach that price.'

In our private lives too, that ability to depend on a brand continues. Given a binary choice, I doubt I am alone in a preference for 'Durex Extra Safe' over a price-reduced bag of budget condoms.

This also relates closely to the discussion about followership in Chapter 2. Unlike for our prehistoric relatives, the consequence for choosing your own path at work is not a death sentence. However, trailblazing puts you in a vulnerable state compared with following the pack: even assuming that you can attract followers, you lose the protection of the wider group and miss opportunities to learn from other leaders.

Theme 2: 'We can't (or I don't want to) go back'

Once we have made a decision about a direction – especially where we have sold the option as the right choice – it takes courage and humility to admit a mistake. Imagine that you are the decision-maker who has driven a radical restructure of your organisation. You are convinced that your high management headcount is slowing down decision making, preventing teams from doing their best work, and – to add insult to injury – costing you a good slice of your budget. Accordingly, the change will remove 250 management roles to flatten the hierarchy, and by making half of that total redundant, will redirect salary budget into service and development. Three gruelling months later, much of the employee-relations part is over and you can put your full energy into supporting the teams and tuning workflows to suit the new layout. Job done.

However, by month six, the wheels are coming off. Your vehement position that 'We don't need all these managers!' turned out not to be a smart choice, and performance is obviously suffering. Teams are not self-organising as you thought they might be, customers and peers are complaining and the few managers remaining are swamped. Morale is low, in part because of the loss of colleagues, and also ongoing confusion about how to operate. Being called by the board to discuss what will happen now, do you maintain support for your decision despite the evidence? Do you admit that things are not working out and attempt to reverse the change? Or do you stall and fade into the background until the waves calm down?

In my experience, the second of these – to attempt reversal of the changes – is the least likely. Instead, we might conclude that we just did not go far enough (think Liz Truss),[88] or that we just need further investment to secure the advantages that we were seeking. This idea of throwing good money after bad – to convince ourselves and others that we should not cut our losses, but rather keep going – is a well-studied social motivation.

Known best as the 'sunk-cost fallacy', a simple example comes from its alternative name: the Concorde fallacy.[89] In brief, despite the failing economic case, the British and French governments continued to pump money into the continuation of the jet's use because of the money already invested. A related consideration here is tied up in our ego, and pride in the things that we have created: the IKEA effect. In a study carried out by the Harvard Business School – 'The IKEA Effect: When labor leads to love' – one group of participants was asked to construct some IKEA furniture and then place a value on it.[90] A second group was given a pre-built version and similarly asked to consider its worth. The study team found that those who had built their own furniture both valued the result at a higher price and were more motivated to purchase it.

It is a fascinating consideration in our organisations: it implies that if we have had a hand in the creation of an initiative, we are more inclined to invest in and maintain it, even if it fails. I have observed many times a leader developing an emotional attachment to their new initiative, protecting it vehemently against critical data and reality.

Theme 3: 'No, boss, there's nothing wrong'

Returning to Hans Christian Andersen's story of 'The Emperor's New Clothes', in our organisations, there are constant opportunities to be unknowingly naked.* Our policy change, sales strategy or otherwise might be failing, but we will still find people deferring to the leader's wisdom. Continuing to say 'Yes' and 'Carry on' prolongs the false sense of security and the confidence held in that position. Soon we are massaging reports and data to show that everything is wonderful, and a cultural norm develops. 'Why didn't you tell me?' is a challenging question to answer, so we avoid situations where we could get asked.

---

* For reference, if you are *knowingly* naked, that probably constitutes some sort of disciplinary breach.

One client's metaphor exemplifies this: 'We have watermelons everywhere here – green on the outside, red on the inside.' Indeed, to tell the leader that they are naked not only makes that leader appear foolish, but it also casts a revealing light on every other person who said nothing. Worse still, like the emperor, the longer the subterfuge goes on, the harder it becomes to break the cycle – the harder it becomes to admit, even to ourselves, that we were wrong.

What does that all mean for us?

Bringing all of that together, this is the situation that we find ourselves in:

- There is no single practice or leadership style that works in all circumstances.
- Degrees of success for any practice or style directly relate to context.
- Contexts change, and sometimes unpredictably so.
- Even when we achieve success, it is difficult – if not impossible – to attribute that success to our chosen practice or style.

> *Even when we achieve success, it is difficult – if not impossible – to attribute that success to our chosen practice or style.*

Cripes. That is a pretty inconvenient conclusion to reach – especially for all those people peddling practices. Unaware of this, or even despite it, many organisations will choose to follow the route of doctrine, and it would be disingenuous of me to suggest that they would achieve no results at all. A leaking bucket can still hold water and people employed to do a job will do their best, no matter how unhelpful the environment. Work will get done, sales will be won, services will be built and customers will be served. There might even be efficiencies gained through commonality of language and a uniform sense of identity. Recall Musk's 2023 purchase of Twitter (now X) that, despite sweeping changes and predictions of self-destruction is still operating. Would it be faring better without Musk's intervention? It is impossible to know.

And so we have two options from here. Option one is to put this book down now, forget all about context and talk to one of the companies out there that will tell you that they have the answer. Please go ahead. Attend their training, get certified and hire their consultants. If you find out that things are going wrong, I have even prepared some excuses in the previous sections that you can share with your executive team. Option two, however, is to embrace the reality that the notion of a singular and correct path for our leadership and practice is fundamentally flawed. From that perspective, I invite you to join me for a look at what we might do about it in Part II of this book.

What follows is a collection of ideas, prompts and techniques relating to leadership, strategy, delivery, teams and change. These are a convenient grouping, rather than a formula to use, and can be used as component parts however you wish. Thus, in 'Delivery, delivery, delivery', for example, you will find content that is applicable in other areas. My hope is that with a wide palette of choices for you to dip into, mix and adapt, you can take your team and organisation to new heights.

PART II

A credible alternative

CHAPTER 4

The sense-making leader

'Nothing has meaning without its context. Meaning doesn't exist.'

— F<small>RITZ</small> P<small>ERLS</small>[1]

In this chapter, I am going to look again at leadership, think further about context and explore the essential skill of sense-making. Sense-making – literally, to make sense of events and situations around us – is crucial for our ability to make contextual choices, and therefore underpins everything else that we might intend.

> *There are two fundamental vectors of influence that you can exercise as a leader: the results you achieve for stakeholders and the environment that your teams work in while achieving them.*

Before I dive into that, however, I will begin with a general and simplified principle. There are two fundamental vectors of influence that you can exercise as a leader: the *results* you achieve for stakeholders and the *environment* that your teams work in while achieving them (see Figure 4-1).

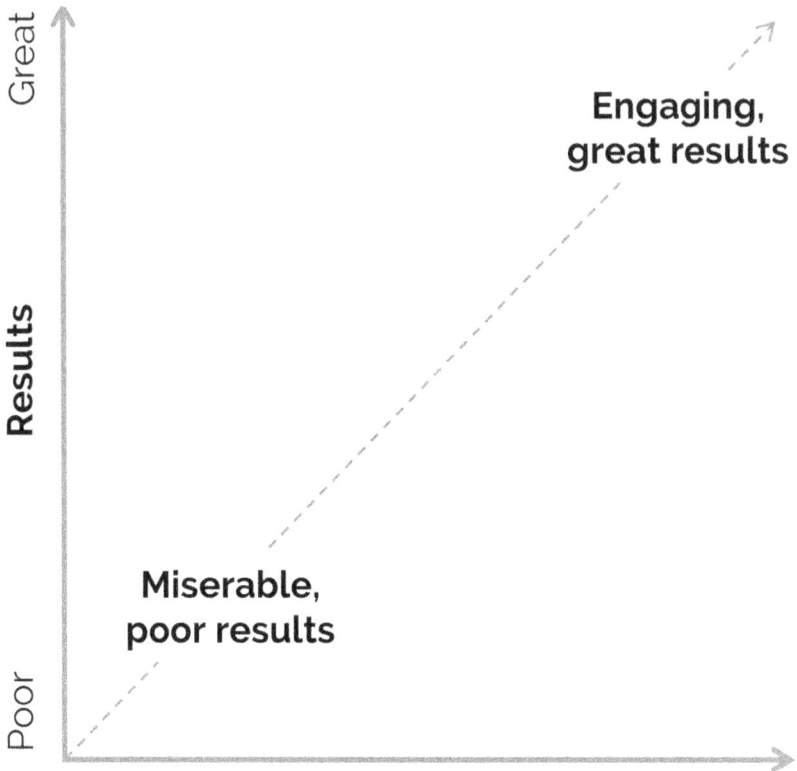

Figure 4-1. The axes of management influence

An ideal position (top right) is one where we achieve great results in an environment that is appreciated by our people. In other words, our customers and stakeholders are happy and satisfied with our work, and our teams are engaged and fulfilled. The opposite in the bottom left – no results and miserable people – is clearly something to be avoided. It is worth briefly considering the other corners too. In the top left, achieving amazing results for our customers, but forcing our people to work to exhaustion for results, is unsustainable and may erode trust and loyalty, pushing staff to leave. Finally, in the bottom right, we may create a broadly engaged and contented team, but without meaningful results for our stakeholders we risk wider commercial problems.

As a leader, you have a key role in balancing these forces using the many variables at your disposal. It is not an easy task, and the styles and practices you choose can both drive and prevent progress. Consider a large mixing desk in a music studio. When a song is being recorded, an engineer adjusts the volume of individual instruments in relation to each other and, in doing so, changes the sound and feel of the end result. Turning up the volume of the drums or bass will inevitably influence other instruments, ideally accentuating them, but at times drowning them out completely. The goal is to achieve balance, and for any given piece of music there will be many mixes available: a few great, many good and others awful.

When we are leading and organising teams, we have many choices about which elements we increase or decrease to adjust the mix. The agile framework called Scrum, for example, is based around five core events:[2]

- The sprint: A set and repeating period of time, typically two weeks, where work gets done.
- Sprint planning: A session at the start of the sprint to decide what the team will work on.
- Daily scrum: An opportunity for the team to check on progress and impediments.
- Sprint review: A session at the end of the sprint to examine value delivered.
- Sprint retrospective: A session at the end of the sprint for the team to examine how they operated and seek improvements.

If we push up the volume on the 'sprint review' to focus attention on the value we create, for example by increasing attendance from customers and interested stakeholders, we should influence planning and prioritisation. That could be important. However, that same spotlight may also cause stress and delay the achievement of internal aims. Similarly, considering a description of authentic leadership with ten 'must-have-attributes', changing the balance between 'listening', 'transparency' and 'lead with heart' will have its own effect. Indeed, I have experienced people becoming so impassioned in leading with heart that they stop listening altogether! Returning to our sound desk, a well-mixed song balances its components for a pleasing result. An effective team is likewise one of the successful combinations of the many possibilities available.

The key questions then are how we identify which sliders to move on our mixing desk and how we detect a result if we do. Before I get to that, however, it is important to dive much deeper into context.

'I can report that Sprint reviews are both improving and worsening our planning and prioritisation'

The criticality of context

Context is broadly defined as: 'the situation within which something exists or happens, and that can help explain it'.[3] As a simple example, and ignoring air resistance or unintentional forces, a cannon-ball dropped from a tower will fall vertically down until it hits the ground. However, if we repeated that action on the International Space Station, the same ball would now 'float' in a stationary position once released.* The behaviour of the cannon ball has been modified by its context.

In Chapter 2, we saw how the Cynefin framework describes environment in terms of predictable and non-predictable contexts, which affect the results we get from the choices we make on how to act. But is that environmental context all we need to think about? What do we *really* understand about the situation that our people, teams and organisations are in? What do we know about how those people are feeling, their experience or knowledge as they enter that situation? Will their starting point be the same today as it was yesterday, or might be tomorrow?

The book *Exploring Context in Information Behavior* illustrates this well, highlighting 15 distinct types of context.[4] For example, we might consider context as discourse, with our thoughts impacted by what we have been discussing and have heard to this point. We may think of context as the person's mind itself, and the state in which they arrive at the conversation. These frames of reference and understanding overlap and intertwine creating a complex, unpredictable starting point, well beyond our environment. A simple game that you can try at home or in a small group can demonstrate.

First, choose an animal and then ask everyone in your group to imagine it for a few moments. For example, 'Imagine a dog', 'Imagine a horse', or 'Imagine a lion'. Next, and one at a time, ask each person to describe what they pictured to everyone else. What you will quickly find is that each person pictures something different, and some of the answers can seem a long way from what you expect.

---

* For accuracy, the ball would not float, rather it would perpetually fall around the earth due to its orbital velocity.

A recent 'Imagine an elephant' exercise I ran yielded these responses:

Person 1: A grey elephant spraying water with its trunk.

Person 2: A family of elephants in desert of orange sand.

Person 3: Sadness.

Person 4: A large bull elephant looking at me straight on.

Person 5: A baby elephant holding its mum's tail as they walk along.

Person 6: The animated Dumbo from the new film.

Here the context of the person's mind, along with their experiences and understandings, joins with any information that is to hand to produce an answer. Had someone in the group been looking at elephants in a zoo before the exercise, I would expect their answer to be influenced by that experience.* For another example, take ten seconds and look at the photograph of the child's very muddy hands opposite (Figure 4-2). Once you have done that, turn over the page.

---

* When my mother thinks of elephants, she will recall a trip to India, or a family-famous story from when we were children when an elephant reached over a fence and took my brother's sou'wester.

Figure 4-2. Photograph of a child's very muddy hands

Look at this word. What is the missing letter?

SO_P

In the times that I have run this exercise, the overwhelming answer is 'A' (giving soap), with very few opting for 'U' (for soup). Repeating the test with a photo of a bowl and spoon, the opposite is true, and we get more soup than soap. What we are doing in this example is priming the participants with some information so that they are more likely to pick a certain answer. This is an extremely common trick in magic, film and marketing, where we aim to influence a person's context with cues or nudges.

Another more serious example of context, in this case context as a role, is the infamous 1971 Stanford prison experiment, led by Stanford psychology professor Philip Zimbardo.[5] The experiment was intended to be a psychological study of prison simulated life over two weeks. An advert offering $15 per day to recruit 18 men was placed and the selected volunteers were then randomly assigned prisoner or guard roles. Guards were given military-style uniforms, a set of instructions (notably that they must not hit the prisoners, but should aim to create feelings of fear and powerlessness) and the role of preventing the prisoners from escaping. The prisoners meanwhile were picked up from their houses by local police, handcuffed and taken in cars to the local police station. There they were given fake charges, fingerprinted and then blindfolded for transit to the experimental prison. On arrival they were stripped, deloused, dressed in plain fatigues, allocated a prisoner number, chained by one leg and then locked in cells. If that already sounds horrific, the experiment was stopped less than half-way through following the devastating effects of the psychological abuse carried out and incited by the guards. To give a sense of what this involved, their actions included removal of beds, hot meals and toilet privileges, solitary isolation and a continuous dehumanisation by use of prisoner numbers only.

In 2002, the psychologists Alex Haslam and Steve Reicher created a similar experiment. The study developed from an interest in themes of tyranny and resistance and aimed to explore the social and mental effects on people assigned to groups of differing power.[6] It was televised by the BBC and, like the Stanford experiment, a mock prison with guards and prisoners was constructed. Over the course of eight days, the play for power and influence twisted and turned. The groups went through conflicts, rebellions, changes in roles, the establishment of a new order and the creation of a commune spanning both the prisoners and guards. Ultimately, as a move towards a strong authoritarian and military-like order started to take hold, the experiment was again stopped by the researchers.

While the Stanford experiment continues to be described as one of the most unethical in history, both it and the BBC prison study have contributed to our understanding of group dynamics and the question of why people behave as they do in context. We will come back to group identity again in Chapter 7 but, for now, we can see in both studies how behaviour develops from context in a way that seemed implausible before the experiments began.

A leader is often portrayed as different, even elite. We saw this in Chapter 1 and we see it again in the expectations around guard-to-prisoner relationships. Indeed, when I first took a management position, the first conversation I had with my boss went something like this: 'Don't expect people to like you. Don't try to be one of the team. Focus on your goals and make sure everyone else is too.' Heartening, it was not, but plenty of publications still support those ideas. *The Harvard Business Review*'s bluntly titled 'You're a Leader Now. Not Everyone is Going to Like You' or their '5 Things That Change When You Become a Leader' are two such examples.[7]

The point is that no matter how meticulously you have thought about your environment, the variables that can come from the people, their relationships and feelings towards one another, will sometimes trip you up. Imagine that we have decided, because of a changeable and high-speed market, to use more complex-appropriate approaches under the philosophy of systems and enablement. Those involved have been encouraged to self-organise and use frameworks with limited governance so that they can adapt more quickly to change. Moreover, we have actively connected the team with stakeholders and have told them they are fully empowered in terms of strategy, decision-making and final product scope. On paper, this appears reasonable, but we have addressed no other context than environment. Do the individuals we select for the team have the skill, experience or capability to work in a self-organised team? Will common patterns of behaviour in the organisation – for example, hierarchical habits – impede the progress of the team despite what they were told? Does the team understand the same thing about the approach being used or what they have been empowered to do? Has the team spent any time discussing these questions together or with the people who have empowered them?

> *Saying that a team is self-organising . . . is categorically not the same as having that self-organising team available and effective with the click of your fingers.*

Saying that a team is self-organising, even if we determine that it is a good option for a situation, is categorically not the same as having that self-organising team available and effective with the click of your fingers. In reality, creating the structures, skills and space needed to make this happen is a perpetual and ever-present task for any such team. As a thought experiment, can you imagine the confusion and loss in productivity caused if an entire organisation were told that it should now be self-organising, without any understanding of what that means or how people might execute upon it? That it should flatten its structure like Spotify. Thank goodness that kind of thing never happens in the real world, and it is not the kind of thing recommended by large consultancies.

What is sense-making?

To work with the contexts that affect us – to discover them and consider what to do next – we can make use of sense-making concepts. Sense-making, a term initially used by Karl Weick, is an idea in social psychology for how we organise with the information and perceptions we have available.[8]

There are many papers that discuss sense-making, and while I intend to demonstrate that the ideas can be transformative in teams and organisations, much that is published should come with a language health-warning. Terms can include scientific and philosophical definitions which, while accurate, are not always accessible. For instance, epistemology (what people know, and what it means that they know it?) and deontological pluralism (how we determine what is ethical) are interesting in the context of sense-making, but less easily applied. If you are more scientifically-minded, Matteo Cristofaro gets to the core with his superb systematic review of 402 organisational sense-making papers, but I will attempt to be more down-to-earth.[9]

Sense-making is not something new or inaccessible and is something that we naturally do. Sense-making helps us to engage with others in our environment, and in our past, present and future realities, to decide on our actions. In other words, we gain a better understanding of the landscape, and going back to our sound desk, it helps to reveal and then monitor the sliders available as they are moved up and down.

Individually we all sense-make. When we are lost in a city, we look for landmarks and information to help us work out which way to go. When we consider a party to vote for, we use a combination of beliefs and facts to weigh our choices. Playing chess, we consider the situation on the board, the potential moves, and even moderate our approach based on our understanding of our opponent's ability.

However, the power of sense-making as a discipline comes from discussion in groups, or the collation of separate data and conversations. By drawing in facts and viewpoints and by observing and discussing contrasts, we can organise that thinking into a consensus of understanding – as Weick alluded – and choose a next action. The result will never be a deterministic, perfect and detailed description of everything, but an invaluable shared exploration of perspectives.

To aid this intention, many sense-making tools and 'frames' exist that lightly constrain discussions to allow progress. Frameworks may include minimal rules. However, with experience, you will quickly learn their use and be able to create your own frames to work with. Following are examples of frames and a walkthrough using Cynefin.

My recommendation is to attempt a few exercises with your team or a group of peers and observe what happens for future use.

A few general notes about sense-making tools and frameworks

- Every situation will be different, and the discussions, outcomes and insights found are often unpredictable. Hearing phrases like 'I didn't realise that!' or 'I didn't understand what it meant for you' is common in these exercises.
- A single discussion with one frame may be sufficient or it may reveal a

need for a different perspective. That could require additional stake-holder views or the use of different frames.

- Results will not be perfect descriptions of reality. Even if you could achieve that feat, the movement in our people and organisations would quickly make conclusions inaccurate. Therefore, a principle of diminishing returns applies, and unless there are significant open concerns, you should halt the sense-making and pick it up again later if needed.
- Discussions in sense-making exercises are extremely useful, but not always comfortable, especially if strong, differing opinions are found.

Sense-making frames

The following are examples of sense-making frames, organised for ease into some broad categories. All frames can be used and adapted for multiple circumstances. If you are unfamiliar with any of the names, details can be readily found by searching online.

Frames that relatively compare A with B and with (n)

- Relatively positioning items on a linear scale (importance, value, cost, urgency, impact or similar)
- A two-axis plot, for example an Eisenhower matrix
- A three- or more-pointed shape to plot information

Frames that consider events or activities in time or priority

- A project plan
- A project evaluation and review technique (PERT) chart or other dependency map
- Value chain mapping
- A story map

Frames that examine situational context

- Cynefin (David Snowden)
- Confluence (Cynthia Kurtz)
- Agreement and Certainty Matrix (Ralph Stacey)
- Wardley Mapping (Simon Wardley)

Frames that encourage targeted reflection

- A retrospective
- Ecocycle planning (Liberating Structures)
- A value status check (sprint review, quarterly progress review)
- A project lessons-learned event

Frames that examine relationships and understandings

- What I need from you (Liberating Structures)
- A human network map (who works with whom and how information flows)
- The clean-language elephant game (with your subject replacing the elephant)
- Six Thinking Hats (Edward de Bono)

Frames that consider potential futures

- Future Backwards (David Snowden)
- Celebration-5W (Agendashift)
- Crazy 8s (design sprints)

Sense-making in practice

To illustrate using such frames, imagine that we are deciding on the future of a product development function in our organisation. The basic flow could be:

1. Pick a high-level description or theme for the discussion – for example, product development.
2 Run an initial sense-making exercise using a frame. For example, to consider potential good and bad futures for product development, and what events might take us there, the Future Backwards frame would be a great start.
3. Consider and discuss the results to decide on next steps.
4. If needed, run a second sense-making exercise using a different frame – for example, Cynefin.
5. Consider and discuss the results and decide on next steps.
6. If needed, run a third sense-making exercise, and so on.

In the first step, the description sets the scene for what you will be discussing, and that choice requires some thought. If the description is set as something broad, participants will be free to think openly and share their own varying perspectives. By contrast, finely targeting the description will do the opposite and restrict conversation and potential topics of discussion.

Consider the range of options in Figure 4-3, with product development in the middle of the list as an example.

High-level
description

Our organisation
Our current and future organisation
Our products
Product development
Development of Product X
Development of Product X next year
Development of Product X, Component Y

Low-level
description

Figure 4-3. Levels of description for a sense-making discussion

Starting with 'Product Development' I would expect elements like product scope, quality, delivery practices and approaches, team organisation, product inter-operation and customer engagement to come up. By contrast, setting the theme to 'Our current and future organisation' could still identify those themes, but the conversation is now wide open to other concerns across our company.

Going in the other direction to the 'Development of Product X next year' narrows the field of discussion. I would now expect to only focus on the ambition for that product and the more practical aspects of delivery: budgets, people, process, technology and tools. This is why the choice requires some thought. Too broad and conversation could end up a long way from what you want to discuss, and too narrow can prevent useful ideas being shared. For instance, if someone had an idea for cutting delivery costs across all products, but the discussion was fixed to a component, they may not speak up or be listened to in that forum.

Thus, as a rule of thumb, aim to set the theme at the highest level you can without losing the identity of the thing you are discussing. Doing so encourages wider and more diverse contributions, and from my experience, this is the area where hidden insights and assumptions are most found.

Let us assume that one of the outputs from the first discussion was a decision to prioritise the launch of a new product to market. To make sense of the work involved and which approach to take, we have created a list of the main components and actions that we know about (some intended, some unplanned):

New product launch actions and issues

1. Book reception venue
2. Define success metrics
3. Harry the developer has quit!
4. Schedule social media posts
5. Decide pricing strategy
6. Test customer experience
7. Database performance problem
8. Execute social media campaign
9. Search engine optimisation
10. Publish product information
11. Invite customers
12. Train the sales team
13. Update products on our customer relationship system
14. Complete front-page design
15. Document launch strategy
16. Update website content
17. Obtain executive approval
18. Order banners and posters

In discussion, the 18 product launch actions are considered using a Cynefin frame, plotting items according to their predictability, into areas of clear, complicated, complex, chaotic and confused. To plot them, we start with the extremes (most complex, most complicated, and so on), and then the remaining actions are plotted relatively to those. Only once complete are the dividing lines added to produce a picture of the situation (Figure 4-4). In this diagram, numbers are used for reasons of space on the page. In practice, sticky-notes or cards are used on the framework so all of the information is to hand.

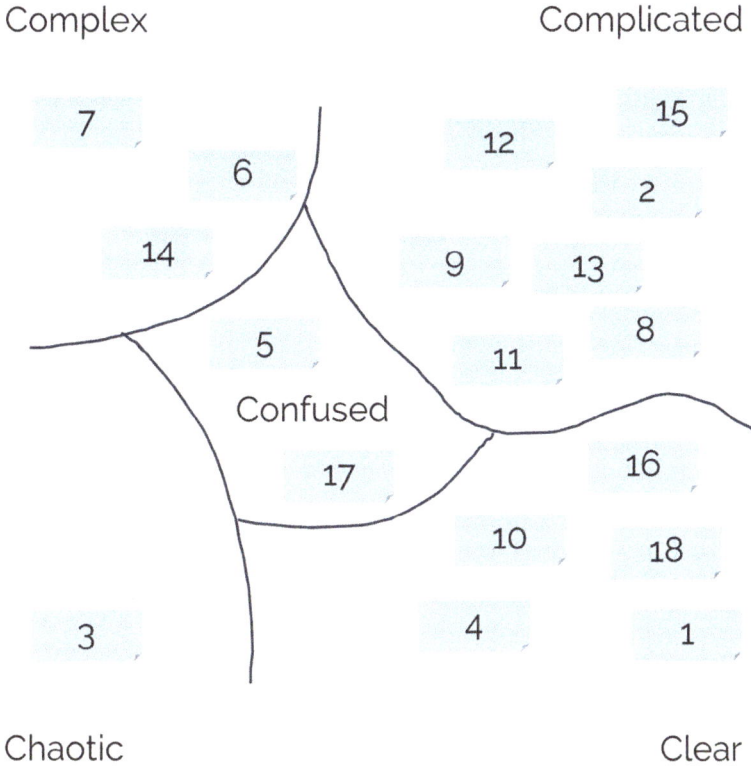

Figure 4-4. Cynefin diagram for the product launch example

What does this tell us? First, we have more tasks on the right (in other words, predictable) than on the left. That offers an insight into how we might plan our work. We can also see that there is one chaotic item, relating to a developer quitting, and that needs some immediate action. For the complex items where we cannot plan accurately, we need to think in terms of experiments and trials, and finally for the centre, a conversation with the executives involved seems appropriate to clarify pricing strategy and obtain the necessary executive approval.

Now imagine that a second group carried out the same exercise. It is unlikely that its views will be identical, and so we could see a different result (Figure 4-5). This group has interpreted the situation as being more unpredictable, with most items in the complex domain. This implies that there is more uncertainty in the launch, and that we should organise ourselves accordingly.

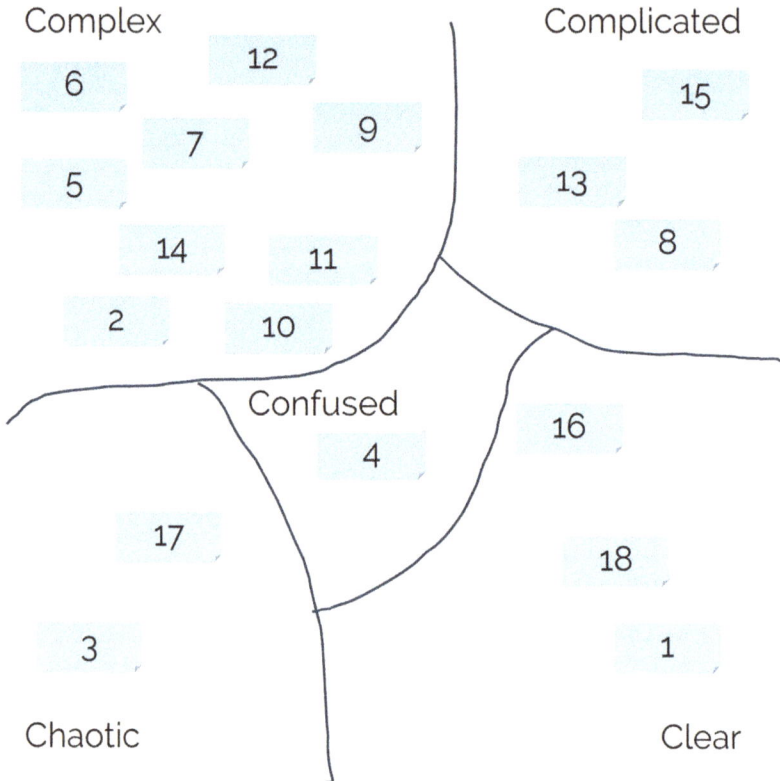

Figure 4-5. Second Cynefin diagram for the product launch example

Which perspective is accurate? We cannot answer that question, but what we can do is to discuss the results together, and this is where much of the potential in sense-making emerges. By talking about why a task is considered differently, a deeper and shared understanding of the situation can be achieved. Moreover, by merging the perspectives, the overall picture created is likely to be much more accurate. Thus, the insight we generate gives us a good steer for decisions, strategy and policy.

Relatively speaking

In this example using the Cynefin frame, items have been positioned relatively. This technique is invaluable. Say that we have 100 marbles, and we sort them into four fixed quadrants based on their size. Dividing them, we discover that 85 of the marbles end up in the top right quadrant, with 5 in each of the others.

That might be interesting, but if we change the frame to the classic Eisenhower matrix (categorising tasks according to their urgency and importance), and we discover that 85 of our tasks are both urgent and important, it could be an extraordinarily long day! A better choice would be to repeat the exercise, but this time to plot items *relative* to each other. The most extreme top right item is our must-get-done-now action. All the others relatively positioned to it give us a good sense of what needs to happen once that is complete or we have the space to look at a second item (Figure 4-6).

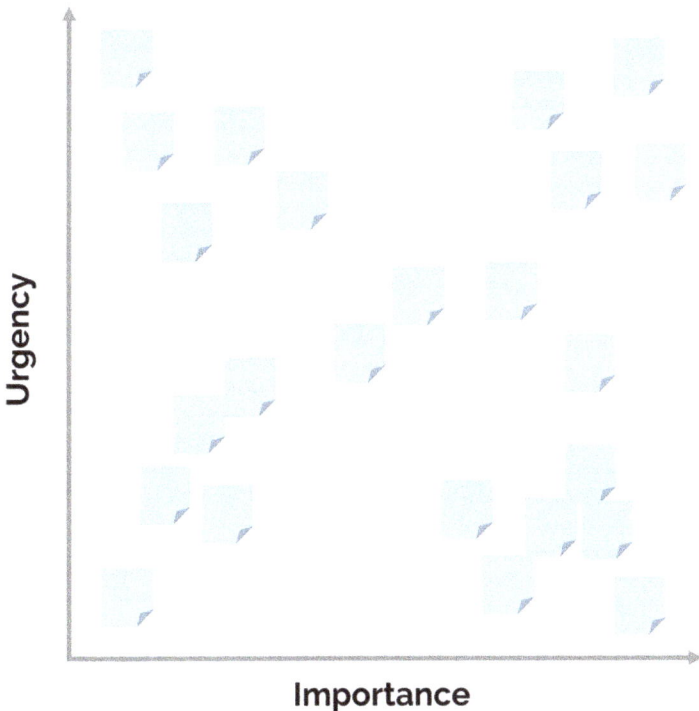

Figure 4-6. Assessing the relative urgency and importance of tasks using an Eisenhower priority matrix

There are no restrictions on the labels or number of axes* you might use for such an exercise, and I have only briefly modelled Cynefin and the Eisenhower matrix. As an example of a three-axis frame, consider a decision about which policies we might use to engage and motivate teams. Plotting them on a three-axis frame of things that might encourage self-governance (autonomy), deep learning (mastery) or a connection to why (purpose), we can learn more about which options to choose (Figure 4-7).

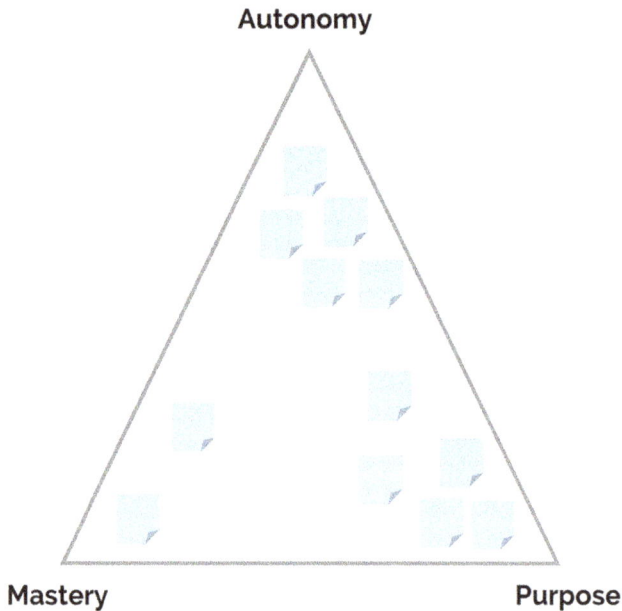

Figure 4-7. Assessing the potential of actions to increase motivation against autonomy, mastery and purpose

Who should make sense?

Finally, I would like to consider who should join a discussion like this. You can benefit from using any of these frames on your own, however, given our

---

* Note that more than three axes can be hard for participants to complete. Excluding decisions about relative positioning, a two-axis frame has three choices – A, B or both – and a three-axis frame increases the number to seven.

difficulty in agreeing exactly what an elephant is, the real power of sense-making comes in when you work in a group and compare multiple perspectives.

> *Given our difficulty in agreeing exactly what an elephant is, the real power of sense-making comes in when you work in a group.*

To bring those together, review the stakeholders for the theme you are interested in. For the product development item above, we might include development teams, product managers, customers, finance, leadership, sales and operations. Each of these stakeholders and stakeholder groups will have a unique perspective on product development, and the collection of their perspectives could be very insightful. With limited resources, there is clearly a balance to be struck between the cost of gaining additional opinions and the value of that potential insight, but you cannot predict how conversations will go. Open themes can become very narrow through discussion (or vice versa), so keep the door open to further exercises with other audiences whenever you can.

To increase the value of working with a diverse group of stakeholders, do not mix stakeholder groups together, where possible. That is, if you have sufficient people, keep the customers, finance or sales people separate until their perceptions are recorded. This can feel contrary to ambitions about 'breaking down barriers', but it is worth it.* Keeping the initial conversations partisan preserves those differing perspectives until you are ready to interpret the results. Only once you have captured those different views do you come together as a diverse team to discuss and explore why opinions may not align.

In contrast, if you mix the different stakeholders together early on, it tends to promote interpretation and efforts to persuade others in the small group discussions. Ideas and perspectives get filtered out and compromises are

---

* Every non-mixed group has commented afterwards about how useful that was, even if sceptical in advance. You may need to persuade people to try it and reserve judgement until then.

adopted too early in the process. I have also experienced many times that if a senior leader meets with different working groups, those teams share different and more carefully curated information.

As a rule of thumb, always aim to generate insights in partisan groups during the data gathering stage – subject-aligned, role-aligned, seniority-aligned and so on – so that you capture as much insight as possible.

Sense-making and decisions

Making effective and context-relevant choices is one of the core reasons to use sense-making in the first place. There is plenty written about the art or science of decision-making. However, in context of this chapter, let us examine two decisions against the major domains of Cynefin:

- Choosing when to restock the coffee.
- Picking a new organisational structure.

First, and as a recap, let us look at the kinds of decisions that we might place in those domains.

- Clear: Simple decisions, for which there is an obvious answer, like following a known process to resolve a problem, or whether to switch the lights off when leaving an office.
- Complicated: More difficult decisions that have more than one credible option, like a choice of hardware supplier or the layout of a new office space.
- Complex: Opaque decisions, at least in terms of knock-on effects, like moving offices to a new city or committing to an acquisition.
- Chaotic: Urgent decisions, like the response to a cyber-attack, critical press enquiry or office fire.

No doubt you will have already forged an opinion about which of those two decisions go where. The choice of when to restock the coffee is undoubtedly in the clear domain. There is a clear answer, and a convincing case for an autocratic – even 'JFDI' – response. Consulting around the organisation, or seeking wide consent would create delays and waste, and risking a coffee drought could have devastating ramifications for local productivity. At the other end of the scale, choosing a new organisational structure is firmly in the complex domain and is better suited to a consultative and experimental response. Arbitrarily and autocratically making such a wide-reaching decision could cause long-lasting consequences, where as engaging with those people involved is more likely to yield refinement and support for the ultimate organisational design.

Finally, a word about decision timing. Deciding early removes uncertainty and allows people to get on with the next activity, but a rushed decision can have its own fair share of adverse consequences, especially if it turns out to be a poor choice. To find the balance, you may have already come across the concept of the 'last responsible moment'.[10] The idea, often cited by agile coaches, is that there is a theoretical and *perfect* point between rushing and uncertainty. That is, we decide with enough information to be accurate, and our teams never stop work because of a delay. While this is a nice mental model, I think it is practically flawed. Decisions in organisations are often complex due to the people, hierarchies and processes involved, so an attempt at precision is inevitably guesswork.

Perhaps Jeff Bezos's wisdom on this is more practical. In his 2016 letter to Amazon shareholders, he included a perspective that: 'Most decisions should probably be made with somewhere around 70% of the information you wish you had. If you wait for 90%, in most cases, you're probably being slow.'[11] 'Probably' being the operative word, as we can never know what would have happened with a different choice. We do not have a control to measure our decision against, and even if we reverse a mistake, it does not reset the space-time continuum. People will still remember, and impact will have been made.

Chapter summary

Context is fundamental to everything we attempt, whether we choose to understand and adapt, or risk the success of our actions in spite of it. To discover and work with your specific contexts, sense-making frames and discussions facilitate interpretation, and thus choice of situation-appropriate action.

- There are two fundamental areas of influence in teams: the *results* you achieve for stakeholders and the *environment* people work in while achieving them.
- To exercise influence, think of a mixing desk. Try things out to adjust the sliders, increasing and decreasing the effects of different components. Many combinations will yield results – some will be great, others not.
- An understanding of which sliders are available, and an ability to see their effect, comes from awareness of context through sense-making.
- Context can take many forms, from the predictability of a situation to the mood, skill and relationships between individuals. Each exerts influence on the actions we can take and their results.
- Sense-making is an innate skill, and the frameworks we choose will help guide the flow of conversation.
- Sense-making activities are more valuable when they are undertaken with homogenous groups of similar stakeholders. Somewhat surprisingly, this method reliably highlights different opinions and beliefs, resulting in a shared and more comprehensive understanding.
- Sense-making discussions centred around broad topics invite wide-ranging and creative perspectives. Narrow topics do the opposite, allowing discussion to go deeper into the chosen subject.
- More than one – even several – sense-making exercises may be needed to get to grips with a situation. Early discussions often lead to new questions or open the door to participation from other groups, so keep your eyes open!

CHAPTER 5

Direction and strategy

'Even William Tell would miss a target he knew nothing about.'

— STEPHEN E. MORRIS

A sense of direction

We turn now to direction and strategy. Both concepts, on the surface, are simple. Direction is where we are going, and strategy describes how we intend to get there. However, the breadth of related labels that we use, and their nested nature complicates the picture.

Consider this list of concepts: mission, strategy, plan, method, outcome, vision, purpose, goal, objective, tactic, policy, approach and output. Now add one of these terms alongside – organisational, sales, marketing, technical, product or finance. Bearing in mind that we cannot agree on what an elephant is, do you read those words or phrases with clarity about what they mean and how they apply in your organisation? My assertion, and not a controversial one, is that no matter what you call these things, teams with access to where we are intending to go and how we plan to get there have an advantage.

Knowing our direction can:

- Align efforts and focus delivery
- Make it easier for people to make decisions in context
- Allow for autonomy and ownership behaviours
- Help us spot when we are moving the wrong way
- Support and cement group identities and a sense of team

During the early stages of the Covid-19 pandemic, I witnessed a good example of this with an on-site user support group in a large organisation. It was the spring of 2020, as the first lockdown was beginning, and the IT team was under pressure to deliver continuity of services and provide answers and decisions about how people would be able to work. Users tend to have an expectation that laptops, phones, email and connectivity will always be available.* Indeed, when they stop working, escalations and complaints can be fast and unfriendly until service is resumed.

The team responded with a rapid change in priorities and a singular focus to keep things working. Other tasks were deferred while remote-access systems were bolstered to help remote workers, online collaboration platforms were fast-tracked, and engineers experimented with methods to onboard new staff and service the machines of existing employees. The energy and drive were palpable, and many staff continued to work beyond their normal hours to design and implement novel ideas to help their colleagues. Within only a few weeks this global organisation had effective methods of remote operation that had not previously existed. Understandably, the IT support team were praised and lauded for their quick action, innovation and customer care. Moreover, morale went up and teams reported enjoying their work through this period.

In terms of direction and strategy we might describe this as:

- Direction: Keep people working as the pandemic situation evolves.
- Strategy: Divert all effort from other work to find a solution.

The direction was obvious – but other strategies could have been adopted, bearing in mind relevant government guidance. They might have reorganised office space for controlled social distancing, or diverted a small percentage of effort to keeping people working while continuing with existing work, or simply done nothing for several weeks to see what would happen. The clarity of the strategy gave the team boundaries and an environment in which they could act freely to make progress.

Unsurprisingly, most leadership frameworks emphasise a need to do something in this space, to be 'visionary' or 'lead with purpose'. My own framework, *The Open Leader Method*, that I shared in Chapter 2, began with 'Purpose' as part of the Visualise segment. In the remainder of this chapter, I

---

* IT support of this kind is typically a 'hygiene factor' – in other words, like oxygen, its presence is expected and only noticed when absent. From Herzberg's Two-Factor Theory Of Motivation-Hygiene.

will take us through these concepts, starting from vision and strategy before looking at objectives, stakeholders and the all-important task of communicating what we create.

Vision

Vision is a description of where we want to go, assuming we achieve our aims. It could refer to our organisation, our industry, our team, or another group. It sets out a picture or vision of the future. A vision does not need to be precise or inspirational, and it does not describe the plan of how to get somewhere, but it should be good enough for those working towards it. As such, clarity is more important than glitz, and while clever-sounding visions and flowery language are tempting, messages will get lost behind them.

Some examples of visions are:

1. To be the world leader in transportation products and related services.
2. To establish a self-sufficient human colony on the moon by 2050.
3. To organise the world's information and make it universally accessible and useful.
4. A computer on every desk and in every home.
5. To separate the real from the imagined through flight.
6. Shape the future of the internet by creating unprecedented value and opportunity for our customers, employees, investors and ecosystem partners.
7. To build the web's most convenient, secure, cost-effective payment solution.
8. To be earth's most customer-centric company; to build a place where people can come to find and discover anything they might want to buy online.
9. To be the best financial services company in the world. Because of our great heritage and excellent platform, we believe this is within our reach.

Some are clearer and more inspirational than others, and I expect that you recognise which companies a few belong to.*

---

* 1. General Motors, 2. Fictitious, 3. Google, 4. Microsoft (at founding), 5. Armstrong, a NASA project looking into atmospheric flight research, 6. Cisco, 7. PayPal, 8. Amazon, 9. JP Morgan Chase.

Purpose

If the vision is *where* we would like to be (e.g. 'a computer on every desk'), then ther purpose is our *why*, or our *so what?* Unlike the visions above, which are mostly about being a profitable company, purpose can represent a bigger and longer-lasting idea, giving meaning to the actions we are taking.

Some example purpose statements are:

1. In business to save our home planet.
2. To further scientific endeavour, inspire generations, increase the chances of long-term human survival.
3. To better humanity through software and help drive the creation of a socially and economically just world.
4. To kickstart the demise of the disposable cup.
5. To advance the way people live and work.
6. Toward a world in which no child's life is torn apart by war.
7. To discover and spread ideas that spark imagination, embrace possibility and catalyse impact.
8. Nourishing families so they can flourish and thrive.
9. To help people achieve their ambitions.

Once again, you might have recognised a few of them.*

Connecting with vision and purpose

There are some statements above, like 'Toward a world in which no child's life is torn apart by war' for War Child, that I genuinely believe are core to their organisation. Others, however, invite some cynicism and smell of 'purpose washing'. I wonder how often a conversation comes up at the $13-billion-dollar Kellogg company about how nourishing their profit-maximising, ultra-processed products actually are. Likewise, I cannot quite place how a bank like Barclays is actively helping people to achieve their ambitions. Is this idea influential in their decision-making about which products are offered to consumers? Given that it is exceedingly difficult to operate without a bank

---

* 1. Patagonia, 2. NASA, 3. Thoughtworks, 4. KeepCup, 5. HP Enterprise, 6. War Child, 7. TED, 8. Kellogg, 9. Barclays.

account, it feels disingenuous to connect such an essential service with individual ambitions. Of course, I might be wrong and perhaps there are board-level meetings dominated by purposeful conversation, even when it means a hit to profits.

The point is that no matter what we write, a vision and purpose are interpreted. No matter how genuine you might be in your belief about the good you are trying to do, how (and if) that message lands around your organisation is mostly out of your control. To illustrate, when I am working with a new team or group, I will often ask questions like: 'What are you working towards?', 'Why is that important?' and 'Who will benefit from your work?' Answers vary dramatically across and within teams, from detailed links to stakeholder needs to general statements.

Others are unable to answer the questions, as one recent example demonstrates. The team was a delivery group of 15 people, made up of internal staff and external software developers. They had been working together for over a year, producing supply-chain software, and were organised using Scrum. In response to my questions, I received varying answers about stakeholder identities, what the team was trying to do for them and why that mattered. Some people were not sure what stakeholder value was being created, nor for whom, and the clearest description I received was that the team was replacing a manual process. Members of that team could, however, point me to the tasks and cards they were assigned to work on and some suggestions of people who might know more.

Compare that situation to the story of President John F . Kennedy visiting NASA's launch operations centre in Florida in 1962. Kennedy had reportedly asked the janitor what role he was doing at NASA, and instead of the response that we might imagine, the janitor replied, 'Well Mr. President, I'm helping to put a man on the moon.' While that story is likely to be apocryphal, a zeal and national pride was clearly being displayed throughout the 1960s. The idea of winning the space race against the Soviet Union – or rather, the fear of losing it – was central. To beat the Soviets and triumph over the seemingly impossible technical challenges was close to the heart of many Americans. Indeed, in his famous speech on 12 September 1962, Kennedy had attempted to galvanise national support for the programme. The speech cleverly set out the consequences of not winning the race:

No nation which expects to be the leader of other nations can expect to stay behind in the race for space ... We have vowed that we shall not see space filled with weapons of mass destruction, but with instruments of knowledge and understanding.[12]

Kennedy also included the intrinsic value of the challenge itself in the speech, with one of the most quoted lines, being: 'We choose to go to the Moon in this decade and do the other things, not because they are easy, but because they are hard.' It is difficult not to find something in that speech to rouse a nationalist spirit, and that everyone 'down to the janitor' was connected to that outcome is a compelling idea.

This prompts a question: does it matter if a team is unclear about why their work is important? Would it have mattered if the IT team during the pandemic did not know the importance of their work? The answer, unsurprisingly, links to context. With a task-driven team in an ordered, predictable system, we can conclude that a clear understanding of direction is unnecessary to achieving results. The NASA janitor could carry out their given tasks to a set quality and schedule without an awareness of the moon mission. By contrast, a creative or innovative function where tasks are variable and emergent, will be obstructed by a disconnection to a why. Team members will be unable to confidently decide on actions and policies if the aim of the work is unknown.

Outside of those clear extremes, a challenge appears with the myriad of cases in between. My own perspective is that having a team aware of its purpose is more useful than one that is not, and the investment in communication and engagement is not onerous for the return. An awareness of the overall purpose provides context for people in how to contribute, make decisions and respond to others. That awareness might not change the world, but it will smooth progress and prevent a few own goals.

Let's go back to the example of writing software to replace a manual process. If you are not clear about who your stakeholders are and why they need the software, that will limit the chances of people offering ideas and improvements. It will also open the door wide to producing something that no-one really wanted in the first place.

In leadership training we are advised to engage and connect people with *why*. That is logical. We all find extra time and elective effort to put towards a hobby we love. And Friedrich Nietzsche was right when he wrote that 'If a man knows the wherefore of his existence, then the manner of it can take care of itself.' In other words, if we have a why to live for, the how matters much less.[13]

So, let us imagine you want your teams to be aware of your vision and purpose. You carefully create some slides and a narrative that seek to explain it all and plan an all-hands meeting. What are you expecting to happen? It would be amazing if the whole organisation engaged wholeheartedly in your endeavour, but no matter how compelling an idea might seem to you, it will not carry the same weight with everyone. Alongside those connected people, there will be others that only take away the basics and some that will not recall what the purpose of your organisation is at all. Some 42% of UK employees do not know what their organisation's purpose is – even though 86% say that their employer has issued some form of purpose statement.[14]

Even if we put our carefully constructed ideas right in front of someone's nose, it does not mean that anyone else will be interested.

Let us say you run an environmental charity. A staff member who is wholly motivated by those same environmental concerns could be working with you because it chimes so beautifully with their beliefs. Meanwhile, someone else might be fascinated by the technology you use, or just need a job so that they can pay the rent. In other words, even if we put our carefully constructed ideas – those in which we deeply believe – right in front of someone's nose, it does not mean that anyone else will be interested. As the saying goes, 'You can lead a horse to water, but can't make it drink.'

What could go wrong?

Before I move on from vision and purpose, a few words of caution about unintended consequences.

- The NASA story benefits from nostalgia and the success of the mission. Had the mission failed, would we be able to find Kennedy's speech so easily? That was one of many speeches he made in 1962, and one of a great many more during his presidency.[15] Today we might recall a rallying speech, but it is easy to imagine engineers at the Jet Propulsion Laboratory exchanging glances: 'He's just committed us to what, exactly?' We also seem to forget that there was and continues to be notable opposition to the mission and its costs. Ten years after the successful launch in 1979, an NBC News poll found '53% of Americans saying the costs [$177 billion] were not justified'.[16]
- People that rally entirely behind a purpose or vision are likely to come to work with enthusiasm and apply pressure to themselves and colleagues to succeed. However, that same drive can give them more to lose. As discussed in Chapter 2, we make trade-offs when we choose to follow, giving up authority and potential rewards for protection or a belief in a greater idea or capability than ours. Imagine someone – our janitor, perhaps – discovering that the purpose was a lie or that the team was being prevented from achieving it. Since people continually assess those trade-offs, we can end up alienating the very people who wanted to give the most.
- As noted above, not everyone will work with you because they believe in the purpose you represent. For those that have different reasons, a constant attempt to pester and persuade them to be more engaged can be frustrating and cause resentment.
- Belief and honesty. There may be times when you are put in a position of representing an organisational vision with which you do not agree. That puts you in an awkward position with your teams. Do you tell a convincing story and keep your views outside the conversation, or should you be honest? I will return to teams and identities in Chapter 8, but for now, suffice it to say that the truth might win local kudos with your team, but there are stakeholders in and around an organisa-

tion. The right thing to do can only be governed by your moral compass and the culture you are working in.

- Evolution. As markets, organisations and relationships change, so can the purposes and visions towards which we are working. Pay attention to the cues. Hearing that 'we can't make that work, because…' might be painful in the short term but sticking rigidly to a target that is no longer valid is wasteful and demoralising.

A compelling strategy

The Cinderella fairy tale provides an opportunity to build on what we have discussed so far. At a turning point in the fable, the prince is left guessing after the beautiful princess has left him standing at the ball. Distraught, he is possessed with the urge to find her and has one clue: a glass slipper. In our terms – and since this is the world of Disney – the prince has a vision to marry the mysterious woman with whom he has become smitten. We can assume he also has a purpose to live happily ever after. That is a start, but he also needs something to bridge the gap to action, and he does not disappoint because he has an idea – a strategy – to find her. Our prince is going to knock on doors until he finds the woman who fits into that glass slipper. Genius. Ignoring continuity errors that the shoe still somehow exists after midnight, and that many feet would be the right size,* our prince has something. He has a way of making that vision a reality and satisfying his purpose.

By contrast, some teams I have met have had no strategy at all. They had a vision and some identification of purpose – normally told to them – but decisions about how to plan to tackle the problem at a macro level were missing or vague. Where strategy was discussed, it was implicit, and if great strategy is akin to Hannibal's military genius in his defeats of the Romans, these teams probably had about enough to order lunch.

Conversations about strategy are often complicated by a belief that strategy is something grand: military plans, global trade discussions or at the very least something that executives do. Accordingly, leaders, being

---

* Unless the would-be princess sported enormous clown feet, the prince is going to need more than a slipper to identify his beloved.

expected by their teams and colleagues to think of something, end up couching their intention in abstract language. Take this for an example of corporate strategy:

> *Our strategy is agile. We will lead a sustainable effort of the market through our use of culture and leaders to build a digital business. By being both customer-focused and open, our cloud-based approach will drive internet of things throughout the organization. Synergies between our design thinking and value will enable us to capture the upside by becoming collaborative in a networked world. These transformations combined with ecosystem due to our social media will create a competitive advantage through growth and data leaders.**

That is certainly safer for the owning executive than saying something like 'Put all energy into product 1, deprecate product 2.' The simple latter statement would leave the owner vulnerable to later review and criticism, when compared with the former impenetrable cloud of words. More importantly for the organisation, that car crash of ideas and buzzwords is certainly not a strategy and does little or nothing to help anyone with the day-to-day.

Instead, the critical and central thing we want in a strategy is something *intentional*. Intentional in what you plan to do, and intentional in what you will not do. For example, if our strategy for the sale of our product is to focus on the private healthcare consumer space, that is where we are putting our bets. If an opportunity comes up in manufacturing, that should be an easy choice: we will not allow ourselves to get distracted unless we decide to change our strategy. That is why the generated words above are not a strategy. They indicate an effort to be everything at the same time, and the prince's approach for finding Cinderella's foot (and we hope the whole of Cinderella) is more worthy of the label.

---

* This particular paragraph was created using Simon Wardley's strategy generator, and the tool will happily churn out randomised versions at the touch of a button. See strategy-madlibs.herokuapp.com.

Two whys

The need for strategy to be intentional and thoughtful fell further into place for me with Simon Wardley's description of 'two whys'.[17] Referencing Sun Tzu's *Art of War,* Wardley describes that behind any action that we might take, there will be two distinct 'whys'.[18] First, we have a *why of purpose*, familiar from the previous pages. This is your why of destination: Why are you seeking to land on the moon? Why do you want to launch your new business? Why are you moving abroad? This is then partnered with a second why, a *why of movement*. Explicitly, why – given your circumstances – are you taking your chosen actions to reach your purpose? Why are you planning your trip to the moon in *that* way? Why carry out *these* things to launch your business, or relocate abroad?

To illustrate, consider the acquisition of two AI companies by McDonald's,[19] whose 'big' purpose is stated as: 'To feed and foster communities. As the leading global foodservice retailer, we believe it's our responsibility to make a positive impact on the world.'[20] The purchases, in 2019, follow only two previous ones: Donatos in 1999, a pizza company through which it sought to diversify, and Boston Market in 2000, a restaurant chain purchased initially for its real estate. Even acknowledging a nearly 20-year gap in acquisitions, the AI companies, Apprente and Dynamic Yield (the latter purchased for $300 million), represent a sizeable and new investment in the digital space. This is not menu or real estate related, so why would these purchases make sense? The answer to that is their why of movement. *Wired* suggests it is a desire by McDonald's to become a tech company, and we can speculate that Dynamic Yield's expertise in algorithmic content mapping (targeting of offers) could bolster McDonald's app and ordering experience. For Apprente, a developer of voice-based conversational agents, we might imagine the technology being used for drive-through orders, perhaps eventually replacing all humans at the till. The buyouts might even be a power play, seeking to prevent competition from gaining an advantage.

The why of movement highlights a crucial need in strategy: that our intentions are sensitive to the realities of our environment and situation – to our context – and are not anchored only in desire. As an example, let's go back to the prince and his chosen path for finding his beloved Cinderella.

He clearly had his why of purpose nailed: he wanted to live happily ever after. His vision, to be married to the mysterious woman, was also clear. What of his strategy to knock on doors and see if he could find a match for the slipper? Why did *that* make sense? The prince could have chosen any number of strategies, like distributing posters, rewards, interviewing guests, holding other dances, meeting every woman in the kingdom, or even asking the fairy-godmother herself. Perhaps his choice – his why of movement – was both practical and easy to execute. Perhaps it was the only option tabled. Maybe it provided an opportunity for the prince to demonstrate his charm and romance to Cinderella and his subjects in a way that putting up wanted posters could never achieve.

Sometimes, we just have to climb

I want to be careful of what this might imply, however. It might appear that with careful analysis of the environment and conscious action we can pick the correct strategy to deploy. But we know from the mixing desk that we will have any number of more or less successful strategies available to us. It is possible to give ourselves better odds by taking time to observe context and consider our actions based on that, but there are no guarantees.

There are plenty of commercial and military examples of picking a flawed strategy, from the British assumptions of limited German resistance at the Battle of the Somme leading to devastating losses under machine-gun fire, to Kodak's decision to hold back on a launch of digital cameras even when film was in serious decline, or Blockbuster declining to purchase Netflix for $50 million.

In each of these cases, the strategies employed had their own justifications. In the same situation, many would have made the same choices. In the end, a good strategy may follow on from several bad ones, developing from the insights they created. As such, I propose an addendum to the well-known Stephen R. Covey quote. Alongside his words, 'If the ladder is not leaning against the right wall, every step we take just gets us to the wrong place faster', we should add the caveat: 'Sometimes we don't know whether we have the right wall until we start climbing.'[21]

Objectives and outcomes

While our vision and strategy alone are valuable, many organisations seek to break them down into smaller components or objectives that are easier to handle. Since the 1950s, there have been at least eight popular objectives-based concepts (Figure 5-1), and it is unusual to find an organisation not using one of them or a derivative.

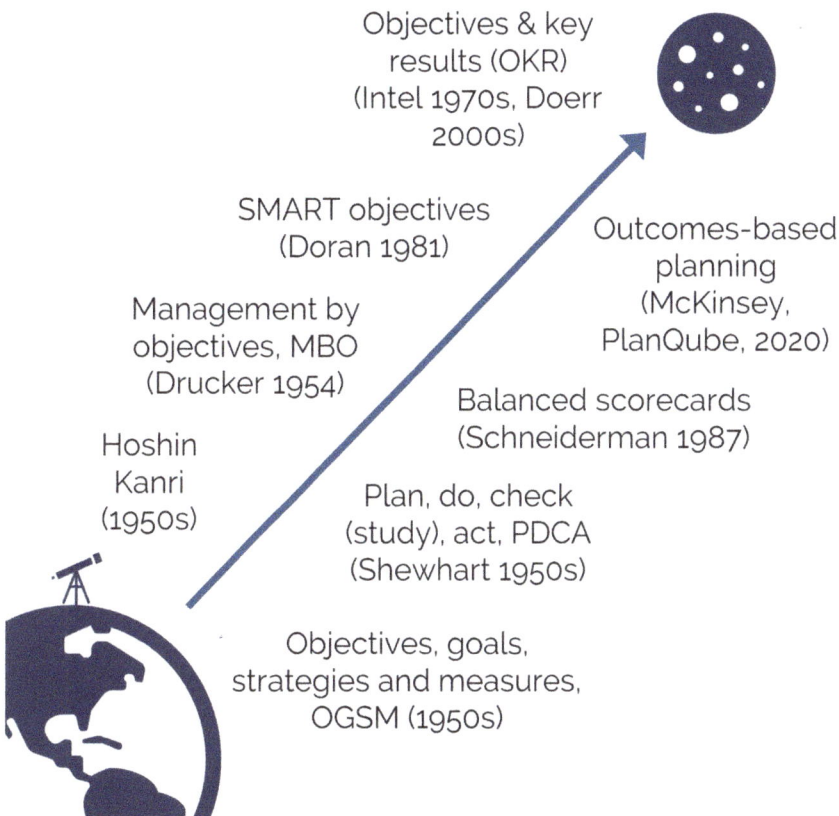

Objectives & key results (OKR) (Intel 1970s, Doerr 2000s)

SMART objectives (Doran 1981)

Outcomes-based planning (McKinsey, PlanQube, 2020)

Management by objectives, MBO (Drucker 1954)

Balanced scorecards (Schneiderman 1987)

Hoshin Kanri (1950s)

Plan, do, check (study), act, PDCA (Shewhart 1950s)

Objectives, goals, strategies and measures, OGSM (1950s)

Figure 5-1. A selection of objectives-based concepts

If our goals are likely to take many years to achieve, tools like these provide a practical middle ground between that ambition and our day-to-day plans.

Here are examples of some objectives to represent a massive – and invented – vision for moon colonisation, 25 years out. With the scale of such an aim, the long-term objectives are huge, so they have been broken down in a hierarchy, long-term to short-term. This is a core practice in the Hoshin Kanri process and is common across all objectives methods, like MBO and OKRs.*

Vision: A self-sufficient human colony is established on the moon by 2050

25-year objectives

> O1. Permanent goods corridor from earth surface to moon surface active
> O2. Primary and backup sites established and inhabited
> O3. Constant supply of qualified and mission-ready astronauts
> O4. 50% of water and food requirements produced on the moon
> O5. Always-on communications between earth and moon online

These 25-year objectives offer information about our plans but are still very large. To address this, each objective can be split further, for example into ten-year targets, five-year targets and smaller, as necessary. This nested set of objectives tells a story back to our vision (Figure 5-2). It does not mean that we know we will hit these objectives, or that these will continue to be the right ones, but it does give us a sense of the strategy and major steps we plan to take to achieve our ambitions.

---

* Hoshin Kanri, translated as 'policy management', defines long-term goals or a 'Company Hoshin' which are then broken down into departmental, group and individual activities.

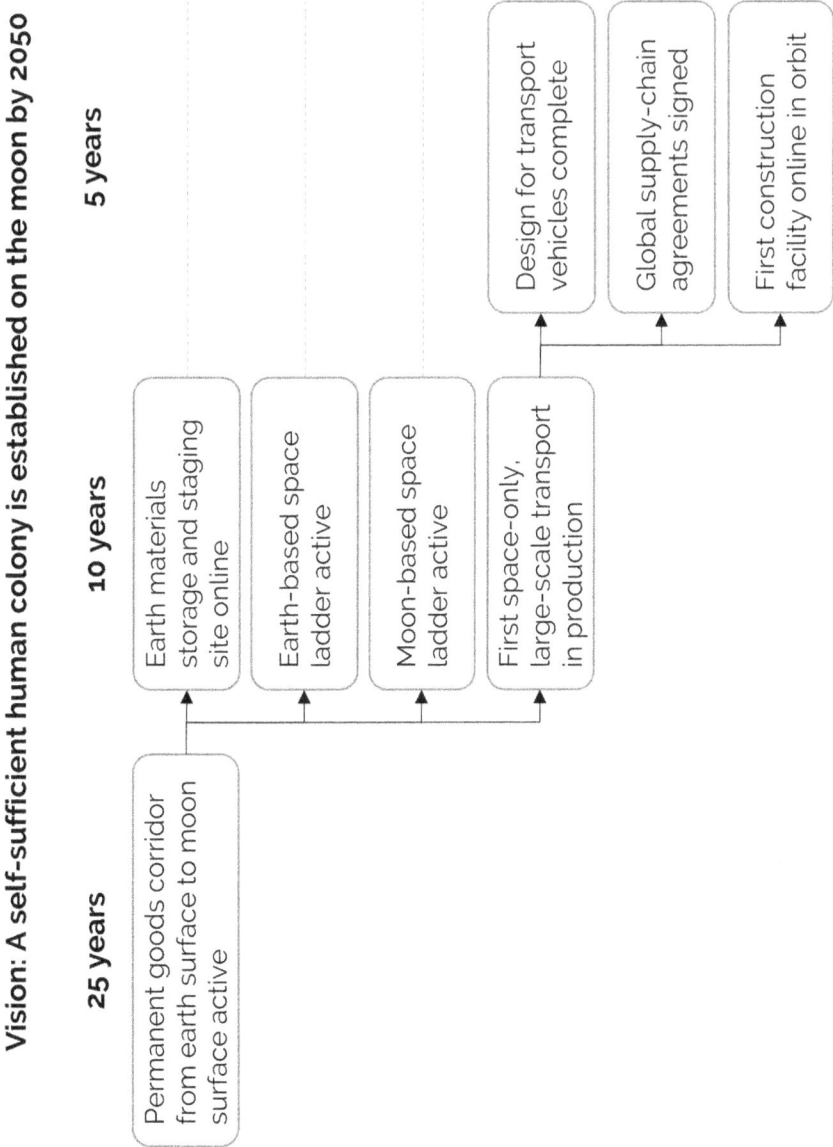

Figure 5-2. The nesting of objectives based on the moon colonisation example

Objective obfuscation

If we use nested objectives as a high-level execution plan, and therefore a link between vision and day-to-day, it follows that we want them to be clear and widely known. Loosely written objectives with ambiguous language open the door to wide interpretation and subjectivity, in turn growing misalignment, inefficiency and waste.

A favourite example of mine, and in part because I was asked to deliver it, was an objective to reach 'world-class customer service'. To be recognised for our service sounds like a positive thing, but the goal was not defined in any useful way. How we would go about measuring where we were, or whether we had crossed the line to 'world-class'?

Objectives like these regularly get shunted around organisations: 'Put the customer at the heart of what we do,' 'Make it simple!' and 'Adopt an Agile mindset' are just a few I seem to hear often. In each case, what does the phrase mean? More practically, how would they influence what we work on today? As general principles or values, they certainly offer a nudge, but no specific intention is described. If we take, 'Put the customer at the heart of what we do' as an example, that could mean we prioritise customer-related issues at all costs. It could also encourage us to invite customers to join product development panels and discussions, or less favourably for the organisation, that we limit our profit margins to give customers the best value for money. With these vague statements, what do we actually want to have happen?

To make objectives clearer and perhaps even measurable, there are many approaches we could choose. We might add some success criteria to the phrases above to give them some boundaries, or we could choose to write them in a particular format. One very well-known layout is that of SMART objectives. The idea, published by George Doran in a 1981 article, was to specify some formal dimensions for objectives.[22] His original criteria were:

Specific: What is needed is clear and explicit.
Measurable: Success or failure can be identified.
Assignable: Enough information so someone could start work.
Realistic: Can it be done with the resources available to us?
Time-related: When is it intended to be completed?

With these dimensions Doran asserted that, 'You will also know that you have taken a step to introduce management excellence in your organization.' They certainly help to challenge or replace statements like 'world-class' or 'customer centricity'. Later iterations, reflecting less task-based management, replaced Assignable with Achievable, Realistic with Relevant and Time-related with Time-bound.

My first experiences of working with objectives were inspired by Peter Drucker, the American management consultant, and his management by objectives or MBO practice (Figure 5-3).[23] The process went like this. At the start of the year, and based on their understanding of the market, and demands from the board and clients, the executive team set high-level, organisational objectives for the next 12 months. Once set, they cascaded through the organisation so that lower-level objectives could be written in alignment. The objectives remained fixed for the cycle, with performance evaluated at the end and results feeding into the next cycle. Individual performance against objectives was then considered in pay and reward discussions.

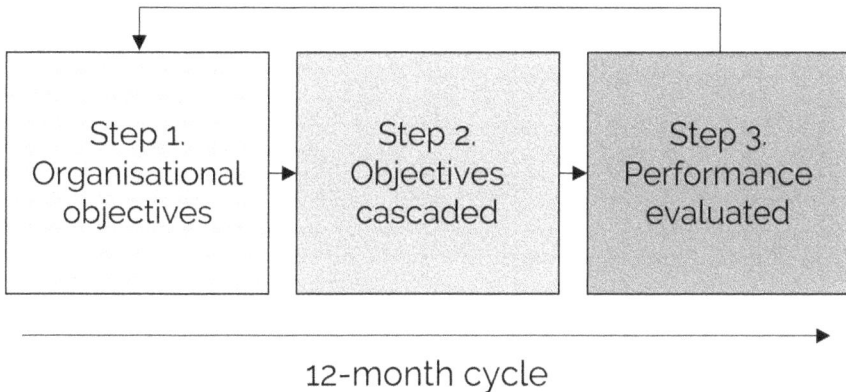

Figure 5-3. A management by objectives (MBO) process

On the upside, this approach helped people within the organisation understand their targets and how their work fitted in with the bigger picture. It also provided a high-level plan for the year which was easy to communicate, and it allowed some performance evaluation against our intentions.

Unfortunately, this approach to objective setting also had some downsides. Firstly, sticking with objectives set at the start of a period does not go well with change. If customer demands change, our competitive landscape shifts, otherwise, we might continue to work on something no longer relevant. One way to address this risk of change was to use those general, wide-scope objectives from earlier, like 'world-class service' or 'innovate to be number 1'. We know that does not work well, so a more practical adaptation was to review objectives quarterly, at least providing an opportunity to make amendments if there was a strong enough argument.

Secondly, cascading objectives from above made several assumptions about the knowledge of the leadership team. The process required them to know and bet on the right targets, while simultaneously limiting the contribution of insights, knowledge and ideas from others. Thirdly, and arguably most damaging, was the connection between objectives, appraisals and reward.

In my first year as a manager, I was penalised in a review because, while I had delivered a number of customer-demanded outcomes, they did not match targets from the start of the year. My manager was apologetic as he scored these results poorly, suggesting to me that I set more general and readily attainable targets in the future. This recommendation and a system that constrained people from changing course inspired targets that were easy to attain and written with ambiguous wording. Crudely described as 'sandbagging', some specific examples include a salesperson setting low territory targets for the year by over-stating its difficulty and a development team committing to small enhancements for a product. The most common sandbagging I have seen, however, is in project management, with one ex-colleague habitually doubling every delivery estimate he was given when planning. There is at least a recognised bias, the 'hard-easy effect', that has us believe complicated things are easier than they are (and vice versa).[24] In this context, however, it was all about protecting his own backside.

Finally, it is worth noting that the Achievable and Realistic elements of SMART directly address this habit. I once asked what we should interpret with these terms – inside the known laws of physics, anyway – and clearly remember being told that 'there's no point starting a job you can't finish'.

Shifting the philosophy

Thinking back to the historical development of leadership and practice in Chapter 1, it is important to acknowledge that these practices and their authors lived in different contemporary circumstances. The full title of Drucker's book from which MBO emanates is *The Practice of Management: A Study of the Most Important Function in American Society*. Likewise, Doran's article on SMART is wholly focused on the top and middle managers writing the objectives, with the rest of us doing what we are told. As much as it might seem an odd habit for organisations to prioritise achievement over value, both practices are born from managing outputs rather than a target of systems-driven quality. How about we switch that around, and emphasise the *value* we generate, more than the work we get done? Take a moment to think about this question:

> *In 2019, Toyota produced 10,740,000 cars, while Ferrari produced 10,131. Based on this data, who makes the better car?*

The answer is that it depends.* It depends on what you are trying to get done. For example, if you want a car that helps you to carry your family around and has ample luggage space for shopping and holidays, then a Toyota is likely to be the better car for you. If instead, you want a car that helps you to get away from your family as quickly as possible, then the Ferrari is going to be the better choice. I doubt Ferrari will hire me into marketing any time soon, but you get the point. The number of cars is merely a data point, and may or may not be relevant.

The distinction that this sets up is an emphasis on *outcomes*, rather than *outputs*. That is, the number of lines of code that we write, the complaints we resolve or the hairdryers we manufacture matter much less – in the end – than the value of the application, the customer engagement or revenue reached. If, before implementing agile, launching our product, or investing in a new technology, we get clearer about the outcome we are trying to reach, we may discover that these are not the logical steps to take. Indeed, we may not actually need to do anything to achieve our outcomes.[25]

These shifts in philosophy are easier said than done, however. If the habits and culture of your organisation praise busyness and applaud those that start project after project more than those who complete them, it will take sustained effort to create a new normal. If you think that you want to move in this direction, I have seen that objectives and key results (OKRs), and specifically the *framing* of OKRs, helps as a vehicle for this change.

---

* It depends unless, I have found, you ask an Italian team this question.

The origin story for OKRs is well publicised: they developed first in the 1970s as a method of objective-handling at Intel. Ex-Intel employees then spread the idea to other companies, and their current popularity comes through their use at Silicon Valley firms, notably Google. The story goes that Jon Doerr, who started as an intern at Intel in 1974, later became a prominent Silicon Valley investor. In 1999 he became one of the early investors in Google and at a board meeting was asked by founders Larry Page and Sergey Brin for practices to help manage the fledgling operation. Doerr suggested OKRs and the rest – according to Doerr, at least – is history. He has since gone on to introduce OKRs to – among others – HP, Amazon, Intuit and Slack.

Regardless, the key to understanding OKRs as something different and contributory is their philosophy, which is well summarised in the words of the late Andy Grove, Intel's first employee and later president and CEO. Following a diagnosis of Parkinson's disease at age 63, Grove invested time and money in research into the condition. Frustrated by the limited results, he famously noted that 'There are so many people working so hard and achieving so little.'[26] This is not someone used to slow progress nor wasted effort, and immediately we have the opposite attitude to the notion of sandbagging objectives. We want to get valuable things done. We want outcomes, not actions and busyness.

A specific example from Google comes in the form of targets being set by now-CEO, Sundar Pichai, in 2008 for the use of the Chrome internet browser. The year 2008 may not feel that long ago, but at the time Chrome was the new kid on the block with a handful of users in a market dominated by Netscape Navigator and the freshly released Internet Explorer 7. Google wanted to do something about that, and so Sundar's team set a target of reaching 20 million 7-day active Chrome users in 2008. With less jargon, that means 20 million users of the Chrome browser worldwide, using it every single day of the week. By the end of the year, the team got numbers well above 10 million, but failed to reach its initial target. So, what did they do? Was the team berated for the result and counselled to 'limit their objectives' next time? Not Google. In 2009, it revised the target to 50 million 7-day active Chrome users, more than doubling the original target. At the end of that year, it had again failed to reach their number, with only 38 million achieved. Regardless, the 2010 target was revised up again, to 111 million, which was reached before the end of that year. This example reveals three important points.

First, I was intentional with my language above saying that google *failed* in 2008 and 2009. But did it really fail? For 2009's target of 50 million, it is technically accurate to say anything less than 50 million is not a success: you either did it, or you did not. In a classic MBO-driven objective, the output did not meet its stated target. But did it achieve any kind of outcome? Yes. We might assume that Google has higher expectations for results than some organisations, but 38 million does not read like failure to me. It seems a decent outcome, and a very meaningful step in the direction it wanted to go.

Second, there seems to be confidence, a sense of adventure or entrepreneurship, accompanying these high targets. Cast your mind back to Kennedy's appeal for support for space exploration and try to apply the logic of a SMART objective. Where do ideas of achievable or realistic fit in to choosing to go to the moon? Perhaps if achievable and realistic mean 'damned difficult, but inside the laws of physics', we are fine, but if we take the path of 'choose something easy so you don't get marked down if it fails', our wings are clipped. As Michelangelo is reputed to have said: 'The greatest danger for most of us is not that our aim is too high and we miss it, but that it is too low and we reach it.'

It is going to take more than some off-the-shelf parts and an oil change for our family hatchback to overtake a flat-out Aston Martin Vanquish. It is going to need rockets.

Third, the stretch in the target itself creates a change in behaviour. To illustrate, imagine that you have a task to increase the 106-mph top speed of a 2004, 1.4 litre Ford Focus hatchback by 5 mph.[27] To achieve this, we can look to several relatively easy changes. We could take the seats and other trim out to reduce the weight, we could upgrade some components like the exhaust or air filters or reprogram the engine control unit. If, however, the task was to double the top speed to 212 mph, we have a very different situation. It is going to take more than some off-the-shelf parts and an oil change for our family hatchback to overtake a flat-out Aston Martin Vanquish. It is going to need rockets. And so, we are into the territory of innovation and (crazy) ideas that might well fail, but with the potential for interesting and game-changing results all the same.

Practically speaking

The idea that OKRs as a practice might encourage ambition and unlock creativity in our teams is compelling, but please do not get carried away. Given a chance to repeat a core theme of the book, I will lay it on thick.

First, if OKRs helped innovation and drive to happen at Google, it was because of a whole heap of effort well beyond the mechanics of a method. Everything from their culture, virtues and vices, and their people and skills, to their resources and environment played a part.

Second, no organisation deploys OKRs – or any other method – into a predictable and non-complex system. Teams will already be experienced in other methods and will be having some success with them (given that the organisation has not folded). Practically, the inertia from any existing system has influence, and we must acknowledge that, for most people, the 'new thing' is not the 'main thing' occupying their thoughts. Changing the system jolts people from relative stability to an unknown, and I have worked with plenty of people that consider changes to objective systems a cynical move to control and hold back reward.

Therefore, if you are tempted to think that OKRs will make your operation better, they might. However, like a running machine that is never switched on, implementation of OKRs without an intentional and active effort can yield hugely different and disappointing outcomes.

Stakeholder relations

Through the discussion of visions and strategies so far, an indispensable element has been implied but not discussed: stakeholders. They could be groups or individuals, even organisations, societies and countries that have some relationship with the work that we are doing. Our purpose and vision will inspire and benefit some, while discouraging and disadvantaging others. The strategy we choose will commit the energy of individuals, teams and colleagues; proponents and competitors will seek to influence our ambitions. It is crucial therefore to think about who we impact in our plans. Beginning at the trivial end of the scale, like sharpening a pencil, we may have only ourselves as a stakeholder. At the other, we could think of the 45–50 million people able to cast a vote in the UK as stakeholders of government policy, or all eight billion of us in the world as stakeholders of global environmental policy.[28] There is a vast difference in consequences and our ability to influence the outcome in these extremes. In our own context, we should spend time establishing relationships with those that matter.

Immediately, a subjective idea comes up: those that matter. Looking at our projects, if you think about who is involved and who might need to know something, the list gets long. Since we have limited time and energy, however, we need to make some decisions about where our focus goes. Most approaches we take will come under the broad heading of 'stakeholder management' – literally actions to manage our stakeholder relationships, perspectives and engagement.

In the first step we take our list of stakeholders and categorise, map or grade them to help us understand where our priorities are. In case you are not familiar with the common frames to visualise this information, I have included three here. The first maps stakeholders based on their level of interest and ability to influence. The greater a stakeholder's interest and ability to influence, the more important it is to engage and maintain an effective relationship with them (Figure 5-4).

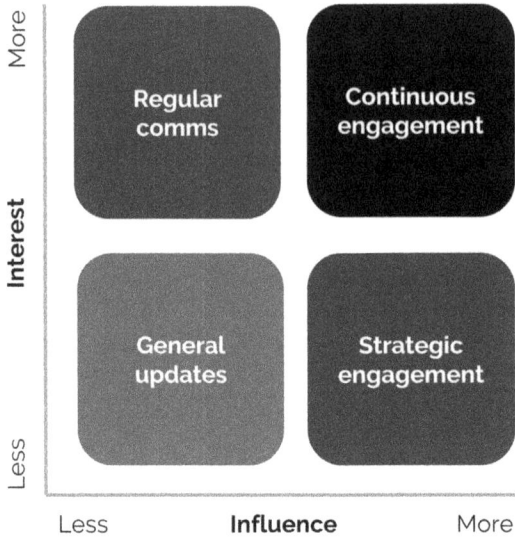

Figure 5-4. Stakeholder level of interest and ability to influence map

The second frame plots stakeholders based on their area(s) of interest, allowing us to highlight what we think people would like to know about (Figure 5-5).

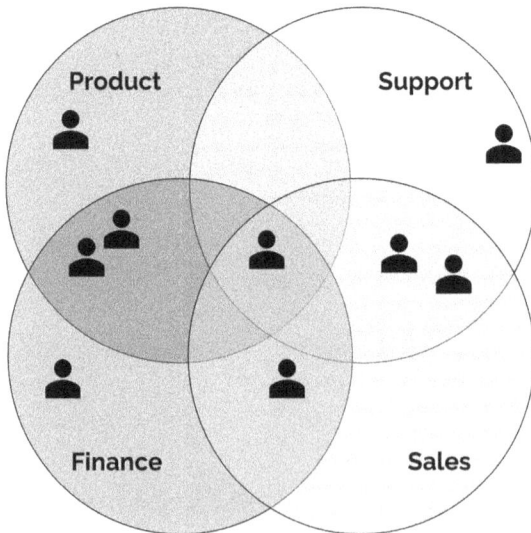

Figure 5-5. Stakeholder area or function of interest frame

Finally, the onion diagram offers a different approach, with stakeholders mapped from most important in the centre to the least important on the edges (Figure 5-6).* It is vital however that, as a group or team, you are clear about what 'important' means. To clarify, this frame can be used in a sense-making exercise, comparing different opinions about who and why people are important.

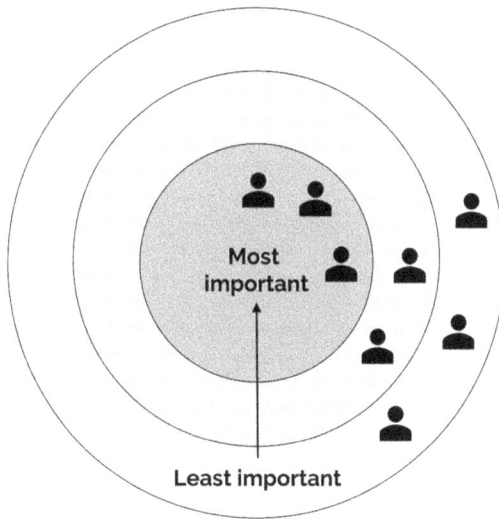

Figure 5-6. Stakeholder onion diagram

What a beautiful map!

By creating diagrams like these, we can make better sense of who is involved and who we need to engage with. This understanding, particularly for those people involved in creating the diagrams, builds understanding and will immediately start to influence decisions and actions that people take. It is a valuable activity, and much more valuable than passively waiting to find out who might care.

But flawless stakeholder management is impossible. You will miss stakeholders or forget to engage. You will delight, annoy and trouble them. You

---

* I have found this 'target-shaped' version makes it easier to plot relative weighting between stakeholders.

will disagree with their opinions and decision-making and they will delight, annoy and trouble you right back. If it was not already obvious, stakeholder engagement is another complex humans-trying-to-understand-other-humans activity. Believing that you know your stakeholders is not the same as handling them when the project starts, changes or closes. Therefore, we should recognise from the outset that stakeholders, and our relations with them, are unpredictable, which always represents opportunity and risk.

For all that context, criticality and value, I am often surprised to see pretty diagrams stored in project folders, rather than active stakeholder engagement. Thus, I offer a few thoughts:

- Actually engage with your stakeholders. As obvious as this may seem, relationships mean getting off your (metaphorical) chair, going to where your stakeholder is and spending time with them. Put meetings and reminders in your diary and then seek to understand what makes your stakeholders tick. Understand what they need and how they would like their relationship with you to be. Listen to what they have to say, find out who else to engage with, and answer questions you get asked. If you have not read Dale Carnegie's famous *How to Make Friends and Influence People* book, join more than 30 million people since its publication and order a copy now.[29]

- Use the contacts you have. It can be tempting to allocate the role of stakeholder management to one person, for example a product manager. While it makes some sense to have someone with overall responsibility, that does not automatically mean they have the best connections or relationships to leverage. A brief exercise to map connections between the people in your team may yield more appropriate points of contact. In Figure 5-7, I have mapped three members of a team, A, B and C. Taking B as an example, they have direct relationships with G and J, and through G to H, I and L. Knowing these connections will inform your choices.

- Sense-making. Working with stakeholders is an excellent opportunity to use sense-making tools. As an example, stakeholders of a CRM project I was part of had a disagreement about delivery priorities. Not unusual, but to address it we met with representatives from each 'side' of the argument and ran a number of discovery exercises.* The result was increased mutual understanding, clarity in areas of commonality and conflict, and agreement on immediate priorities.

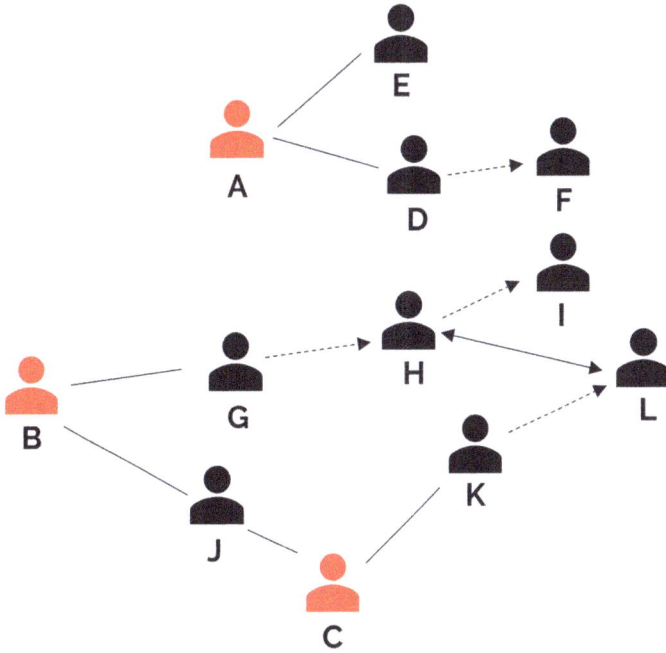

Figure 5-7. A relationship map

Communication and engagement

In the final part of this chapter, I am going to turn my attention to communication. It is wonderful that we have created all these visions, strategies and objectives, but as a paper exercise they hold limited value. We need to get that information to our colleagues and teams so that people can coordinate and collaborate in those aims. In this pursuit, the first tool that people reach for in

---

* Alongside some bespoke exercises, these included Snowden's 'Future Backwards' to look at perspectives about the future (cynefin.io/wiki/Future_backwards) and ecocycle planning to examine feature 'maturity' and as a comparison to ideal future states (liberatingstructures.com/31-ecocycle-planning).

the playbook is a broadcast – an all-hands or town hall meeting where we tell everyone what decisions, targets and changes are being made. Unfortunately, with so much coming at us continuously, from work demands to those posts on LinkedIn about '4-am-routines-for-guaranteed-success', much will be filtered out. Here is an only somewhat cynical view about how this kind of meeting plays out:

1. The organisation's vision and purpose are broadcast from the leadership team, with much fanfare.

2. Teams listening to the update find it difficult, and doubly so those hierarchically distant from the leadership, because:
   - The content is difficult to understand, possibly described in language that is not readily understood.
   - Assumptions have been made about what people know and how they will interpret the information.
   - The content is not seen as relevant by those listening.
   - Individuals listening may not be followers, so are unconvinced that the trade-off of commitment is worth it (discussed in Chapter 1).
   - More prosaically it is always five o'clock somewhere in the world, and this might be the one thing stopping them going home.

3. The next day, people start to do the best they can with the information they retain, or just carry on until someone tells them to do something different.

4. A few weeks later, a leader observes some misalignment with the announced vision and purpose, perhaps a person making contradictory decisions.

5. The leadership team consider the issue and decide to run another town hall meeting to make sure the message lands.

6. Go to 1.

This situation reminds me of a much-attacked question posed on the Quora platform: 'I have two employees that usually leave work at 6 pm. They are good, but I don't like that their commitment lasts for work hours only. What should I do as a CEO?'[30] Alongside responses like 'This question makes my blood boil' and a few attempting to answer it, my personal favourite was simply: 'What should you do as a CEO? You should quit as a CEO.' The point is, communicating harder and hoping that people just 'get it' is at best unreliable. Moreover, the outcome we wanted in the first place will only come through something other than one-way traffic.

> *Communicating harder and hoping that people just 'get it' is at best unreliable.*

The art of understanding and being understood

In the previous chapter on leadership, we looked at the 'Imagine an elephant' game to demonstrate differences in perspective. In the context of communications this is essential, since understanding more about how others see the world gives us insight into how to get our messages across. In the words of Stephen Covey's habit #5 from *The 7 Habits of Highly Effective People*, 'Seek first to understand, then to be understood'.[31]

With apologies for my French, imagine the vulgar Brit on holiday in France, trying to communicate with the baker by using wild arm movements and progressively louder shouting.

Le boulanger:	Bonjour. Vous désirez?
Le client odieux:	[Pointing wildly] Bread. You know… BREAD. What's the word? Err. Pain?
Le boulanger:	Pardon. Je suis confus. Voulez-vous un pain, ou un lapin?
Le client odieux:	Bread. French stick. I dunno. Speak ENGLISH!
Le boulanger:	[Stares at the customer]
Le client odieux:	[Best sarcastic French accent] Whatever. A la-pan ppp-lease.
Le boulanger:	Merci, Monsieur. S'il vous plaît, attendez.
Le client odieux:	[Walks out with a rabbit]

Without empathy and understanding of others' views, we are likely to be left with plenty of unplanned rabbits. The first step then, is to listen. Whether individually or in groups, the more awareness of different interpretations you can gather, the better. Here is a brief sense-making team exercise you might conduct.

1. Arrange to have people from different teams in a workshop.
2. Keep the teams together in their functions and do not mix them. Keep finance with finance, customer services with customer services, and so on.
3. Invite the teams to discuss the vision, purpose or strategy that you are proposing (or have presented). Offer prompts if needed:
   - What do you understand our vision/purpose/strategy is, in your own words?
   - Does that vision/purpose/strategy go far enough?
   - Why do you think that it is important for our organisation?
   - Why could this be the wrong thing to do?
   - In what ways are we already fulfilling it?
   - Where have we got more work to do to?
4. Teams look at what everyone else has written.
5. In the main group, teams share their observations and questions.
6. Everyone discusses, draws conclusions (where appropriate) and considers next steps.

From the answers and discussion, you will achieve at least three things. First, everyone in the discussion will have the chance to learn and better appreciate other perspectives, developing their own contextual understanding. Second, from the areas of agreement and misunderstanding, communication and content can be revised and tested to increase their resonance. And third, thinking back to the SOAP/SOUP example in Chapter 5, people will have been primed to think in a certain way by the information received. That is, if I understand our strategy is to focus on customer engagement, I am more likely to notice opportunities and act upon them.

If we consider that level of awareness is a passive involvement, something more active could be teams delivering objectives or taking intentional actions to drive the aims. Considering that target of customer engagement, imagine we are seeking 'A big shift in customer perceptions of the company' measured by aggregate reviews, reduction in client turnover (churn) and increased adoption of features. A software team can directly influence that target through improvements to products to make them more effective, higher quality and with customer-desired features. Meanwhile, a finance team focused on increasing speed of enquiry handling, usability of invoices or price structuring can contribute to the reduction in client turnover. You get the idea.

We are faced with a question, however. Should we insist that people adopt the central goals? As always, there are trade-offs. Insisting that every team in the organisation has objectives linked back to a core aim benefits organisational alignment. Indeed, the alternative of leaving things open and risking patchy progress through a lack of interest certainly sounds undesirable. However, thinking about awareness of others' situations, no leadership team can know what it is like to work in, say, finance or software, and it will be blind to local priorities. Indeed, if people are hamstrung by some tool or practice that needs investment, allowing them space to fix it could well be a better choice.

Accordingly, we could add some other questions to the exercise above. We could ask: 'How can your team support the vision/purpose/strategy?', 'What needs to happen before that is possible?', and 'What else is a priority for you?' Unless there is something fundamentally at odds with your intentions (in which case pay attention!), teams will invariably support central aims, so listen to and support what comes out.

A lesson from IKEA

As a last thought on the subject of understanding and being understood, have you ever left IKEA with something you did not think you needed? I have my own furniture-shaped experience here and watching someone attempt to magic a sofa into a Fiat 500 recently makes me confident that I am not alone. That couple must have known which car they arrived in, and yet they still bought the thing anyway. Why would they do that? The brilliance of IKEA is that as you walk around, there are not just shelves of goods to purchase, there are multiple room layouts that you can walk through, sit in and imagine are yours. You see the items in context, not as isolated and abstract objects. It is much easier to start picturing your house with the sofa, desk or lamp you have just been admiring. The context makes some kind of deep connection and desire, so that before you know it you are hooked. This is a notable example of engagement, and while such a physical model might not be an option, narratives, images and experiences can be powerful tools to help teams sit on your own virtual sofa.

This can include inviting people to spend time with customers – ideally in their own setting as they engage with your services – or by sharing notable stories and use cases about your impact. In one of my roles a few years ago, a large genomics project took out a trial on our platform. During their tests using clinical data, the customer identified a specific genetic trait in one of their cancer patients, leading to more suitable treatment. The human impact that our platform made resonated very well with our engineering teams and became a source of both pride and renewed energy.

Waking up after the engagement party

Active in the late nineteenth century, the psychologist Hermann Ebbinghaus was fascinated by learning and memory. In a variety of experiments on himself, including attempts to learn and recall strings of random letters, he studied patterns for absorbing and then retaining that information. His conclusions and discussion were recorded in *Memory: A contribution to experimental psychology*.[32] Notably, this work included the first mention of a 'learning curve', and experimental figures to demonstrate how information is forgotten. It is now known as the 'forgetting curve' and is represented in Figure 5-8. Further, his work examined approaches for absorbing information and differences between the types of information that we might learn.

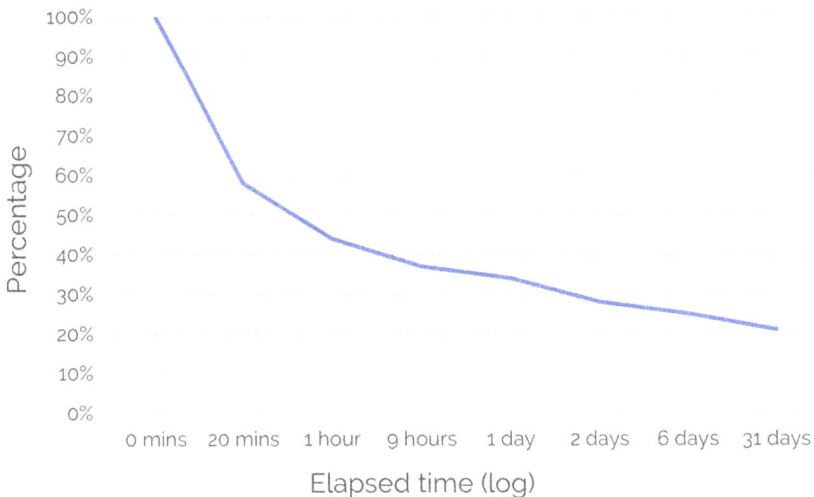

Figure 5-8. Ebbinghaus forgetting curve

There is something intuitive about these findings. There is an onslaught of information across our senses that we need to filter and prioritise, and even in the quietest of rooms, thoughts and ideas flash across our awareness. With the brain's vast energy needs – it makes up 2% of our weight but consumes up to 30% of what we eat – it makes sense that we are both selective about what information we take in and then limit the amount we retain.[33] We have evolved efficient ways to manage a wide range of stimuli, including the use of patterns and biases to help us quickly categorise, calculate and navigate the world around us.[34]

It follows that when we are attempting to communicate and engage, even if messages land, they can get lost and replaced in already-busy minds. The implication is a need for more sustained engagement, and clearly a one-off broadcast of information will have limited mileage. Instead, you might take inspiration from the marketing 'Rule of Seven' and take every opportunity to discuss, demonstrate and link back to your messages.[35] You might tell stories and share anecdotes, show progress (or a lack of it), and get people in front of the customers. You could use any of the hundreds of tools and alternatives available and try out what works for your audiences.

Intuitive or not, however, the headline loss of 40% of what we learn within 20 minutes, according to Ebbinghaus, should be treated with caution. Predominantly because the experiment was completed on only one person – himself – and also as his method of memorising random letters and text bears only some resemblance to our day-to-day subjects.*[36] Imagine delivering a 30-slide presentation about the state of the marketplace and your ambitions for the next ten years. It is true that people will miss and forget elements of the content, but for many audiences in your organisation the information will not be wholly new, nor require everyone to understand everything.

As I said at the start of the chapter, how your messages land around your organisation is mostly out of your control. Ultimately, therefore, whether using my exercise above or simply in conversation, the key task is to listen and observe how things are playing out in reality so you can respond.

---

* This is another example, like Maslow's hierarchy of needs in Chapter 1, of a popular idea becoming normalised and unchallenged despite its limited grounding in scientific fact.

Chapter summary

A broad understanding of where you are going, why you are going there, and your plan of approach is intrinsically valuable information for all. There are many ways that we can articulate these ideas, but in the end, what matters is that the people and teams you are working with understand enough about the intended direction. Saying things like 'we want to be customer-centric' or 'agile' is unlikely to provide sufficient context to coordinate and steer efforts, especially across a large team or organisation.

- Our plans and decisions are shaped by our circumstances and surroundings – our context. In other words, 'Sometimes we don't know whether we have the right wall until we start climbing.'
- Consider your 'big why' of *purpose* and your strategic why of *movement*. I also recommend you read Sun Tzu's *The Art of War*, a short and excellent book.[37]
- Purpose, vision, and strategy can all evolve, and sometimes very quickly when the landscape around changes.
- *Outcomes* can provide more efficient and greater results than *outputs* because they separate what you want from how to achieve it.
- Engaging customers and stakeholders inside and outside of our team gives us important additional information and context to guide our choices and actions.
- Like IKEA, demonstrations and direct experience of your situation, your customer's situation, your goals, strategy and visions for the future will help people to connect.
- Ultimately, due to the vast array of individual context, how your messages land around your organisation is mostly out of your control.

CHAPTER 6

Delivery, delivery, delivery

'Everybody has a plan until they get punched in the mouth.'
— MIKE TYSON[38]

So, we know where we want to be (our vision), and why that matters (our purpose) and have decided on a high-level approach to achieve it (our strategy). This already has value in clarity, organisation and communication, but at some point, someone needs to deliver something. The promises we made now need to be fulfilled – and, in short, we need to move from lofty ideas and presentations to getting stuff done.

In this chapter, I will cover that journey, looking at project techniques, operations and measurement. Given that many objectives we write will have something to do with a product or service offering, I will present these in the context of a product development life cycle.

Product development life cycles

A typical product development life cycle starts with an idea, moves through design and delivery to operation, before ultimately reaching end of life. If you look up the term, or consider your own experiences, you will discover plenty of other stages or sub-stages that you could include. A short list might include analysis, prototyping, strategy, validation, planning, marketing, maintenance, testing, integration, transition, handover, retirement or recycling. You get the point.

For our purposes here, I will limit the stages to six: idea, design, deliver, operate, improve and end of life (Figure 6-1), and a brief explanation follows.

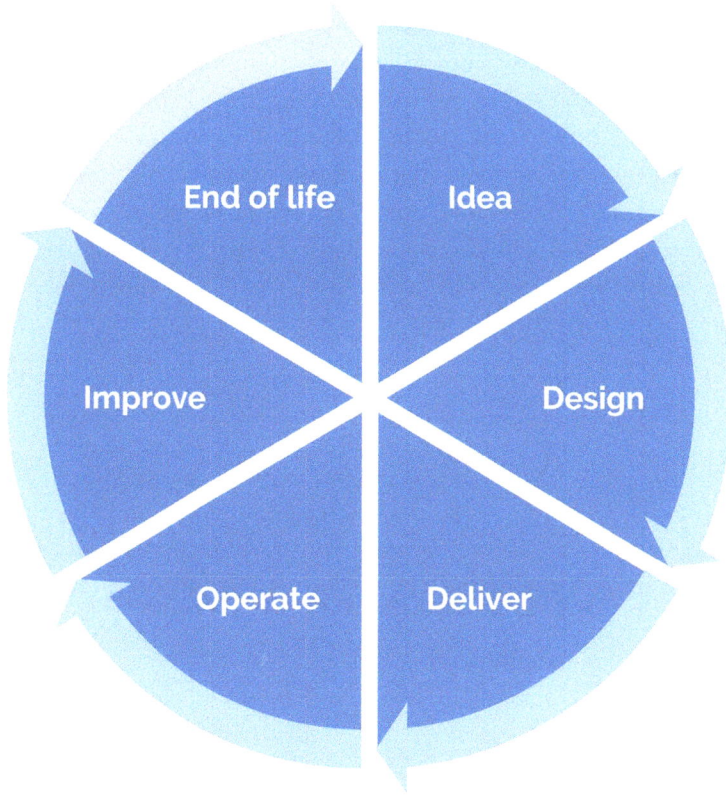

Figure 6-1. A product development life cycle

Idea

For our new product, or the betterment of an existing one, we need a spark of creativity or demand that drives its development: some words to complete the sentence 'Wouldn't it be great if …'. This starting point could come from our strategy, customer or team feedback and research, or through a change in the environment. The details do not need to be fleshed out. However, some light market analysis and screening could be necessary where there are competing ideas. That may include discussion with customers about need and fit, or with teams, engineers and suppliers to get an indication of cost. Ultimately, a successful idea will get people motivated to engage and invest further.

Design

We will often need more than an idea before we commit teams to delivery, and certainly if budgets are out of our control. Design is where we get into detail about how the idea could look and how processes might work. We may invest in prototypes and MVPs* to test that thinking.[39] Additionally, this stage gives us a chance to think about our strategy for creating the product, the tools or practices we would use, and where to start developing or building. The sum of all of those things lets us test if the idea is still viable and secure investment for its delivery.

Delivery

With the initial design and funding in place, we can get on with making the idea a reality. This is where we build whatever we intended, and test whether it does those things. The delivery phase can include marketing to notify and engage customers, alongside training and awareness for teams that will offer support once the product is live. The next section will cover much more about delivery and delivery methods.

Operation

The idea we had is now delivered and in the hands of our colleagues and customers, moving us into an operation and maintenance phase. After some handover,** operational teams take over from the project team to support and manage the product's use. During this stage we have an opportunity to learn more about how the product is used, what works well and what could be improved or changed.

---

* A term popularised in *The Lean Startup* by Eric Ries. An MVP, or minimum viable product, is a concept that invites us to invest the least amount of people, resources and time to help us prove whether our idea is worth it. In other words, cost-effective prototypes – from sketches to actual products – to find out early on if we are wasting our time.

** 'Some handover' can mean a detailed, integrated and caring transfer of knowledge. Unfortunately, it can also indicate a project team suddenly and wholly tasked on something else. In such cases, the emphasis shifts. 'Oh my, that was *some handover*.'

Improvement

Assuming that our product was not perfect first time (or that we ran out of money), changes and enhancements are made. Broadly, these will either be small enough for operations teams to execute alongside support, or drive a project team to cycle back to the idea and design stages.

End of life

Eventually, even the most innovative and successful products no longer have a market. Depending on the infrastructure involved in delivering the product, closure could involve archival, migration to a new solution, deletion of data, decommissioning or recycling of assets.

Three choices in delivery

Let us start to look at delivery in more detail. Imagine that we are about to embark on a project that will turn all those glitzy slides into something that people can actually benefit from. Before we run away with ourselves, there is an elephant to name first, and that is: 'Which approach to delivery should we take?' With a feeling of déjà vu for the choices available, it is easy to get lost.

Should you work with the more popular Scrum or PRINCE2 (Projects in Controlled Environments)? How about picking up PMI's Project Management Body of Knowledge (PMBOK) and applying that to your world-changing idea? Perhaps you should get someone who is certified in Kanban, SAFe, LeSS, MSP, PMP, CAPM, PgMP, PfMP, PMI-ACP, PMI-PBA, PMI-RMP, PMI-SP or OPM3?

To make some sense of what to do, I will reduce the choices to three.

'Just do it' may conjure up an inspirational and affirmative swoosh, but 'Just f'ing do it' is probably the experience you're more likely to have in the office.

Choice 1: J(F)DI

'Just do it' may conjure up an inspirational and affirmative swoosh, but 'Just f'ing do it' is probably the experience you're more likely to have in the office. Something like:

You: 'Here are three infallible reasons why this won't work.'

CEO: 'JDI.'

You: 'They really are infallible, though.'

CEO: 'J.F.D.I.'

If the work is small enough (although what 'small' is, is of course, subjective), we can take it in our stride and deliver it alongside everything else. Indeed, repetitive, well-documented and well-established activities are less likely to need close governance and risk management, so we can just get on with them. Simple, obviously.

In the meantime, for larger and more complicated work with different moving parts, we will need something more coordinated and sensitive to events. As the US Department of the Army saying goes: 'Prior Planning Prevents Piss Poor Performance.' Very sage. Not to be outdone, the US Marines include an additional P: 'Prior *Proper* Planning Prevents Piss Poor Performance.' Pardoning the imagery, there is something golden in those phrases. Both explicitly state that you can plan your way to good performance. While there very much is value in planning, the idea that we could have avoided every disaster or secured every ambition with better planning is false and something you should be wholly sceptical of by now. And so, here enter the two main schools of thought around project delivery.

Choice 2: Waterfall-like, predictive project delivery

This is a reductive approach to delivery and what most people I meet started with. In essence, predictive project delivery assumes that we know what we want to do and how we want to do it. Therefore, we can create a detailed plan up-front and choose to fund its achievement in entirety. This is why you may hear the term 'waterfall', or waterfall project management, in these situations. Just like water flowing down a mountain, the path of the project is sequential: we carry out A, then B, then C and so on. Water does not flow up the mountain, and neither would we carry out C before A.

During the project, our progress is managed according to the dependent, and often rigid, triangle of time, cost and quality. For instance, if we find ourselves behind schedule (time), our options are to look at cost (adding more people, buying a resource) or, deep breath, reduce quality ('We don't really need to test the seat belts, do we?') Similarly, if we want quality to go up, it will inevitably lead to an increase in time, costs or both.

At a high level, a predictive project method runs through steps similar to the following:

1. Proposal: A documented summary or business case to describe the reason and intended benefits of the project and to secure necessary funding.
2. Project initiation: Detailed review of feasibility and methods, development of a plan, and setting of controls based on the proposal.
3. Delivery: Management of the tasks, deliverables, risks, issues and changes following the plan.
4. Progress checks: Regular status reports, and for larger projects, formal 'gates' to separate stages and allow opportunity to check on value and change direction if needed.
5. Close and handover: Verify recipient satisfaction, review the benefits realised and transfer ongoing support to normal operations teams.

Interlaced within these steps are various registers of information and analysis, including risk and issue logs, quality requirements, stakeholder maps, Gantt charts, staffing rosters, communications plans and project budgets. To help ensure we get to where we want to be, and to 'control and protect the project's products', a change control approach is also defined.* This sets the policy for how we respond when something happens that we did not see coming. As you might imagine, that can be quite a stack of paperwork, but involved in

---

* This is language from PRINCE2, and much of the language implies a hierarchical and managed environment. We should have a mandate to initiate, from which projects are directed, controlled, managed, accepted and finally closed.

something with a billion-dollar budget, I can understand why people sleep better with words like 'control' and 'plan' being emphasised. Unless they have spotted the repetition, the PRINCE2 wiki still doubles down on this idea:

> *Remember, without a plan there is no control, so a plan is required for the project. Failing to plan is planning to fail. The very act of planning helps the project management team to think ahead and avoid duplication, omissions, and threats. And remember, failing to plan is planning to fail.*[40]

> ## Involved in something with a billion-dollar budget I can understand why people sleep better with words like 'control' and 'plan' being emphasised.

Choice 3: Agile-like, adaptive project delivery

Adaptive project delivery, as the name suggests, is less rigid and more experimental. That is, we know approximately what it is that we want to do but are not certain about the final detail or much else. The latter will include trivial things, like the colour of a button, through to whether our customers want and would pay for our product. A high-level path may be plotted out to get somewhere but we are actively checking the value of our progress, and the funding we make available, with contemporary information. A is probably followed by B and maybe C, but we will not know until later. Since this is probably a project that someone somewhere is funding, we likewise have time, cost and quality concerns, with the new addition of 'features'.* The thinking goes that since we cannot guarantee what's going to happen during the project or development, being asked to spend more or sacrifice quality are not ideal. Instead, we prioritise the things that the project is intending to do and – if it becomes necessary – delay or cut lower-ranked features. In other words, even if we cannot deliver everything that we thought we wanted, we have delivered something on the right date and to the right quality, and the feedback we get from that will be invaluable.

---

* Time-cost-quality-features is the basis for DSDM, the Dynamic Systems Development Method. DSDM was developed in the 1990s to bring discipline into early get-stuff-done application development approaches, like RAD, Rapid Application Development.

At a high level, an adaptive project method looks like this:

1. **Proposal:** A documented summary or business case to describe the reason for and intended benefits of the project and to secure necessary funding.
2. **Project kick-off:** Team discussion of approach, creation of a backlog of work, and identification of the first 'slices' of value that could be targeted. Prioritisation of the slice(s) that will get value into the hands of stakeholders the soonest.*
3. **Delivery:** Work through the backlog, regularly checking for progress, acting on risks and impediments, and adapting when necessary to deliver greater or earlier value. Verify recipient satisfaction with delivered slices as they happen.
4. **Close and handover:** Verify overall satisfaction with the delivery, think about ongoing support (if not already in place as each slice has been completed) and review the benefits realised.

Without spoiling the punchline, I hope you can already see some broad overlaps in these methods. While some people will guide you to the idea that you must do only one of these things – as we have seen, agile good, waterfall bad, and JFDI worse – my view is that we are doing all of them, all the time. The rest is merely marketing, and to demonstrate, I will take a deeper look at agile.

Agile! Oh, agility!

Agility (or agile-something-or-other) is a zeitgeist word. We are encouraged to be *agile* in almost everything: agile in projects and delivery, in HR, in finance, in government (and governance), in procurement, in resource planning, in marketing, in sales, in strategy, in service management, in account management and more.

Agile has spread outside of work too, and people are openly and delightedly

---

* A brief note on slices. Imagine a loaf of bread as the product being delivered. A valuable increment of delivery – something we can use – is a slice of bread. Delivering a component, like the yeast or salt, is no value even though it is part of the final product.

using agile techniques to conduct parties, weddings,* funerals and other ceremonies.[41] We are using agile in schools and education. We even have companies selling specialist knowledge to churches to help them become 'More Agile'. From this list, it might appear that agile is some kind of new, shiny panacea. That becoming more agile will cure all ills. Indeed, it is easy to find blogs and articles that hint at a cult-like following for agile as *the* fix for your team's productivity, *the* answer in your organisation or *the* obvious choice. That warrants some further thought.

What is agility?

For an event some years ago, I was asked to provide a description of agility. I chose the metaphor of a guided missile, as opposed to a rocket. In the case of a rocket, we design and calculate everything up front and – based on the accuracy of our sums – we hit or miss our target. However, if our target starts moving, or we decide too late that we should not have launched, we are at a loss. Step up the guided missile. Once we have launched, we still have some opportunity to redirect and update our flight path and destination while en route. We hold some level of control and choice until the last moment.

> *In the pursuit of some goal, 'being agile' simply means that we give ourselves more opportunity to make changes along the way, based on the newest data we have.*

While that definition is crude, that is all that agile is. In the pursuit of some goal, 'being agile' simply means that we give ourselves more opportunity to make changes along the way, based on the newest data we have. In changeable environments, or those where we begin with limited information, being able to regularly adapt hopefully sets us up for a good and cost-effective outcome.

---

* 'Manage your wedding with Scrum' seems quite a common idea recently. However, as Scrum is, by design, an iterative approach to discover and create a well-fitting product, my assumption would be that we would attempt multiple (and hopefully increasingly satisfying) weddings. OK people, once more, but this time with feeling!

The implied alternative, to make all of our calculations up front and commit to an unchangeable course of action, regardless of feedback, could mean we achieve neither.

These ideas are anything but new. Travelling to a country for the first time, do you expect that everything will work out as you plan, or are you open to things working out differently? Taking a route to work, would you try one route, and one route only, forever, or might you attempt more than one to see if there are advantages? When your sports team (or army!) is losing against the opposition, do you stick fast to the game plan or reflect and change? When you are attempting to sell to a new market, do you rigidly commit to your planned sales and marketing strategy come what may? Of course not. We attempt something based on an idea – 'we *think* this marketing campaign will work' – and then adapt using the results we receive.

In other words, we are following the scientific method where, based on the things we observe, we create a hypothesis, test it and then respond to the results. Considering agility from this perspective, we see it everywhere. Here are three short examples.

1. Roger Bacon, scholar, philosopher, and friar (1220–1292): Bacon advanced the use of empirical scientific methods in Europe, noting the importance of experimentation over reasoning alone. In *Opus Majus* he notes that, 'There are numerous beliefs commonly held in the absence of experiment, and wholly false … The natural philosopher forms a judgement on these things: the experimenter proceeds to test the judgement.'[42]

Moreover, he records what is thought to be the first formal abstraction of experimentation as a discipline: 'Inventions of the greatest utility may be discovered, as perpetual fire, or explosive substances, or modes of counteracting dangerous poisons, and innumerable other properties of matter as yet unknown for want of experiment.'[43]

2. *Crime and Punishment* (Dostoyevsky, 1866): A philosophical conversation between Razumihin and Pulcheria in the classic *Crime and Punishment* that could be the direct inspiration for Eric Ries's *The Lean Startup*.

'What do you think?' shouted Razumihin, louder than ever, 'You think I am attacking [my uncle, others] for talking nonsense? Not a bit! I like them to talk nonsense. That's man's one privilege over all creation. Through error you come to the truth! I am a man because I err! You never reach any truth without making fourteen mistakes and very likely a hundred and fourteen.'[44]

3. OODA Loop, 1986: The OODA loop is a decision-making cycle attributed to Colonel John Boyd of the US Air Force.[45] Boyd proposed that pilot decision-making is carried out in a cycle, where we:

- Observe: Take in unfiltered information about the situation and environment.
- Orient: Understand the relevance of information to knowledge and previous experience.
- Decide: Choose what to do based on that orientation.
- Act: Take that action and go back to observe.

If, for example, two jet fighters are engaged in combat operations, both will be executing their own OODA loops. Boyd noted that 'in order to win we should operate at a faster tempo or rhythm than our adversaries'.[46] In other words, the fighter that can process the loops more quickly can get inside their opponent's loop, changing the situation before their opponent has decided what to do next. Interestingly, in a later version from 1996, Boyd expanded 'orient' to include elements such as cultural traditions and genetic heritage. This speaks directly to our discussions on the differences in our individual interpretation and their origins.[47]

In all three examples, there is cyclical behaviour based on the results and data that we have. That sets up a better description of agility: because we do not know if what we are attempting is possible, we know changes will happen, and we might be wrong, we organise ourselves so that we can appropriately observe and respond to circumstances.

Connecting this back to the idea of domains, you may have already (and correctly) identified that this experimental approach is better suited to unpredictable contexts. In a complex domain, for example, we will be dealing with multiple, independent actors where cause-and-effect relationships are only knowable after the fact. We might have an outcome in mind, but until our action, decision or otherwise is in progress and we make observations, we cannot know if it will help. Working in this context, committing to an inflexible plan relies – perhaps recklessly – on the correctness of our implicit and explicit assumptions. Instead, we will be better served by responding to new data through the results we get, testing our assumptions and adapting our strategy. Conversely, in a clear, *predictable* context, where there is a known cause-and-effect relationship, fast-cycling principles make less sense. Using upfront plans – especially those that have been successful previously and sharpened into precise methods – will be significantly more efficient. If we plot these ideas on a graph, we can see that we would be better served with more agility when we have less predictability (Figure 6-2).

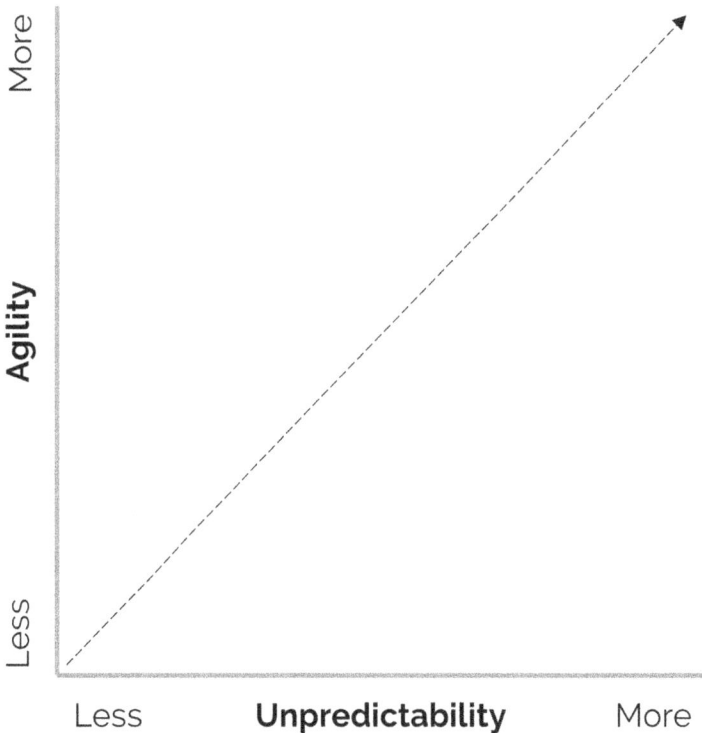

Figure 6-2. Relationship between agility and unpredictability

It is worth expanding the idea of being more or less agile before we continue. I define something as operated or delivered in a *more* agile way if we have a greater number of opportunities to reflect, decide and redirect work through its duration. By contrast, something *less* agile will have fewer opportunities to adapt in that same time – or even no opportunities at all.

To illustrate, imagine that we have two teams tasked to improve our website over the next 12 weeks. The target that they both have is to a) increase the time an average visitor stays on the site and b) increase the number of 'clicks' through to other pages. To achieve this, Team A spends three weeks on analysis, stakeholder engagement, design and the creation of a detailed project plan. This plan includes all of the work they want to do to achieve the design, and with that written, they focus all of their efforts on delivery. The team then works to finish testing so that they are ready for release in week ten, giving a two-week window for aftercare and troubleshooting.

Meanwhile, Team B, looking at the same objective, spends one week reviewing data available, connecting with stakeholders and producing working theories to pursue. Within a two-week block, they deliver lightweight prototypes for three of their ideas, and collect data about the potential impact of each. They discuss the results of these with relevant stakeholders, then refine their aims before planning their next two-week block. The team repeats this two-week cycle, sharpening their design and release a production pilot at eight weeks. The remaining four weeks are spent on improvement and a push to full production.

Based on my definition, Team B is operating in a more agile way since they gave themselves a greater number of opportunities to change course and adapt, based on interim results. By contrast, Team A did not have any clear opportunity to change course once their design and plan was in place. There were trade-offs, however. During the 12 weeks, Team B spent much more time planning and meetings, where Team A was able to use all their time to do 'actual' delivery work once the plan was created. That means if Team A were right in their design and plan, they would have delivered more, but crucially if they were wrong, they could have delivered something ineffective – or worse, something that no-one wanted. Team B's approach meant that even if they sacrificed some delivery time, they did not have to be correct in their design or planning upfront. They gave themselves space to test these assumptions and tune designs based on interim results.

To show that visually, let us also add some broad cost ideas to that graph. As Figure 6-3 shows, applying more agility when there is no need could cost us more (additional exploration, planning revisions, meetings and disruption to work-time). Alternatively, applying non-agile practices to uncertain, complex and changeable contexts could also cost us (failing to deliver something valuable, paying more to cover assumptions, potential over-delivery). If that representation is true, there will be a point at which the costs of being agile or not are equal, and it truly does not matter which path you take.

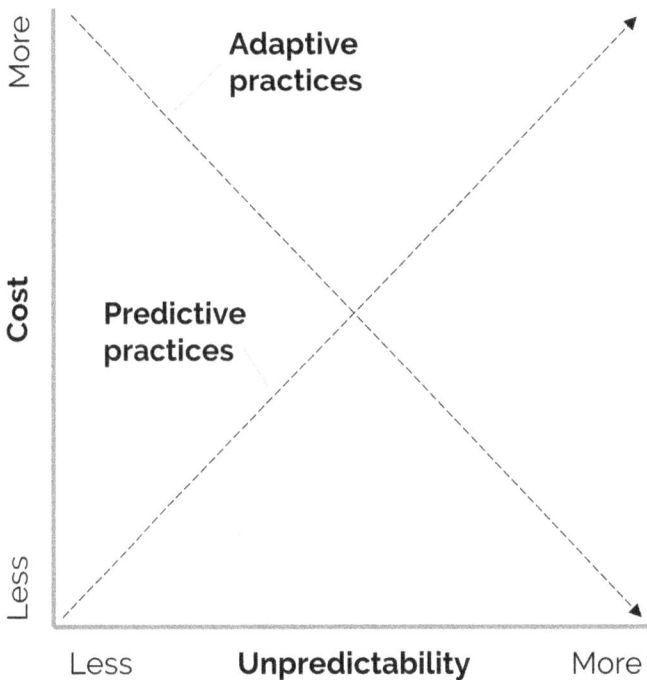

Figure 6-3. Relationship between practices, unpredictability and cost

Agile culture

I can imagine the voices of previous colleagues at this point, calling out, 'Agile isn't just experimenting and adapting, Stephen, it's a philosophy!' They are also likely to point out that *doing* agile is quite different from *being* agile – so I will respond in advance. The modern idea of an agile culture, and something that some would recognise as a change in our ways of working, is rooted in the Agile Manifesto published in 2001.[48]

The story is well told, so I will keep it brief. In essence, a group of software engineers and leaders from across development methods came together to craft a set of principles to fight against the heavyweight documentation and process-driven standards of the time.* The group produced the following statement:

Manifesto for Agile Software Development

We are uncovering better ways of developing software by doing it and helping others do it. Through this work we have come to value:

Individuals and interactions *over processes and tools*

Working software *over comprehensive documentation*

Customer collaboration *over contract negotiation*

Responding to change *over following a plan*

That is, while there is value in the items on the right, we value the items on the left more.

Assuming that software development is typically unpredictable and (Cynefin) complex, that aligns with the discussions so far. In these environments, which demand adaptation to succeed, we will be much better off without strict plans, onerous processes and litigious customer engagements. The implication for teams is a freedom to evolve their work in partnership with each other and their customers, while keeping an eye fixed on value creation. As the last line of the manifesto clarifies, this in no way means that we also abandon all controls, documentation and processes, but seek a 'left'-leaning balance.

Compare this description with the Taylor and Sloan management of outputs approaches discussed in Chapter 1. If our organisational culture

---

* To be clear, not all software was being written in a 'heavyweight' way.

(more in Chapter 8) is one that favours that kind of control – the right-hand side of the manifesto – we are going to be hard-pushed to make ground with adaptive practices.

A brief example relates to a software project my team was working on. In previous predictive projects, with complete analysis and design up front, we would state costs with a relatively small variability for sign-off. Starting its first slice, and with many unanswered questions to be solved as we progressed, the range of potential costs this time was extremely wide. To the finance director this was both baffling and unacceptable, and we were asked to provide tighter estimates. We could only do that with much more analysis – effectively making us a predictive, waterfall-like team – or by making something up. I will let you decide which path we took.

Hang on a moment, something smells

This all makes it sound like there is a correct approach for all the activities we do! It implies things like:

- Predictive waterfall projects cannot change course once started.
- Predictive waterfall should not be used to deliver software (or anything else in a complex domain).
- Every team working with agile is experimenting, deeply customer-engaged and adapting to client needs.
- Using agile for a straightforward task is a sort of deadly sin.
- Because of collaboration, agile teams are more 'customer-centric'.
- Successful agile teams exist only in open, non-bureaucratic organisations and successful waterfall teams in hierarchical, cautious organisations.

That is ridiculous. In reality, the area of 'it does not matter which approach you use' is far wider than the intersection point in Figure 6-3, and actually looks much more like a Venn diagram's overlap (Figure 6-4). Complex, multi-faceted and pioneering initiatives would *probably* be more efficient with adaptive approaches. Likewise, core, well-known and repetitive initiatives would *probably* be more efficient with predictive techniques. However, we would make progress regardless of which path we choose. Since we may not know when we start if a project would be better with experimentation or procedural rigour, that is a good thing. It is also a good thing for our teams that will have capabilities and preferences across the whole diagram.

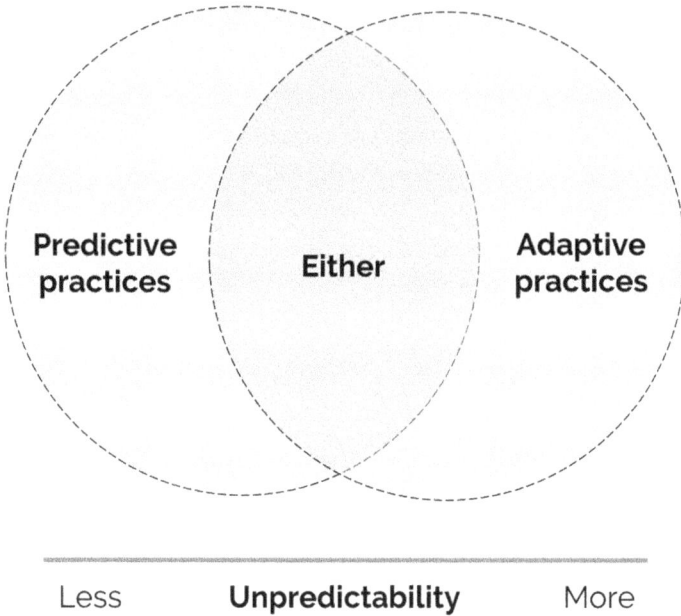

Figure 6-4. Relationship between practices and unpredictability

Lastly, in our choices about which practices we use, we will inevitably be influenced by the culture of our organisation. Coming back to the two delivery philosophies from Chapter 1, our organisation may default to controlling task and process (management of outputs) or aim to relinquish control with more open and egalitarian options (systems and enablement). That will affect our options and choices, but it is not a fixed relationship. Not all bohemian-West-Coast-USA organisations run agile-like operations, and neither do all heavily regulated, established and conventional ones stick to fixed procedures. As above, the areas of the Venn diagram overlap a great deal and, if it is not already apparent, agile working is often 'rooted in practitioner advocacy, *not* academic purity (Figure 6.5)'.[49]

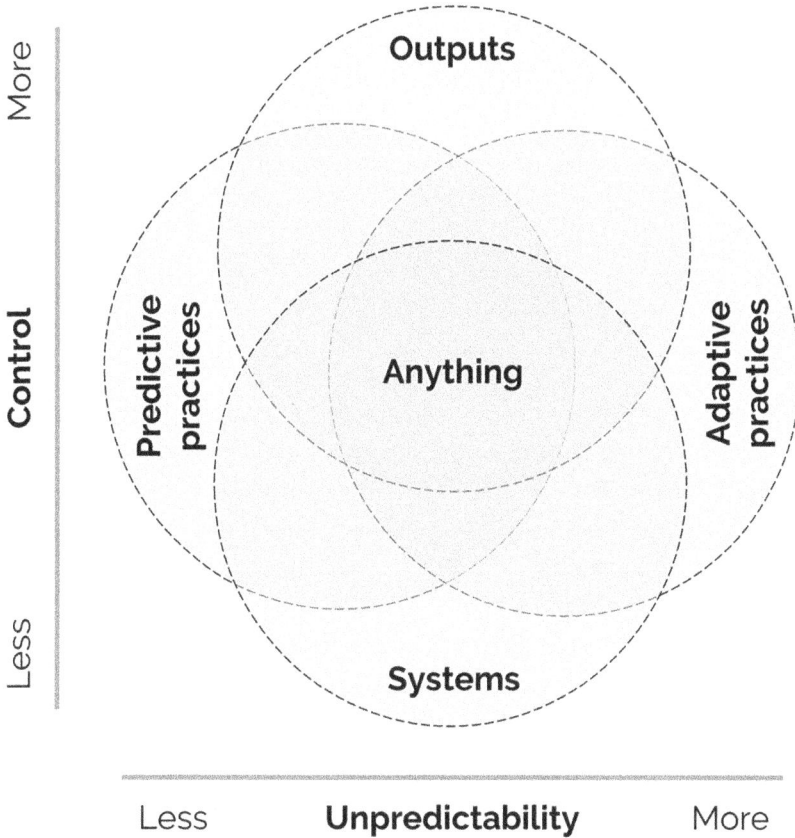

Figure 6-5. Relationship between practices, control and unpredictability

Scaling delivery

From the standpoint of 'it does not matter what you use', we can argue the value of rolling out a homogeneous organisation-wide practice. A hypothesis would run something like this:

If we accept that our work exists on a spectrum of predictability, and that it can change over time, we can gain advantages by using standard skills, language and processes across our organisation. For example, standardisation will mean that when new teams are created, they can get started immediately; there is no need to explain the rules. Additionally, at a more macro

145

level, this decision will mean an organisational shorthand will emerge for how-we-do-things-around-here. That second-nature familiarity should outweigh any disadvantages we might get for working out of ideal context.

Although a single practice is much easier to implement – one set of skills to recruit, train and sharpen – with many tens, even hundreds of teams needed, which side of the metaphorical fence do we come down on? If you have 1,000 people in front of you, 'Should we use PRINCE2?' is suddenly much harder to answer than for one independent team.

Let us imagine part of an organisation with a function and a project (Figure 6-6). The function operates in a relatively stable environment and its teams can work in a predictive way (P). The project, however, faces volatility and complexity, inviting the teams and the overall project to work in an adaptive way (A). Providing that these functions are independent, it makes little sense to force either to work in a way that is out of context with their environment. At the organisation level, we can set our objectives with a mix of both, accounting for what each function delivers.

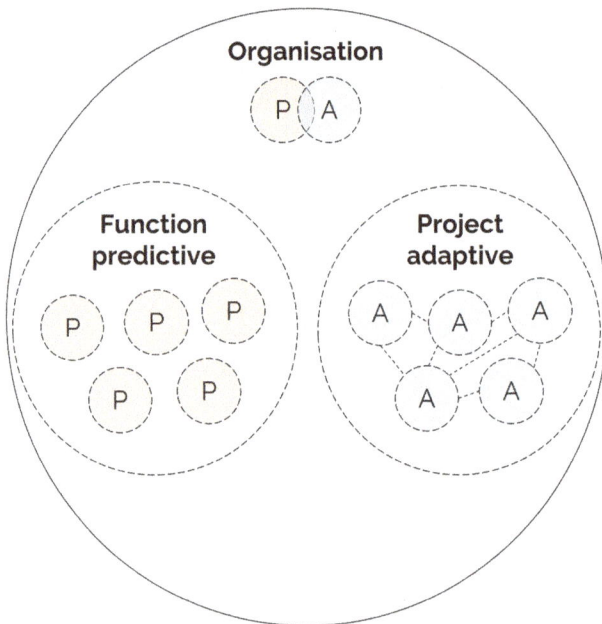

Figure 6-6. An organisation with a predictive (P) function and adaptive (A) project

Now consider a setup with unpredictable contexts alongside predictable ones (Figure 6-7). In this example, the function could represent an IT group delivering cutting-edge software alongside maintenance of a small desktop and laptop estate. As before, if these teams are independent, we can support them working in a context-sensitive way. By contrast, in the project we have mixed teams who *do* need to coordinate, likely requiring compromise from all groups involved.

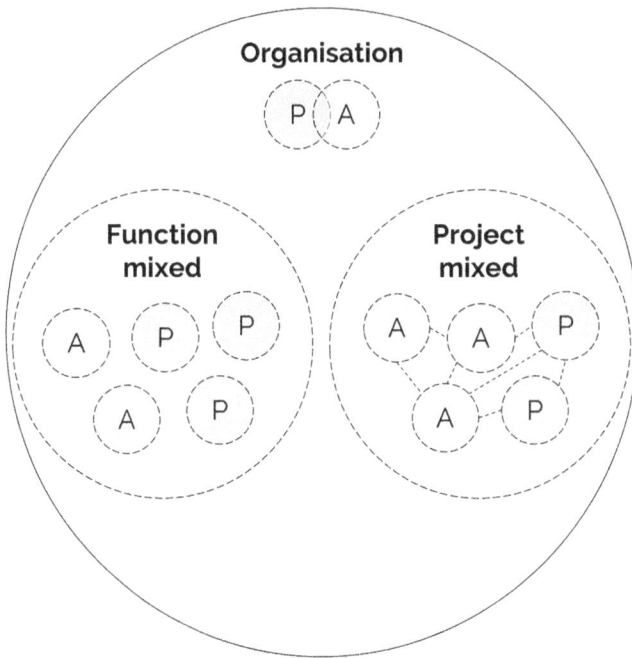

Figure 6-7. An organisation with a mixed function and mixed project using both predictive (P) and adaptive (A) elements

To illustrate, imagine the adaptive teams set up to release changes weekly and the predictive ones quarterly. With dependencies between them, the adaptive pace could cause planning headaches for the predictive, and in return, the adaptive teams could be sitting on their hands waiting for a necessary component. Broadly we have two options.

- Change the approach so that everyone works in the same way. Teams could coordinate themselves, or we might bring the work under a scaling framework, for example Large Scale Scrum (LeSS), Scaled Agile Framework (SAFe), or Managing Successful Programmes (MSP).
- Leave the team methods intact, instead coordinating at the programme or portfolio level, 'above' the teams. This capability could be drawn from the teams, or externally, and would seek to manage dependencies and bridge gaps in timing and expectations.* To achieve this, regular engagement between people from all teams would be essential, with visual maps, plans and current data to assist conversations and sense-making.

There are advantages with each. A single approach to coordination of plans, backlogs and dependencies can aid planning and communication, but must be weighed against levels of skill and suitability for each team's task. Mixed modes, by contrast, are context-suitable but require more continuous efforts in planning and dependency management. Assuming no organisational rule, a typical approach to decide what to use is a product- or value-based lens. By mapping the major components and known dependencies of the thing that we are trying to do, priority and approach decisions can be informed. In other words, with some facts and paths identified, we can discuss which option we think gives the highest value to our stakeholders.

It is also worth noting the intrinsic behaviour that these options regarding practice reveal. In all cases, we must have some kind of coordination, whether from the teams themselves or something dedicated. This will entail plenty of conversation and discussion with regular evaluation of position and velocity.** Indeed, with more moving parts, we are compelled to act when a team is blocked by another, we discover the order of events could be improved, or an outside influence changes our plans.

---

* As it was once described to me, programme management provides the tallest pole in the tent. It cannot hold up on its own but allows all others some space.

** Velocity in the mathematical sense of a magnitude and direction, i.e., are we going to the right place fast enough?

While there is variability in how much people think they can control (Figure 6-5), our programmes will fail if they do not adapt to circumstances. Moreover, this behaviour continues beyond the project and programme environment, to the functions, organisation and board. Of course, you will not normally see a boardroom reviewing corporate strategy on a fortnightly basis, but each will conduct adaptive discussions at its own tempo.

Operations and management

Now that we have delivered something, let us take a look at the next stage of the product development life cycle: operate. This is the product stage where we are managing, maintaining, and servicing the product so that (hopefully) our users, customers or otherwise continue to receive its desired benefits. It will not surprise you to note, once again, that there are plenty of different approaches to this. Within the IT sphere where I have spent much of my life, frameworks and movements come and go, with some of the most talked about being the IT Infrastructure Library (ITIL) and, more recently, DevOps (a portmanteau of 'development' and 'operations', which can also sometimes include security, in the form DevSecOps). To demonstrate the breadth of choice, here is a list of some other practices and ideas that also exist in this ecosystem:

- Control Objectives for Information and Related Technologies (COBIT)
- Microsoft Operations Framework (MOF)
- Kepner-Tregoe's Problem Solving & Decision Making (PDSM)
- Site Reliability Engineering (SRE)
- The Open Group Architecture Framework (TOGAF)
- Six Sigma for IT
- Kanban
- Lean IT
- ISO/IEC 20001 (Service Management)
- ISO/IEC 27001 (Information Security Management)

Conveniently for us, many of these approaches tend to fall into predictive and adaptive arguments like the delivery methods. Frameworks like ITIL, COBIT and anything ISO come from a perspective of predictive process and control of outputs, while DevOps, SRE and Lean invite greater collaboration and adaptation.

Let us look a little closer. ITIL[50] is a collection of practices and guidelines for the management of an IT service. Version 4 of the framework includes tested best practices for 34 processes, from the financial aspects of service management through to management of capacity, handling of incidents and problems, and the control of change. In the collection of processes under the heading of service transition, one process will be useful in comparison to DevOps, i.e. 'transition planning and support'. This process provides a bridge or a gate, if you will, between the development or update of a service and its live use. The process examines and documents the needs for live service into a plan, include people and roles, stakeholder engagement and criteria for execution. That plan then feeds into associated change control and release processes to put the new service into the hands of its users and production support teams. Think of it like a relay race when we are releasing services, with each separate function or stage handing over ownership to the next.

DevOps, as the name suggests, blurs those edges of responsibility. Rather than a handover of responsibility, team to team, with a DevOps approach, the teams overlap and run together with a shared goal. This intends to allow all involved – from developers to operational staff and others – to collaborate and flex to deliver value for the end-users and remove back and forth if there are bug fixes or process updates to be made. For the customer or operations team engineer that spots a problem or has an idea, the prospect of being able to discuss and prioritise this from the inside of a multi-disciplinary team can be much easier and faster than the formality of official change requests and lobbying to get back onto the development schedule. Indeed, trying to get a problem resolved when the original development team has already been reassigned to some other project can be slow or even futile.

The implication is that ITIL is more suitable when we are working with more predictable, less changeable products or environments, and DevOps the opposite. While the philosophies of these approaches are different – in ITIL, to say what we are going to do and do it, and in DevOps, to collaborate and support one another with business value in mind – that is not the end of the story. Service management activities, like managing capacity, incidents and problems, do not go away if we are using DevOps. ITIL is not intended as a strict rule book that you must adhere to.* And there is nothing to say that a problem or enhancement with a release cannot go straight back to the top of the development workload. The reality is that you are going to need both kinds of approach, blended, based on the situation you are in. Yes, it is that word again: context. As a simple example, let us consider two separate products being released into operation.

Product 1: Email platform (migration)

The first product is an update of an existing email platform to which users will be migrated overnight. There are experienced people in operations ready to receive the new update, and the engineers doing the migration are following a trusted plan from previous releases. The level of certainty in this exercise is high, but to mitigate risk a transition window has been added to the plan, when the migration engineers will be on standby to handle incidents. Once live, there is little or no need for the engineering teams to continue working with operations and they will go back to their normal work.

Product 2: Customer self-management tool (new)

The second product is the release of a new self-management tool for customers. The tool, requested by customers, will allow them to carry out several tasks independently of a phone or email request. The transition plan is simple, making the service available to customers in batches, but there is uncertainty about how customers will respond. Moreover, as a completely new product, operations teams have no experience of handling incidents or support requests, and documentation is incomplete. The risk of embarrassment is high, so rather than a relay-like handover, a new team has been created using people from both development and operations disciplines. For eight weeks initially, this team will work together to support customers and handle

---

* Unless you pick up ISO 20000 and get audited. Like ISO 9000, the expectation from an assessor will be wider adherence to the outputs required, more than the picking and choosing of aspects that generate the most individual business value.

any problems and changes. Its single goal will be to make the new tool a success, both for customers and internal teams.

We could, of course, switch the approaches around, and still get our products released. In either case, specialists will eventually go back to their original teams, and operations will end up in charge of service management activities. However, in line with the theme throughout this book, working with methods appropriate to context is important. Choosing a linear process in a wildly unpredictable environment, or a highly collaborative one, for something known and predictable is unlikely to be as effective nor satisfying for the teams involved.

Measurement and reporting

While Vic Reeves dryly concluded that, '96.2% of all statistics are made up on the spot', essential measurements exist in almost every aspect of our lives.* From civic to professional, from personal health to property, they help us to track our progress, identify patterns and inform. Measurements provide irreplaceable context, inviting us to comprehend, converse and make sense. To illustrate, here are a few statements that alone suggest something of the situation:

- A state election was won with a 99% majority
- Website visits and 'click-throughs' on our website have been zero for two days
- 980 hours of flight time in the last 11 months
- Waiting lists for heart operations have doubled
- A person walked more than four million steps in 2022

In business, without understanding how much revenue we make, when our products should be ready, or the costs of goods and services, we are flying blind in our decision-making. However, despite this necessity and the prevalence of measurements, if you ask people for their thoughts, many have stories of misuse, mistrust and scepticism. Indeed, while a measure is ideally a cold and factual description of something, how it is interpreted and used can be wildly different.

---

* The fact that I found several different numbers when looking up the quote is just wonderful.

The good side of measurement

To get us thinking more about measurement, consider a rower preparing for a 2,000-metre Olympic single sculls race. The current world record for that class and race was broken in 2017 at the World Rowing Cup II by New Zealand's Robbie Manson. Manson achieved the record time of 6:30:74, with the second place rower nearly eight seconds behind him, and the last placed 30 seconds back – a full 8% slower.[51] For a rower to achieve that kind of pace requires exceptional physical and mental condition, with years of experience and training. Moreover, that training does not track a standard formula for each rower. Every individual will be following a continually refined regime, influenced by environmental and performance data, with the goal of reaching peak performance at exactly the right time. Knowing six months out from a competition that our season's best is 6:40 will lead to different activities than if it were 7:00. The kinds of performance information a rower will be tracking include:

- Average 2,000 m time (seconds)
- Average speed (km/h)
- Peak speed (km/h)
- 500 m split times (seconds)
- Stroke rate (strokes per minute)
- Distance travelled per stroke (metres)

Alongside this information about progress towards their goals, rowers will also monitor their training activity, nutrition and general health, including:

- **Weekly training:** On-water training (12 x 1 hour), gym regime (6 x 3 hours), 2,000 m practice races (x 3), strokes at 25 strokes per minute (1,000)
- **Nutrition and well-being**: Take on 5,500 calories per day, 7 hours sleep (10 pm lights out), daily meditation (30 mins), vitamin supplement mix
- **Health**: Lung capacity (litres), body weight (kg), average heart rate (bpm), peak heart rate (bpm)

By correlating these two sets of data – the results they are getting and the work they are doing – the rower will have a view of current performance and hopefully of the impact of training changes they make.

By contrast, if we only measure our performance, we miss insight about how we are achieving it, and if we only measure our effort, we miss insight about the effectiveness of that work. All the measurement of outputs, inputs and outcomes is feedback to drive better performance and results. Statistics may not always look great, but to improve and develop, the facts are essential.

Personally, I am a keen competitive archer, and the value I get from tracking inputs (what I practice, how often, how I fuel myself during and after competitions, how I set up my equipment) alongside scores and event performance is invaluable.

Scaling this to a team, for example players at a Premiership football club, we have similar considerations. For each player, personal performance will be tracked (goals, work-rate, clean sheets, tackles), alongside managed nutrition, exercise and recovery schedules. Beyond the individuals, we use data at a team level with indicators including tactics, positions and roles (who and how they play), and with output data like number of goals, shots on goal and percentages of possession. With the data in hand, we can tweak our strategy or activities,* and ideally get the edge on our competition.[52]

> *By the very act of monitoring metrics around inputs and performance, we are more explicit with ourselves and our teams about what we are trying to achieve.*

As an additional benefit, measurements are not just indicators of what has happened. By the very act of monitoring metrics around inputs and performance, we are more explicit with ourselves and our teams about what we are trying to achieve. Briefly returning to the idea of 'world-class customer experience,' we can colour in our intentions with some metrics. If, beneath this aspiration we understand we would like high retention, fix rate and referral scores, we at least have some boundaries to work with.

---

* For those old enough to remember the World Cup of 2006, the England coach Sven Goran Eriksson even banned players from having sex before important matches, so as to improve performance.

For all of the value that these measurements might bring us, there is very much a need for caution. There is a bad side to measurement – in two areas in particular: accuracy and politicisation.

Accuracy (in complexity)

There is a rule of thumb in troubleshooting that when looking for root cause, we should test our ideas one at a time. That is, if we think that A or B might be the cause of C, we should try them independently to see what happens. For example, we notice that an application on our computer no longer opens. We think that a new update to the software could be the cause, but we also think that a change in a security system restriction could be the culprit. Following the rule here, we should attempt to test one of the ideas, and then – should it not be successful – reverse that change and try the other one. The alternative approach, where we do not separate the actions, makes it difficult – if not impossible – to know which change made the difference. In a small system where we are fully in control, this is easy to do, but how well does this work in some of the scenarios above?

Looking again at the football team, let us consider an intentional change to tactics. We have explained to our team what we would like to have happen and have put time into training and understanding for all of the players. The next match comes along, and we win! Does that mean that the new tactics are successful and should be deployed every time? Or that we should consider dropping those tactics if we lose? Of course, we are not in a small system. We are in a complex one – at least in aggregate – with no linear relationship between the change we make and the results on the pitch. In each match, we have confounding elements that include variable player experience with the tactics, an unknown level of opposition performance, different-sized pitches, weather conditions, the make-up of and relationships in our team, the physical and mental condition of our players, and fan support.

In Chapter 3, I wrote about the dangers of mixing up correlation and causation, and we have a substantial risk of that here. It is hugely tempting – and easy – to associate an event with a result, especially if it seems related. English cricket has been dominated recently by the idea of 'Bazball', a style of play that emphasises players making positive decisions. The approach, encouraged by coach Brendon McCullum (nicknamed Baz) and Ben Stokes in 2022, has proven successful with higher than ever run rates. Roll forward a year to the 2023 Ashes series, and we have headlines like these:

Ashes 2023: What Bazball got wrong – and right – in the 1st Test defeat

Ashes 2023: Why England's Bazball style is starting to lose its shine

Explained: How Bazball-led England messed up golden chance to win home Ashes against ageing Aussie side

Bazball vindicated despite England drawing Ashes series[53]

Despite the obvious complexity of cricket, and an Ashes series where England and Australia played five test matches at different grounds over six weeks, these headlines lead you to believe that there was one variable: Bazball. The performance of the England team is directly linked to Bazball, and placed as the true cause of England's performance, not merely a correlation.

Ignoring the press response, we have also seen something else surrounding Bazball. The average run rate while these tactics have been used has been England's best in test matches by some margin. The team has a growing pool of data from performances built up over time, where results are better: X input *tends* to yield Y output. The results in aggregate hint at things that behave more like a cause than a correlation. We can never prove that cause as, yet again, we have no control in this experiment. There is no England team, identical in every way except their choice to play without Bazball tactics, to compare results with. The conclusion is also confounded over time, as there is ample opportunity for other things to change. They may be intentional, like changes to diet or exercise, but many more will occur without control or awareness. I would argue that a key player fed up with their coach and on the brink of quitting will have more impact than the most inspired tactic.

Drawing this back to the office, consider feedback from surveys and engagements with customers. Understanding how customers feel about our products and services is a rich source of information, but what does that mean for our operation? The pinnacle of this is net promoter score (NPS), a popular method for gauging general customer sentiment that asks the single question:

'Would you recommend us?' It is perhaps interesting to know that the number of customers that would recommend us has grown from, say, 65% to 72% – but it gives us zero insight as to why.

Politicisation

Alongside the challenges with correlation and causation of *what* is being measured, measuring teams or individuals can generate emotional and possibly irrational responses to the *why*. The performance of an IT customer services centre in a large legal organisation that I worked with, was measured with two KPIs:

1. Call waiting time: The average amount of time that inbound callers to the service desk needed to wait before their call was answered. The number was measured as an average of the number of seconds waiting, and as a percentage of all callers who exceeded a threshold of 25 seconds waiting time. In both cases, lower was better.
2. First-time fix: For callers into the service desk with a problem – something that needed troubleshooting or another resolution – the team was also measured on the percentage of caller issues resolved in the first call. A customer who needed to call back to resolve their issue would breach this measure, so the higher the first-time fix, the better.

Can you see the challenge? To provide a good resolution for a customer, and therefore increase the likelihood of a first-time fix, an engineer would need to spend time with that customer. However, because of the second measure to prevent waiting time, engineers were encouraged to wrap up calls as quickly as possible to answer the next one. Increasing first-time fix rates risked increasing the call waiting times and vice versa: call waiting times down, first-time fix down. The measures were just statistics, but the team's opinion of them was one of conspiracy. Some thought that the measures had been deliberately set in opposition so that the team 'could not win' and achieve both. One even told me that they thought the situation was engineered to limit increases to their pay in an upcoming review. The reality, as it often is, was more pedestrian. One measure was legacy, but the department leadership had not noticed that it was still being used and somehow the team (and team leaders) had not asked for it to go or removed it themselves.

Unfortunately, in teams, while there are many measures that can help a team tune and develop their own performance, measures are often perceived as having political – and hierarchical – interest. Things like a project being on/off track, utilisation, budgets, sales calls, meetings, service availability and attendance can all be seen as things to control, not to enhance. And what happens if you feel like you are under the spotlight for your numbers, and there's pressure to put on a good show? If you are going to get blamed or lose credibility? Accurate reporting quickly loses ground to favourable interpretation or presentation of data, massaging of figures, and misleading calculations that seem to prove that 1 = 2.*

The world of politics has plentiful examples. Pretty much any sphere you like – from immigration to the environment, the economy to education – has figures being issued that are interpreted to fit the chosen narrative:

- Covid anti-vaccine sites falsely claiming that figures proved more vaccinated people were dying than non-vaccinated[54]
- Ryanair asserting that it was Europe's lowest-emissions airline[55]
- That famous 'Brexit bus' in the UK that stated a saving of £350 million per week by no longer sending the money to the EU[56]

Projects are another rich source. One programme I worked with reviewed reports from various teams in weekly steering meetings. Each report contained highlights, risks, and a RAG (red-amber-green) indicator to summarise the status of the stream. Nothing unusual. What stood out however was the effort put into deciding what to report, with teams meeting for hours to discuss content and present their work in the best possible light.

---

* There are proofs of this, but only by employing mathematical fallacies.

Who cares *how* we deliver?

Who cares is an important but sometimes ego-testing question. If you are delivering results for your stakeholders and are meeting their needs for collaboration and adaptability, who cares what kind of approach you use? For example, does your customer worry whether you are using Scrum or PRINCE2, or if you have flattened your hierarchies? What about those people who are funding or delivering the work? Let us examine some stakeholders.

Customers

If customers are receiving timely results of a suitable quality, often something they need for their own customers, it is unlikely they will care much about your approach. Indeed, if a customer is asking questions about how you are doing the work, then that could highlight something going wrong. It could be a confidence-based question like: 'We trust PRINCE2, is that what you use?'or a policy-based driver like ISO 9000 enforcement. More worryingly, it could be a response to a lack of communication, or poor output, making them uncomfortable. In such a situation, telling your customer you are tightly aligned to Scrum, or have a neatly organised WBS* will not be the conversation they want.

Finance teams

For any project, someone holds the purse strings. Would the primary consideration of such a person or committee be whether you are adhering to a particular practice? No. Their concern will be primarily aimed at whether the money that has been allocated is being spent effectively and will yield results. In such a way, a funding committee would ask some questions if you had spent 12 months delivering something that nobody wanted, just as they would if you spent more than last quarter doing the same work.

An organisation's approach to budgets can be more of an influence on choices, however. For example, in a complex project, by definition, we do not

---

* Work breakdown structure (WBS) is the splitting out of the many sub-components of a project. Literally, a breakdown of the work.

know what is going to happen, nor when. Rather than allocate 12 months of funding to that unknown, it would be preferable to fund an initial small time-box, deciding what to do after that. Finance teams that insist on annual budgets may, unintentionally, force a team's hand to complete more analysis and planning upfront.

Delivery teams

Members of a delivery team clearly care about the approach, as they need to live with (or contest) whatever that decision is. In the software engineering industry, there is a de facto expectation that developers can work in agile environments, typically due to the unpredictability of software development. If we ask our teams to make fixed predictions about delivery dates and features, they face an extremely challenging task and unfair criticism, akin to 'Your estimate about next month's weather was wrong, again!' Simultaneously, with limited exposure to an industry standard way of working, a decision to not be agile can hamper an individual's ability to grow their career.

Delivery leaders also have a stake in the approach too, and choices of techniques across our work includes trade-offs. Multiple methods make delivery more context-sensitive, but make associated processes, hiring and the management of skills more complicated than consolidating to a central method of doing. We also create an opportunity for 'them and us' behaviours between adaptive and predictive practitioners.* I have seen many examples of PRINCE2 experienced project managers refusing to trust agile delivery, and agile teams refusing to do any kind of long-term planning, let alone execute a single mouse click inside Microsoft Project.

Vendors and consultants

While many operate from the perspective of supporting your organisation to deliver its best results, it often seems that vendors can care more than anyone else. On the good side, a consultant observing a team sailing towards an iceberg will step up and offer ideas and alternatives. More generally, a vendor may push an approach because, statistically, it has better results for some kinds of project than others.

---

* Much more on this in Chapter 8.

Unfortunately, on the bad side, some care because that is the only thing that they are skilled in, or more nefariously because they want to sell you tools, training or certifications. And as a reminder, what does a thriving certification system mean? More delivery teams want to use that method to make themselves more employable, and so it cycles.

I invite you to keep in mind that, unless explicitly stated, delivering value for stakeholders is the goal. The various approaches are merely tools, not destinations in themselves. Kai Gilb summed it all up perfectly in Jussi Mäkelä's Scraping Toasts podcast: 'No-one cares how agile you are.'[57] Incidentally, I would pay good money to have that sentence (or better still, that discussion) included at the start of every agile course.

Chapter summary

There are three major choices for delivery – JFDI, predictive and adaptive – and their suitability has a strong, but not infallible link to the context that we find ourselves in. Using a context-specific approach, in an organisation whose culture enables it, and whose people are deeply skilled, is ideal. However, that is not always going to be the position we start from.

More commonly our choice is influenced by elements such as our organisation's tendencies for central control, or simply the level of skill we hold in certain practices. Reassuringly, even if we pick a context-inappropriate method, work will still happen, results will be achieved, and inefficiencies identified can be used to demonstrate a need to try something else.

- Agility is primarily about the opportunity to adapt to changing circumstances and is something that every organisation already does, if only at a slow speed.
- Unpredictable and complex activity is *probably* more effective with practices that can adapt more frequently.
- Well-known and stable activity is *probably* more effective with repeatable and predictable practices that can be refined into tailored and efficient activities.
- Across an organisation, a whole spectrum of styles will be appropriate depending on the situation and context. No organisation is just one thing.
- Measurements are an irreplaceable tool in our ability to see and make sense of progress. However, be careful of unintended consequences based on their use in different circumstances or different interpretation across teams.
- Keeping value front of mind when we are deciding on practices or metrics is crucial. A value view can prevent waste caused by using a method for that method's sake, and it helps focus our choice on what is best for us, rather than what is best for a supplier's bottom-line!

CHAPTER 7

Teams, identity and organisational structure

'One person alone is not a full person: we exist in relation to others.'

– Margaret Atwood[58]

What is a team?

No matter how beautiful our vision, how inspired our strategy and how exceptional our working practices are, they amount to nothing without some people to do the work. This chapter turns our attention to the creation, construction and identity of the teams that will do just that. Apart from the prosaic 'people working together to achieve something,' what comes to mind for you when you think of a team? Examine the following sets of people and decide which are teams:

- **Set A:** A group of people that appears to be uncoordinated. Each person is talented, internally competitive and seems to operate independently. They produce results at the individual level, and long hours are common. Stress and turnover are high.
- **Set B:** A group formed of people who have been together for some time. Results are predictable within a set 'nine-to-five' pattern. Individuals need tasks broken down and repetitive training to embed skills. Changing existing routines is difficult and slow. Stress and turnover are extremely low, with average tenures of more than 15 years.
- **Set C:** A group formed of people who are collegiate, hold complementary skills and operate autonomously. They appear driven and seem to have fun working together. They are reflective, dedicate considerable

time to improving ways of working and regularly make changes based on individual feedback. Stress and turnover are moderate.

To most people I share this list with, set C seems to be the most (for some, the only) 'team-like' group. Undeniably, set C includes some contemporary ideals* for a team: collegiate, autonomous, driven, reflective and a hint that they have achieved a balance between work and life. All good things, probably.

Thus, should we conclude that if set C is a team, the others are not? Or at the very least, while the others also represent people working together to achieve something, the state they are in is not optimal? Yet again, it depends. I will look at five of the characteristics to illustrate.

1. Uncoordinated

Imagine a football team working together towards a common purpose: to score goals and prevent the other team from scoring against them. Uncoordinated individuals with their own agendas and priorities are unlikely to triumph over a group of people acting, wherever possible, in the best interests of the team. By contrast, if our team is instead a research and development function seeking innovation and new insights, central coordination and planning can stifle creativity and reduce speed of innovative ideas becoming reality.

2. Task breakdown and repetitive training

Considering a group of surgeons, rocket engineers or musicians, requiring task breakdown and repetitive training would be a concern. Qualified professionals should not need such intervention, and certainly not repetitively. The same might not be said of a group tackling unskilled or manual work, like fruit picking or other labouring. In such situations, highly autonomous and skilled individuals may well seek to move on.

---

* Ideals in the sense that these characteristics show up in contemporary leadership frameworks, rather than that they are always desirable.

3. Fun

Enjoying the time that you spend with a group of people can make stressful and challenging situations more tolerable, and it might even encourage people to provide more elective effort. After all, if work is *fun* then why would you go home? However, an overemphasis on fun can detract from delivery, will exclude some people or could even be inappropriate.*

4. Reflective

A team that challenges the effectiveness of routines, practices and tools can unlock potential. What we risk, however, is an over-analysis of performance, such that change becomes activity for the sake of change alone. Should a team meet more often? Should they use a different service management tool? Should they change the code base? Should they adopt Kanban? Each of these decisions has a cost which does not guarantee any improvement. Indeed, when considered against current performance, some could be a retrograde step.

5. Internally competitive

If we are all working towards the same goal – as a sports or product team – would do, being competitive with colleagues can be destructive. If a rugby forward selfishly attempts to score all the tries and beat fellow team members, we would likely see a drop in team performance. However, in sales and creative teams, people are not necessarily on the same pitch. That is, if I generate more sales in my region, that does not mean I have prevented anyone else from doing so in theirs.

---

* At one company I worked for, there was an initiative for a 'Friday Fun Day' where there was an expectation that each Friday, people did something fun, silly, or otherwise. What people mostly did was to cringe with embarrassment and try to keep their heads down.

'And I said they need to lighten up'

Back to the question of What is a team? I invite you to think of all of the above, and others besides, as characteristics of teams. They may be different types of teams, and ones which operate in ways more or less suited to their goals, but they are teams. In your own context, the more valuable question to ask is whether the team you have is *appropriate* – or even necessary – for the task at hand. My experience is that this question is asked too infrequently.

> ## Ask whether the team you have is appropriate for the task at hand.

When I started coaching a leadership team recently, they were similar to a Set A team – individually, hugely talented and capable, but when meeting as a group, there was limited shared ground and some confusion about roles. When I asked why they were meeting regularly, it sparked a conversation about purpose and generated three distinct perspectives: that the sessions were for a) information, b) policy and financial decision-making and c) steering collective goal delivery. It is perfectly possible that a team can achieve all three of these aims, but how we organise to make financial decisions is normally quite different from how we do so as a steering committee.

Asking the question allowed the group members to consider their roles, clarify their team's function, and then look at how they were organised.*

In your own context, is your team operating effectively towards its goals or requirements? If that is difficult to answer, spend time with the team discussing what you are aiming to achieve together, then revisit the question. It could be that you do not need a team at all or, if you discover that you do, this conversation will help you shape what happens next.

Identity and groups

As humans, we have a deep and fundamental motivation for group belonging and interpersonal attachment.[59] We act to form groups where there are none, act to stay within group bounds, and worse, actively disadvantage those who are not part of our own group. Here is a short example that I expect you are familiar with:

The business:	*Hey, IT, we need this thing.*
Someone in IT:	*Sure. We'll do that for you.*
[Time passes]	
The business:	*It's late and broken. You can't get anything right!*
Someone in IT:	*We delivered what you asked for! The business never knows what it wants!*
The business:	*You should know what we need.*
Someone in IT:	*We know now. Give us a month.*
The business:	*Don't bother. We've got a supplier doing it next week.*
Someone in IT:	*Good luck supporting it. We're not responsible.*

---

* Ruth Wageman et al, *Senior Leadership Teams: What it takes to make them great* (Hackman, 2008) provides a useful examination of leadership team types.

Here we have two groups, 'the business' and IT, and a case of 'them and us'. Even though IT is part of the business and that implies mutual interest, the relationship and self-identification are almost adversary. Words like 'we', 'us' and 'them' are coupled with a scepticism about capability and motivations.

One popular theory to explain this behaviour is social identity theory, developed by social psychologists Henri Tajfel and John Turner.[60] The theory suggests that all of us belong to 'in' groups that we identify with – for example, our families, friends, teams and those with similar hobbies, religions and political positions. Everyone else is an 'out' group, hence 'we' and 'they' respectively. However, more than just identifying with them, our behaviour, decisions and actions are weighted to favour and prioritise our in-group. We may not go out of our way to disadvantage out-groups, but inevitably, focusing on our own groups creates bias, stereotypes and other social consequences. The psychologist Jonathan Haidt evoked this idea by coining the useful term 'groupish' to describe our actions.[61] I will use that word from now on.

As we saw in Chapter 1, there are evolutionary benefits to being groupish. Consider troops of chimpanzees in tropical Africa, typically living in groups of 20 to 100 individuals. These groups succeed through their relationships and collaboration, creating safe territories that allow their members to thrive. This includes, for example, the stronger male chimpanzees patrolling their boundaries to prevent attack and encroachment from other chimpanzees, often by fighting other groups.[62]

In our human world, we could look to the Manchester football Derby between Manchester United and Manchester City. Two fellow Mancunians with much in common otherwise, but wearing different shirts on match day, can be fiercely loyal, and clashes are not unusual. To say the least, you would not have an easy day if you wore a Manchester United shirt and sat within a crowd of City supporters.

In book and film, the premise of good and bad, privileged and underprivileged, those that know and those that do not is constant: the abundant space-station city above the earth in Elysium, the people aware of being connected to the matrix, or the multiple relationships that Andy Dufresne achieves between inmates and guards in *The Shawshank Redemption*. In politics we have the split between left and right thinking, liberal and conservative-leaning policies – and, looking closely, splits and subgroups within those too. Consider your own political views for a moment on a contentious subject, like abortion, national service or immigration. What do you think about those people who hold an opposing view to you?

Thinking of leadership and the relationships between members of our organisations, this idea clearly has ramifications. For example, if leaders in a room have an identity with that leadership team *and* their own team or function, when a significant issue is tabled, who do they represent? Will each leader approach the issue from the perspective of the wider team and its aims, or from a functional, partisan view?

This weighing up of relative importance is a calculation that we all make in our conversations and decisions, and each of us will belong to many in-groups – personal and professional – capable of exerting an influence.

Not all groups will have the same effect on us, however. When I'm at work, it doesn't matter if I identify with Manchester City or Manchester United (unless I am on the Manchester United board, of course). Similarly, being a member of a team in one department does not automatically translate to a lack of awareness of other functions or of the wider organisation.

A quick in and out.

It might be tempting to think of in-groups being formed over time and due to deep commonality between members. Plenty of literature points to the need to develop bonds, trust and understanding between members.[63] That intuitively seems to be the case. After all, how much will I really care about your needs and believe in your capability if you are all but a stranger to me?

However, in another work by Henri Tajfel, he sought to discover the lowest stimulus for us to identify with a group.[64] In his language, this 'minimal group paradigm' was found to be surprisingly low. They observed in-groups already forming when the group membership was decided merely by coin toss (heads for allocation to group 1, tails group 2), by arbitrary commonality (colour of clothing), or stated preferences from a list of options or artworks.

This finding implies that the urge to connect and identify with a group is greater than any rational assessment of a group's value. In other words, the drive to belong to a group creates an urgency that may otherwise not exist. A few years ago, I also found that this extends to the *replacement* of groups. Due to the scaling of a product and growing ambitions, developers in one of my larger teams were split into two. Within days of the new structure, we heard scepticism in both teams about the work being delivered in the *other* group. People were already choosing them and us language, and shortly after, we observed one of the teams deprioritising work that benefitted the other, but not themselves.

The key point is that it is not easy to prioritise the needs of another group to which you have little or no connection. Thus, assuming that it is harmful to have all teams acting groupishly, this is an important subject to discuss. We all belong to multiple in-groups, and we cannot prevent it. The question is, rather than listening to another executive banging on about how we are 'One team!', what actions can we each take to build identities that bridge gaps between functions and support collaboration when we need it most?

Team structures and organisation

Following on from the idea that we know what our team is for, how then should we organise it to meet that need? Predictably, we are again faced with a proliferation of methodologies. You could choose to be self-managing and organise in circles of expertise. You could keep your team small for easier coordination and focus, allowing no more people than you can feed with two pizzas. You could deploy 'the Spotify model',* be virtual, teal or any of the other colours from Spiral Dynamics. And I promise that it is easy to find someone or some marketing guru that will recommend one or another to you.

To make sense of it all, let us once again bring things back to basics. In an attempt to meet some kind of target, the structure of the team or organisation we deploy will have a few universal components. These are:

1. Roles and responsibilities: divisions of labour to meet the needs and demands of stakeholders
2. Relationships: formal and informal connections between roles and stakeholders that allow them to function

---

* This is not a model per se, but it is how it seems to be referred to, and I have seen it pushed – and lapped up – in consultant/client relationships. The ideas (made public by Spotify in a community-minded gesture) are an interesting read and may inspire experiments – but to imply wholesale that the structure is a model for wildly different contexts is pure snake oil.

3. Regulation: mandatory and legal requirements based on industrial or national policy
4. Processes and practices: intentional and repeatable pathways for achieving our needs

If we are operating a mine, for example, we will need someone to do the mining (1), but they do not operate alone. They will work with other miners, safety teams, engineers, suppliers and contractors (2). In such an industry, general regulations will apply to aspects like safety and the environment, alongside any local government policy (3), and in the spirit of achieving all of these efficiently, some standard operating principles will be applied or emerge (4).

Structure for a particular team or organisation is then how we arrange these components given what we produce, the market opportunity, our available skills and the amount of work we can process. Taking an absolute and cynical shareholder-value view, the structure we want will maximise output and sales while limiting costs: we want our miners to be mining hard and our overheads low. This could translate into efficient or innovative practices to reduce waste – generally healthy things – but it might also mean we equip our miners with cheap tools and burden them with unreasonable responsibilities. Moreover, this emphasis would encourage pressure on suppliers to cut costs, and ultimately impact on the products customers finally receive.

A CEO of mine (not a CEO of a mine!) once gave an impassioned speech to our organisation stating, 'I do not want customer complaints, and nor do I want any customer praise.' In his view, praise meant that we were doing too much for our customers and that was not efficient. Taking the position of a customer, I philosophically understand the idea – I just want what I paid for, after all – but it is an uninspiring and thinly veiled call for teams to do what they can get away with to maximise profit.

Given this can all be pretty torrid for those involved, and at least unsustainable, we should include a fifth and sixth component to our structures:

5. Well-being: the experience that our people have while executing their responsibilities
6. Customers: the experience and value that our customers get from choosing to work with us

For our miner in the earlier example, we might consider varying shift patterns, tools, benefits and consequences (5) – and for our customers, quality standards, open dialogue and collaborative practices (6). We are getting close to all the raw materials we need, but looking primarily at the physical aspects there are two missing:

7. Philosophy: the organisation's general perspective about autonomy, leadership and balance of decision power
8. Culture: the intangible and emergent property from the previous components, alongside the individuals occupying their roles, and the beliefs and ideologies they bring with them

When our miners are at work, how much freedom to act do we expect to be available? Will they work within a strict social hierarchy and defer all decisions to a group leader, or would we want them to act autonomously (7)? How much stake or influence would they have in decisions about what, how and where work was being done or the policies of the mine? What values and behaviours are explicitly and implicitly endorsed, and which are not (8)?

All these components exert forces on the shape and structure of our organisations and, more or less, we have control over their dimensions and detail. That is, we are free to choose our disposition towards our customers or teams, and how information and decisions flow between them. In some cases, that freedom is limited from the outside – for example, a bank or other financial institution needing to abide by the 2002 Sarbanes–Oxley Act.[65] Additionally, if we make the decision to adopt a particular framework (having of course checked that this is an appropriate choice!), we will often find suggestions and templates within for how to organise and structure our teams. At one end, Scrum suggests three main roles – and, at the other, SAFe lists 14 and, by my count, ITIL details 45.

Faced with the abundance of options here, the key question we should hold on to is whether we are organised effectively for the task at hand. The answer to that question will ebb and flow as our situation develops with new customers, capabilities and context, but it does allow us to observe the eight components above and see if they are serving us.

Micro efficiency, macro waste

Imagine a simple scenario in a small IT organisation providing an application to customers. There are three teams involved, organised by their specialisms, and each has two related performance measures. Below is a description for each team, with the two related performance measures beneath.

1. A customer services team, providing a point of contact and support direct to users
   - First-time fix measure: the percentage of customer issues fixed during the first call to the team
   - Customer satisfaction measure: the overall happiness with the services being provided

2. A software team, developing and improving their core application
   - Lead-time measure: how long it takes for an idea to become a reality
   - Fitness-for-purpose measure: how effectively the application meets user needs

3. An infrastructure team, providing the servers and networks needed for the application to run
   - Availability measure: the percentage of up-time for the supporting infrastructure
   - Cost measure: the amount of cash spent on purchase and maintenance of the infrastructure

All three of the teams are doing well against their targets and have improved their results in the last year. Good stuff.

But now consider that a customer experiencing a problem contacts support (Figure 7-1). The customer services team answers the call (A), but in discussion, they realise that they need some help from the development team (B). Unfortunately, the development team does not have anyone available immediately, but they promise to look later in the day. Reluctantly, the customer services agent updates the customer, assigns the ticket to the software team, and looks for the next caller (C). Later in the day, a developer does look at the problem and is certain that it is a network issue, so updates the ticket and reassigns it to customer services (D). That evening an agent reads the update, tells the customer (E), and reassigns the call for a third time to the infrastructure team (F).

The next morning, the customer calls in again, still unable to achieve what they wanted to, and is told that the issue is under investigation by the infrastructure team (G). A few hours pass before one of the infrastructure engineers looks at the ticket. They look at some logs based on the user details and conclude that there is nothing wrong, suggesting the customer might 'try again'. The ticket gets reassigned to the customer services team (H), and they call the customer back (I). It still does not work, so the customer services agent tries a few other things that might help before confirming that it needs to be escalated to the software team again (J).

The merry-go-round spins for a few more cycles, and finally the customer has had enough: they call the CEO (K). Hearing the story, the CEO fires off a few 'JFDI!' emails to the customer services, software and infrastructure teams, to the tune of: 'I don't care who does it. Just fix it.' (L) Spurred on, members from each of the teams work together on the problem and discover a software incompatibility caused by a network change. The group discusses the options and, within an hour, their preferred fix has been applied and the customer is updated with the news (M).

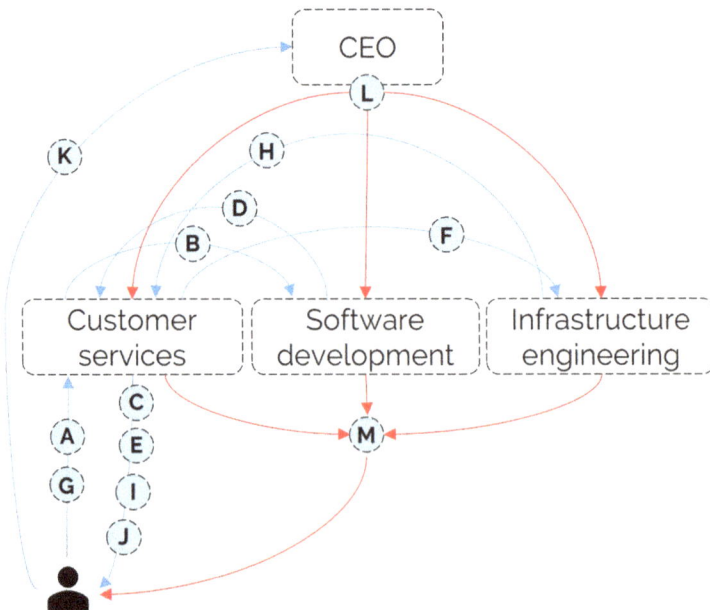

Figure 7-1. Customer problem resolution flow

Sadly, this is not an unusual situation, and it is easy to blame those involved. Perhaps the CEO in the story congratulated themselves on their indispensable leadership while berating the incompetence of their people. Perhaps the teams incriminated each other in a post-incident review. From the little we know, however, can we *morally* put fault at the feet of any of the teams? No. Looking back at the team setups, the only group with any customer-resolution priority is the customer services team. Neither of the other teams has any measure related to fixing problems for customers, outside of the abstracted aims of providing useful applications on stable hardware. That being so, why would they prioritise a customer ticket over their core targets? At a human level, no doubt each would like to help a colleague, but it is not encouraged by the structure.

Examining the structure further, the measures applied invite each of the functions to focus and optimise locally – to create, in organisational short-hand, separate silos. In the case of the infrastructure team, the goal of high availability at low cost will drive innovation and improvements to hardware. For the software team, targets of fit and speed of development push for understanding of customer needs and ideas, and their rapid delivery. For the customer services team, their hands are tied when they need support from peer groups. The target of customer satisfaction and immediate customer fixes will drive local learning and independence from their less customer-incident-responsive counterparts.

In this case, no matter how efficiently these teams operate, when something comes up that needs them to work together, the structures and imperatives will slow them down. This is an example of neglecting system-level optimisation in favour of local optimisation. We would want each part of our organisation to be more efficient or productive than it currently is, but that has to happen in the context of the system.* There are a few structural conclusions we can reach from the previous scenario, and here are two extremes.

Conclusion 1: There is nothing wrong with how we are structured. If we

---

* This is a classic problem for teenage boy racers., where a massive turbo upgrade renders their brakes ineffective. In my 20s I had such a large sound system in one car that the headlights would dim, and my windscreen wipers would stop each time the kick drum thumped. It was cool though.

change things around so that inbound problems like this get solved quickly with our best people, we will not deliver what we need to for our future. We have more than one objective, and fawning over customers each time things are not going their way will detract from our progress.

Putting aside the forthright analysis, there are always constraints on people and resources that demand decisions about how and where they are deployed. If we did assign deeply experienced engineers to the front line, short-term customer experience may be enhanced, but other efforts designed to benefit the long term could halt. Of course, keeping focus does nothing for the experience of a customer calling in, and nor does it save the teams from the effort needed to negotiate and defend their time.

Conclusion 2: This is awful! We should restructure and remove every barrier to collaboration. I can see the tagline now: 'Here at just-another-organisation.com, we've outlawed the silo, and everyone works together in cross-functional, diverse-skilled and happy teams!'

This argument stands up when the alternative is lengthy delays to information and actions between teams. Having people on hand and available so that there are not blocks of wasted time between one function and another makes sense, as does the implied, on-demand, access to the skills needed. However, before we smash all the silos, bear in mind:

- As described in Conclusion 1, efficiency in the short term can harm longer-term aims.
- Silos provide people who have similar skills with a space to specialise and develop together.
- A flat team can slow decision-making due to wide inclusions.
- Silos represent logical divisions of labour and skills that make it easier to see what you have.

Therefore, neither conclusion – to maintain strict hierarchical separation or to flatten structures and invite open collaboration – is ideal. In the end, regardless of how teams are put together, the litmus test for structure is whether our work inputs flow through to meaningful outcomes in suitable time and without too much waste.

> *The litmus test for structure is whether our work inputs flow through to meaningful outcomes in suitable time and without too much waste.*

My mind turns to Peter Crouch's Premier League wonder goal against Manchester City on 24 March 2012. From a goal kick, the ball was headed twice, controlled and then struck on the volley by Crouch, without hitting the ground once. There are few goals so fast and efficient, and evidently something was working well for Stoke City.[66] As we saw, in our own organisations, we rarely have the luxury of such a singular goal, and teams have their own objectives and distractions to account for. A more accurate mental image is perhaps that everyone on the pitch is simultaneously playing another game. Thus, and unlike Stoke, our players might not be there to receive the passes.

To take something from this discussion, I encourage you to experiment with the idea of flow. Working with teams and customers, observe and gather data about how work really flows and then discuss it. By mapping the path of activity – like the diagram in Figure 7-1 – you might discover that experimenting with the way that you are organised is justified or even essential. You could also find that, for now at least, the compromise of priorities you have feels about right.

Distribution of power

Throughout this book, I have made references to egalitarian and enabling styles of leadership and practice, using terms like autonomy, empowerment and self-organisation. With the kinds of prioritisation challenges just described, we can clearly benefit from a group of people responding and adapting directly with contemporary data and without the need for escalation. Indeed, it sounds wonderful that we inspire a team in some vision or another, and that they respond by promptly knocking everyone's socks off. That kind of assumption warrants some examination however, and that is what I will do here.

Empowerment and autonomy

Consider what we are trying to do when we want an individual or team to be empowered or to self-organise. Is our intention to delegate and spread the load, where we might ask a project team to lead on our behalf? Or do we mean to literally share power openly and freely with others, for them to wield it as they wish?

To answer that, take the word 'empowerment', meaning to give or transfer power to an individual, group, or community, from someone who has it. Our democratic politicians are empowered by their voters when given a mandate to lead. Board members are empowered by shareholders, and those same shareholders empower chief executives to be custodians of their companies. I regularly come across phrases like 'We empower our people' or 'I empower you to make the decision' in the teams that I work with, and such sentiments seem to signal good intentions, but there are subtleties.

First, it can be difficult to explain exactly what power is being given. Consider the empowerment to lead a project. Do we share the same understanding about the boundaries? Would I now have carte blanche control of hiring, budget and strategy within the team? I have been in many situations where we have discovered that a choice we made 'should' have been ratified by someone else. In one project, having signed off some supplier completion certificates, I was verbatim told 'Empowerment didn't mean that you could do that'!*

Second, is an empowered person ultimately free to deal with the ramifications of their actions and choices? When a manager is empowered to operate their team how they wish, does that really translate to unequivocal trust, or is it a more conditional 'You can do it as long as you don't f**k it up'? Like the failing politician, empowerment implies that there is always a dotted line back to the source of power. The voters, the board of directors and the people within a business can act if the power is being wielded poorly.

Third, and related to that dotted line, power without responsibility can be dangerous. One argument against limited companies is that the shareholders are merely agents of that company, risking only their original stake in the case of failure. While this protection does not extend to criminal activity, unethical behaviour or reckless decisions that cause debts and collapse generate no addi-

---

* I later discovered that the CEO's concern was that the supplier was then free to invoice, which he wanted to happen as late as possible. I was not empowered with that information, however.

tional pain for the shareholder. Peter Drucker – the management consultant and creator of management by objectives who we met in Chapter 5 – saw this as a risk in organisations, where moving power from the top to the bottom without related responsibility and accountability was dangerous.

Perhaps empowerment then is akin to delegation. We give power or permission on a leash, remaining accountable and holding the ability to withdraw it when necessary. Autonomy, by contrast, is the first time we are set loose. Rather than have power loaned, an autonomous team takes full and independent accountability for what they carry out. That would mean that, within explicit bounds, say regulation and an initial budgetary ceiling, a team can control their own fate and make all decisions for themselves without needing approval.*

Self-organisation and self-management

Extending empowerment and autonomy to teams brings us to self-organisation and self-management, respectively. That is, we can empower a team to self-organise – to choose how they work, what they prioritise and who is responsible for what – where a self-managing team has autonomy. Examples of this are an intentional break-away subsidiary of an organisation, forged to create a new product and free from the parent organisation's controls or as, we will see, whole organisations moving away from traditional hierarchical management.

In recent years, a drive towards greater self-management and complete flattening of structures has gained popularity, notably through the efforts of advocates like Frédéric Laloux. Laloux, a former associate partner with McKinsey & Company, brought together multiple case studies of companies using similar self-managing methods in his book, *Reinventing Organizations.*[67] The ideas presented have their academic roots in research by the psychologist Clare W. Graves. Graves theorised that there are distinct stages of adult development and that our psychological progress moves, both forwards and backwards, through multiple levels of morality and self-awareness. In essence,

---

* It is worth noting that this kind of emphasis is where people, particularly managers and leaders, start to get a little nervous. Indeed, if things go well, the associated leader will be lauded, but just like a dog off the lead, should things go wrong it is very easy for others to point and accuse you of letting things get out of control.

a person at the lowest level of development will have limited and mostly reactive choices in response to a situation. However, if a person can reach higher levels, they gain appreciation for multiple perspectives of social and self-awareness, allowing them a wide and thus more sensitive choice of response.[68]

Later work by Don Edward Beck and Christopher Cowan produced the concept of Spiral Dynamics, extending Graves' work into organisations.[69] Spiral Dynamics presents a similar set of development levels across eight colours, beginning with deep survival instincts, and running through traditional hierarchies before ultimately reaching holistic and unifying perspectives. Like Graves suggested, if our business operates at a low level of development it is unlikely that we will have time or inclination to think about our impact on society or the environmental interests of the planet. To illustrate, this is a simplified set of levels containing five colours:

- Red: commanding, authoritative, with 'alpha' leadership
- Amber: formal and strict hierarchies and controls, traditional, process-driven and bureaucratic
- Orange: objective led, and innovative to be commercially competitive
- Green: enablement, systems, values, culture and stakeholder focus
- Teal: wholeness, self-management and higher evolving purpose*

Comparing this list to the philosophies discussed in Chapter 1, the tendency to seek control in management of outputs would sit somewhere between 'amber' and 'orange'. Heavy use of process, structures and hierarchical objectives to manage work would be common. By contrast, operating in the more open environment of systems and enablement, would align to 'green', with effort directed to relationships, culture and customer-awareness.

Perhaps less familiar, and the focus of Laloux's recent work, are the kinds of behaviours and differences found in organisations at the self-determining 'teal' level. Here we step beyond typical structures. Teams – even whole organisations – may be flattened, with no hierarchy, managers, traditional role profiles or fixed task assignments. Priorities and plans for activities may be decided by all, and decision authority for everything from client pricing, to salaries, holidays and policy can be extended to everyone.

---

* Actually, in Spiral Dynamics it is turquoise, but teal clearly had a better marketing team.

Several of the companies referenced by Laloux, such as Buurtzorg (nursing care), Morning Star (tomato processor) and Patagonia (climbing gear), have unique setups and ways of working, created explicitly to meet their own challenges. Moreover, they are described as achieving significant success, both in terms of the value to and impact on clients and the experience and engagement of their people.

It is not all (turquoise) roses

If you follow the theory, an autonomous, self-managing team has the potential to operate more effectively than one constrained by implicit and explicit organisational control. There are, however, challenges.

The first is about capability, and whether the people in the team have the skill (and experience, ideally) to work without the standard pattern of a hierarchy. Back in Chapter 1, I talked about followers, and the trade-offs that we must make to choose deferral to a leader – for example, lesser spoils but fewer responsibilities. In a truly flat team, everyone is continuously both a follower and leader. People are leaders *together* for global decisions, and leaders *individually* for tasks or themes under their watch. As described in Baird and Benson's 2022 paper, 'effective team members in leaderless teams are likely those who are able to flexibly navigate between the leader and follower role'.[70] Not everyone has this ability, and early enthusiasm can often dry up when the difficult realities bite.

If everyone in the team has the capabilities to flow between roles, a second key challenge is that of peer pressure. In a strict hierarchical setup, it is clear who has authority and, capable or not, we have some kind of arbiter for disagreement. With a flat group, opportunities for confrontation, doubts about motivation and disapproval for decisions and ideas can easily flare. In Laloux's book (and for others presenting their teal organisations), processes are created to mediate when things go wrong or people are uncomfortable, but these things again need aptitude to be successful. This is addressed in another paper, 'Mitigating the dark side of agile teams: Peer pressure, leaders' control and the innovative output of agile teams'.[71] The team concluded that 'Although self-managing teams might experience less bureaucratic control, they are not free from control because peer pressure can often develop' and that 'team peer pressure is a motivational state that can undermine the team's innovative output'.

I make no recommendation either for or against self-managed structure, other than to repeat again the core theme of this book: success is about context, not a recipe.

The names above, and the Googles and Spotifys of this world, have not worked to 'become teal' or any other colour; they have experimented and cut their own cloth.

Learning, performance and skills

For us to be successful, or at least more successful, we need our people to wield the skills and experience necessary to make that happen. Broadly speaking, acquiring those skills falls into one of four categories.

Before I describe them, I would like you to imagine that you are creating a team to compete at the top level in a sport that you follow – football, basketball, cricket, Formula 1, it does not matter which.

Consider these questions:

1. How would you choose which players you want in the team?
2. What key traits would you like to see in the players you choose?
3. Where would you not compromise?

Using football, my own answers to those questions would be something like this.

1. How would I choose which players I wanted in the team? I would select based on capability first – for example, the technical skills of tackling, shooting or passing, regulated by my budget. I would hire the best skilled players that I could for the money I have available.
2. What key traits would I like to see in the players I choose? I want people that can learn and adapt, and those with resilience under pressure or in losing situations. People who can rally, support and encourage each other to a good performance even when things are going badly.
3. Where would I not compromise? Players must have real experience of playing the game, have a record of sporting behaviour (that is, not be sanctioned up to the eyeballs for violence or other antisocial behaviour) and be willing to train hard as part of the team.

That is a quick attempt at the answers – but I can be confident you had something similar and not 'the cheapest we can get away with', 'people who do not think for themselves', or 'people who live locally so they are less likely to quit'. In reality, it is rare to be in a position to create a team from the ground up, and never with absolute knowledge and control over the skills and attitudes we bring together. We do not have computer game character-selection screens to pick our skills and traits, and nor do we have access to a *Matrix*-style knowledge download direct to our brains. Inevitably, the team we have will not be a perfect fit, skills will not be at the level we need, or the team may not come in a readily collaborative and focused package.

'You say you know how to deliver critical feedback? Show me.'

Skills, bells and Pareto distributions

It is important at this point to understand more about the spread of skills in groups, and I will use two distributions to explain. The first is a Gaussian or normal distribution, more commonly known as a 'bell curve' for its distinctive shape of a central peak and tails either side to zero (Figure 7-2). This kind of distribution shows up when we plot general population information, like the number of people with certain shoe sizes in a population or the average sizes of middle fingers.[72]

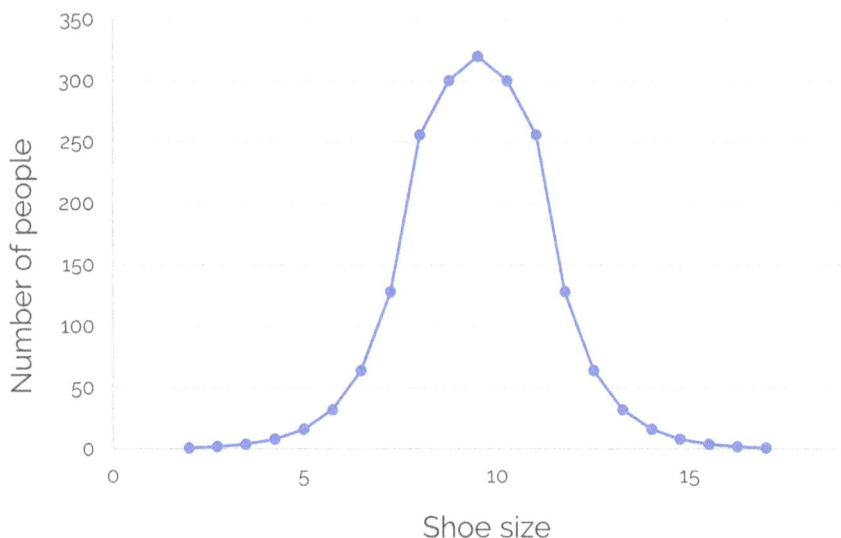

Figure 7-2. Gaussian or normal distribution (mock data)

Outside of mathematics lessons, I first met this curve when managing teams, and especially around appraisal time when we were asked to assign people into performance groups. Typically, there were five such groups, and they started with something like 'not performing' and ended on 'excellent' or 'outstanding'. Our task as managers was to make sure that we did not have many people in either of the tails, and that we – and our teams – should expect most people to be around the middle (Figure 7-3). Those on the left typically received no pay award, those in the middle something modest, and those on the right got what everyone else was expecting that they would get anyway.

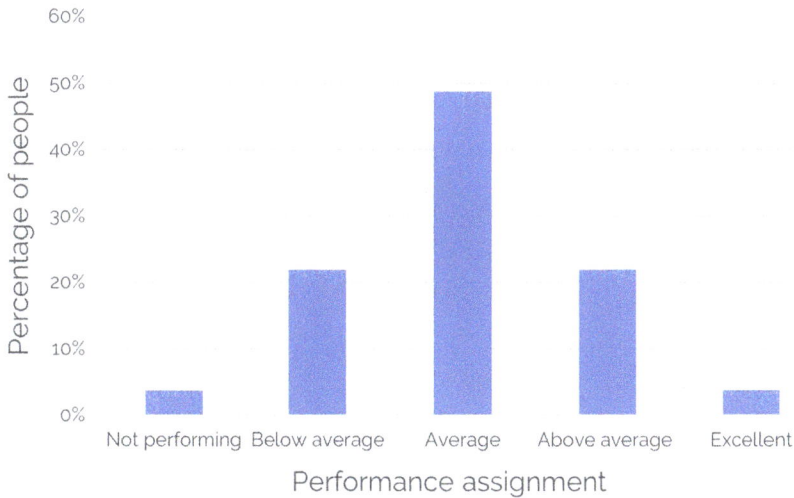

Figure 7-3. Example of desired appraisal assignments from a group of people

However, contrary to this popular view, when we examine skills in individuals, we do not actually get a normal distribution of performance. There is no neat curve with some people above and below average, and the bulk in the centre. Oddly enough, the teams that we rely on day-in, day-out, do *not* always include 30% of below-average performers, and nor do many organisations strive for most of their people to be average. If it is not clear what I am talking about, think about the jet display pilots of the Red Arrows. A standard distribution, like so many of us have endured, would mark one of them as great, one as terrible and the others average.

'That's it, Colin. Fly where we can see you.'

Performance in people actually follows a Paretian or power law distribution, something you may know as the '80:20' or Pareto principle.[73] Instead of the bell curve from earlier, this looks something like Figure 7-4 where we have a few very high performers on the left, with everyone else sitting along a tail to the right-hand side.

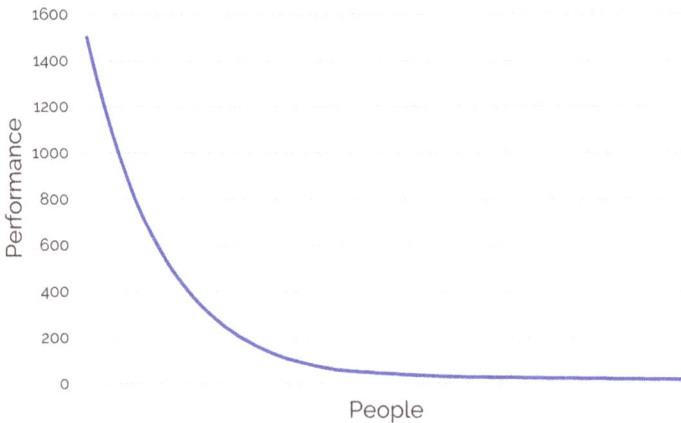

Figure 7-4. A power law distribution (mock data)

This pattern appears in many settings. For example, in 2023, Oxfam reported that 'The richest 1% have pocketed $26 trillion (£21 trillion) in new wealth since 2020, nearly twice as much as the other 99 per cent of the world's population'.[74] Household wealth in Great Britain also follows, where 'in 2022, incomes for the poorest 14 million people fell by 7.5%, whilst incomes for the richest fifth saw a 7.8% increase'.[75] In effect, we have a very small number of extremely wealthy people and a long tail of people with far less.

In sport, this is everywhere too. Of the millions of people who play football in the United Kingdom, only about 550 play in the top-flight Premier League. For those, annual salaries run from £52,000 to £20.8 million, with only 30 players earning over £10 million.[76]

In athletics, the Swedish pole-vaulter, Armand Duplantis had already been Olympic champion, two-time world champion and a three-time Diamond League winner by the age of 24. In 2014, the world record for men's pole vault sat at 6.16 metres, with 6.00 metres broken for the first time back in 1985. Enter Armand in 2020, who took this up to 6.17 metres and then raised it centimetre by centimetre to reach his current record of 6.25 metres.[77] What about everyone else? If we plot the 2023 performance of the top 500 pole vault athletes in the world, Armand's score of 1,576 is 63% better than the 500th position of 969. More remarkably, he is almost 10% better than the second-place athlete, who has 1,443 points. Again, we have a power law distribution (Figure 7-5).

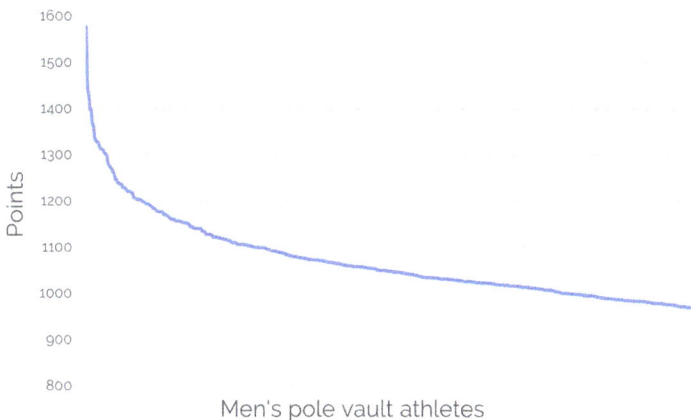

Figure 7-5. Men's world pole vault ranking 2023 (Duplantis on the far left)

To demonstrate that this is no coincidence, I have included three other performance distributions (Figure 7-6 to 7-8).

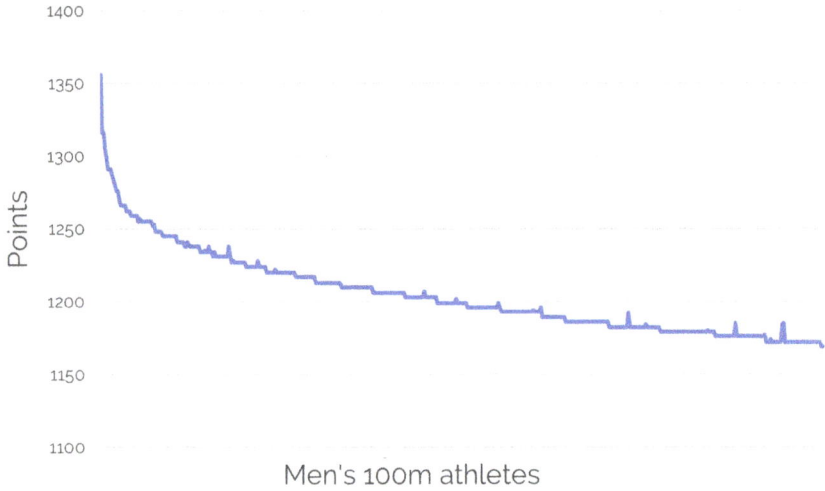

Figure 7-6. Men's 100 metres – all-time best score by athlete (Usain Bolt on far left)[78]

Figure 7-7. Women's marathon – all-time best score by athlete (Tigst Assefa on far left)[79]

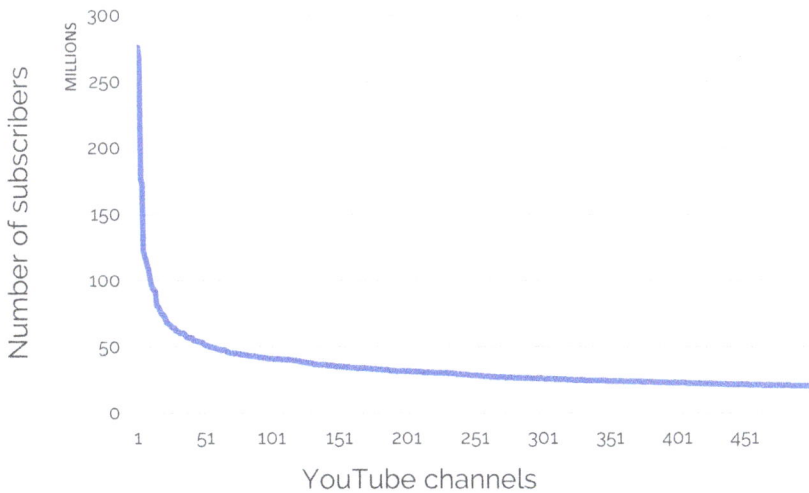

Figure 7-8. Top 500 YouTube channels by number of subscribers, June 2024 (MrBeast on far left)[80]

To bring this to the office, imagine we are hiring a Java developer or a personal assistant. Through probability, most of the applicants we meet will be in the long tail. However, if we happen to find one on the upward stride of the curve, we might get someone *really* special. Not just a little bit better than the others – exponentially so. Having someone like this in a team really does change the game, and those that I have had the pleasure to work with were remarkable.

Four ways

As I teased at the start of the chapter, there are broadly four methods to get the skills you need into your team or organisation: hiring, contracting, transfer and training.

1. Hiring: A long-term solution where we hire skilled people into permanent positions to grow the capability and capacity of the organisation. Finding and hiring ideal candidates can take a long time and be expensive but can be a route to years of experience and knowledge that training and development can never replicate. Real Madrid has not seen success under Florentino Pérez by hiring mediocre players and attempting to train them; it has painstakingly brought in the best players that money can buy, and then invested in their development as a team.

2. Contracting or commissioning: Typically a short-term solution and quick to achieve: we buy the skills directly into the organisation. Whether we hire a contractor with the requisite skill, or we work with a supplier or consultant to deliver the people or the product to us, we do not need to worry about developing our own muscles. If what we need is in a niche, or away from our core business, this makes a good deal of sense. Indeed, if our business makes components for cars, training mechanical engineers in web design so that we can maintain our public presence would be a clear waste of effort. Equally, paying a high price for a contract specialist to look after an activity well within a core team's skill set would also create waste.

It is worth noting that the ramifications for contracting skills are not just restricted to waste. People in your teams will want to develop and grow their skills while they are working with you – indeed, skills are what make people employable in the first place. Thus, if you contract everything you can, you will impact engagement and loyalty from your permanent teams. If your schedules allow, a useful compromise is to bring external talent in to work with and bootstrap your existing teams. Doing this, you gain the immediacy of external skills, but without the effect of sidelining teams to steal a march on the competition.

3. Transfer or promotion: We use someone that we already have within the organisation by moving them to a point of need. This could be a temporary transfer – for example, freeing up engineers working on one project to support a more urgent need – or more permanent, like a promotion. Both can be highly effective in getting some skill and experience to where it is needed, but it is wrong to imagine that it comes without its own problems.

First, it might be tempting to think that people with similar skills are transferable – for example, moving a customer services agent from one team to another. Undoubtedly there will be some crossover – skills in customer engagement, typical procedures within systems, and so on – but differences in products, flows or team norms will mean that a ramp-up is required. This is accentuated if we assume wholesale that a job title is fluid: a developer is a developer, an architect is an architect, or a surgeon is a surgeon. Personally, it would need a special circumstance for me to allow a shoulder surgeon to operate on my heart.

Second, I must also highlight the idea from *The Peter Principle* by Laurence Peter and Raymond Hull, that an organisation tends to rise to incompetence through promotions.[81] That is, organisations will often promote people who are successful to ever-higher leadership positions. Unfortunately, being a stellar engineer does not automatically grant you the skills you need to be a capable manager. Nor can we assume that the manager will perform effectively in a more senior leadership position. In the best cases it all works out, but it is not uncommon to lose a great engineer in exchange for a poor manager. Peter and Hull's conclusion is that when you scale this up, you reach a point where every role is occupied by people without the ability to perform, leading to an organisation that tends towards incompetence.*

4. Training and development: We develop the skills of the people that we already employ, to meet a need. Traditionally, we might think of this as formal study, sending people on courses according to various budgetary allowances.

There are three points about training to emphasise.

- While standard training courses teach concepts and methods, they cannot be sensitive to your context – something that we have discussed repeatedly. Learning that there is an amazing tool or approach does not mean it is necessarily appropriate, nor that your organisation is ready.
- Skilled and 'sharp' people tend to get more done and at a better quality. Unfortunately, I find a common reluctance to allow people space to learn, preferring that time on task is maximised; but by being less well equipped, progress is slow and edges are rough. Stephen Covey included this idea as one of his seven habits, but Abraham Lincoln said it first and best: 'Give me six hours to chop down a tree and I will spend the first four sharpening the axe.'

---

* For balance, I feel like I should congratulate the person who thought that it was a clever idea to make me a manager, and in so doing protect the organisation from a poor engineer.

- Every individual within an organisation is already and constantly developing their skills and experience. This comes from our peers, our own experiences or our own research and reading into topics, and it certainly is not restricted to formal courses.

To expand on this, here are a few further ideas on training and development:

- **Peer learning:** Run sessions to teach and transfer knowledge about things individuals are working on or interested in. It costs little other than time or an occasional pizza to help support these sessions and indirectly you will build networks and bonds between individuals that they can leverage day-to-day. This scales easily from a handful of individuals to informal sharing events that can include everyone.
- **Leverage the left:** Back to our power law graphs, if you are fortunate to have someone on the left-hand side, experiment with ways they can multiply the effectiveness of others. To make the maths easy, imagine you have 21 people in sales, and one of those is exceptional. Instead of getting that person out every day, use some time to teach, coach or mentor the other individuals. A 5% improvement across the other 20 people would equate to another head in terms of output.
- **Pairing:** On a smaller scale to peer learning, pair people to work on a particular output or outcome. Pairing inherently shares knowledge and while I am not going to cover it here, pairing also increases the quality of what is achieved.*
- **Allocated time:** Time available for individuals to spend on researching, reading, watching YouTube – whatever – to help them learn and develop. The hit rate on this kind of initiative tends to be low without regular reminders and encouragement, however. If an individual has a deadline, or there is less support for the time than is stated, other things will of course get prioritised.
- **Meetups and blogging:** As Aristotle said, 'Those that can, do. Those that understand, teach.' I have always found that to be a bidirectional statement, and if you want to really learn something and make it stick,

---

* For a great introduction on pairing in software and its value, search Martin Fowler and pair programming.

teach it. Practically, that could mean people writing a book(!) or article, or presenting ideas and perspectives at events.

- **Guilds and communities:** Especially in larger organisations where people with similar skills work in relative isolation, try out the creation of guilds or communities of interest. This is similar to peer learning, but in this case we restrict the subject matter to that area (a testing guild, a security guild, a customer delight guild, and so on), which supports knowledge sharing. Moreover, these groups help scratch our 'groupish' itch, and can be used effectively to shape policy and practices for the wider organisation.

We really need to talk about experience

When we are looking at performance in an individual, it is important to distinguish between their skills and experience. Having an encyclopedic knowledge of the C# programming language or having the most text-book-perfect golf swing does not make you an amazing developer, nor championship golfer. That skill must also be combined with experience and a smattering of luck. In my years of hiring, it was obvious when a candidate had the certificates, but had spent no time actually using the skills they studied. As a paramedic friend of mine once explained after a callout, there is an enormous difference between the method taught for lifting a dead-weight body and actually responding to a 120 kg man unconscious in a bath.

> *There is an enormous difference between the method taught for lifting a dead-weight body and actually responding to a 120 kg man unconscious in a bath.*

And that is the doozy. Those years of experience, the adversity overcome and the realisation that what it says in the manual is neither the beginning nor the end of the story. This is the difference between our internal tacit knowledge, and our explicit knowledge that we can actually articulate. Referring to David Snowden again, he beautifully summed this idea up by saying, 'You know more than you can say, and you can say more than you can write down.'[82]

In those few words he encapsulates the challenge that is really in front of us. If you drive, you will have had the experience of hearing an unfamiliar noise – a noise that is new and clashes with your expectations of what you should be hearing from your car. How do you know that it is a new noise? You are unlikely to have a recording or catalogue of all the noises that your car was making up until yesterday, so why did this one stand out? How would you explain your thought process for reaching the conclusion that there was something new to be heard? Indeed, when was the last time you even paid attention to the noises that your car was making?* Transfer this idea to the person somewhere on the left of our performance chart, and we are faced with the situation that they cannot readily explain what they know, how they know it or how they apply it. It is only their experience and knowledge, learned, lived through and absorbed, that leads them to the conclusion.

How can you possibly begin to transfer that information to colleagues when the person themselves does not know what they tacitly know? Unfortunately, the question is rhetorical, and you cannot teach experience. Acquiring knowledge is a continuous and non-linear process, and despite an understandable desire to attend a training course and leave it as an expert, the best we can guarantee to take is theory. That theory alone has limited application, and so to turn those ideas into something more, we must practise the new knowledge in real life.

As the Ancient Greeks would put it, we need praxis: the process of putting the theory into practice to realise the value of the lesson. We need to alloy ideas with experience, feeling and developing intuition for what happens when we act. As much as I understand that insisting on ten years of experience in job advertisements can lead to age discrimination, no graduate – no matter their potential – will be ready to succeed as an international sales director on day one out of university.

---

* This could of course apply to the noises coming from the heating in your home, your pet, partner, or anything else.

Turning a tanker on a sixpence

A further reality that faces teams – even if we have good coverage of skills today – is that tomorrow is likely to bring change. Loss or gain of team members, the beginning or end of a project, a move in customer behaviour, the launch of a new technology, or another shift in the environment. In turn, such shifts will impact the skills needed and will push teams to adapt.

An approach that we can take some inspiration from will already be familiar to you – that of the handling of peaks and troughs of demand in a supermarket. Being simplistic, let us imagine that there are three roles in our supermarket of choice: checkout assistants, who scan and take customer's payments; shelf stockers, who make sure that the shelves are full and present-able; and finally warehouse workers, who operate the back room, receive deliveries and organise stock. In general, the roles are balanced – in equilib-rium with each other – and the flow of customers and stock through the supermarket is smooth, with limited delays.

In periods of peak demand – for example, a high volume of additional customers or a large delivery – we will experience bottlenecks. There will not be enough people to take customer payments, and queues will build up, or stock will not be available in time to make sales. To manage these periods, supermar-kets have the option of moving people around to different roles to support the peaks – to rally people for deliveries or enlist help when queues start to build up: 'John to checkouts, please!' and so on. This is not to assume that anyone could do any of the roles, and there will be specific training and practice in each. To help this fluid movement, a number of people in each discipline will need training and experience – praxis – in other areas, so they can help.

This concept of individuals with combinations of relevant and overlapping skills was conveniently abbreviated to different 'shapes' – the shapes they make on an organisation chart – by IDEO CEO, Tim Brown.[83] In Figure 7-9, there are three columns representing specific skills. They could indicate the super-market or, in a technical team, perhaps software engineering, networking and infrastructure. In the first row, we first have 'I-shaped' people, and those that are specialists in one area. Second, we have 'T-shaped' people, who are special-ists in one area and generalists in others. Next, we get 'pi-shaped' people who are specialists in two areas, and finally 'M' or 'comb-shaped' people, who are our polymaths, able to specialise in several areas.

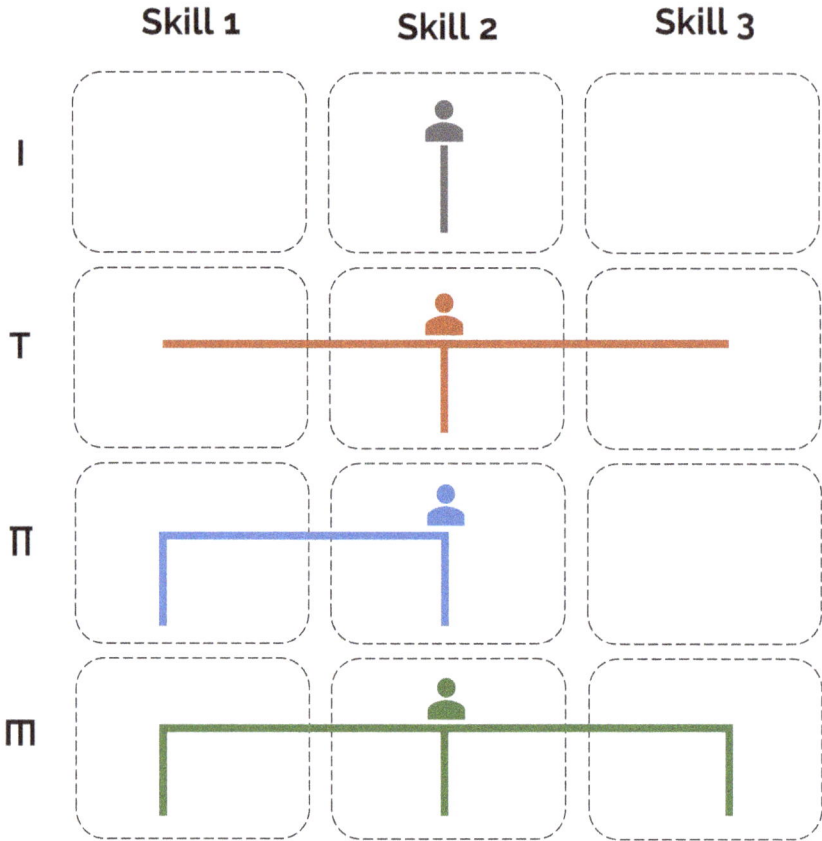

Figure 7-9. Four shapes to represent skill diversity of individuals

In our teams, there is no right answer to the number and configuration of skills across a team, but these concepts give us some building blocks to work with. Taking an IT example, where our function is responsible for networks, storage and email, we will need specialists for each. Being literal with the above terms, that could work as three I-shaped or T-shaped people, two pi-shaped people or even one 'comb-shaped' person covering all of the disciplines. If we choose individual I-shaped specialists, they may bring exceptional knowledge in their fields, but will not be transferable to support others at peak times. If we choose a single polymath, we can sleep knowing that all the bases are covered, but it is going to be tense when they are on holiday.

Perhaps best in this artificial case would be some small overlap between each of the disciplines so that we have some coverage and backup using T-shaped people. To build on that, let us think about this at a larger scale and imagine this time each of our three disciplines has ten people each. Now we can aim to have a number of I-shaped people with genuine specialisms and deep knowledge, coupled with a few pi- or comb-shaped people to provide fluidity when needed.

Money and reward

To make sure that we recruit and then retain those people with the skills and experience that we need, we are probably going to have to pay them something. The concluding section in his chapter thus relates to reward, a contentious subject if it is spoken about at all.

To get started, let me create some context with an imaginary family bakery. The bakery has only three full-time employees: husband and wife Douglas and Karen, and their daughter Mollie who is an apprentice in the business. Since she started, one of Mollie's successes has been the creation of a popular cupcake line that the bakery sells. Each morning before the bakery opens, Mollie makes the cupcakes and artistically finishes them with various decorations. The cupcakes are then sold to customers throughout the day before a new batch is created fresh the following morning. To make sure that waste is limited, Mollie keeps a record of sales and alters the stock of each type of cupcake in line with demand. Where there are leftover cupcakes, these are donated to a local food bank. Mollie continues to experiment with different flavours and designs, seeking feedback from customers coming through the shop. She has also spent time developing the online presence of the bakery and has built a strong following for the cupcakes on Instagram. The combination of these actions over the last year has increased footfall into the shop and grown its sales. Of course, it takes more than some excellent cupcakes to make a successful business. Sales of cupcakes are not exclusive to Mollie and are influenced by the presentation of the shop and the cross-sales that Douglas or Karen make. Critically, no cupcakes would be sold at all if the orders for ingredients were not placed or paid for, and far fewer without the bakery itself.

So, is Mollie performing? Common metrics for a product, like cost of goods and sales, are being managed. She is innovative, doing market research on the products, and finding ways to increase awareness of the products. In the context of the bakery and her parents, Mollie is contributing and helping the overall business to thrive, so it seems so. Now we have performance out of the way, the bakery turned over £275,000 this year, a figure that was £25,000, or 10%, more than the previous year. Costs for the business have remained static, so this means some profit was made. Should Mollie get a pay rise and if so, how much? Should Mollie make more, less or the same as her mother and father? We could try and make that decision based on direct financial value and give her a slice of the cupcake revenue. We could set a number based on the industry normal pay of a bakery apprentice. We could choose an arbitrary salary increase based on what feels right. Would Mollie feel disenfranchised or even leave if her pay were not increased?

The answer is subjective, of course. What Mollie would earn depends on all these things, plus the relationships and dispositions of her parents. Apart from national minimum wages and the influence of industry normal salaries, there are no rules. Even the connection to performance is optional, and ultimately it is up to Douglas and Karen – the people with the purse strings – to decide. So, if it is difficult in a three-person bakery, what happens when we scale up the question of reward?

Traditional management

To insert some rationale into these decisions when many more people are involved, many organisations look to an appraisal process.* Appraisals, run quarterly or annually, typically use a mixture of peer assessments, supporting evidence and discussions to help – hopefully fairly – to get a picture of performance. This process can be informative and support an individual's own development, and crucially provides organisations with a framework, and in the end, a neat bell curve to describe contribution and therefore reward.

---

* There are of course plenty of changes to salary outside of appraisals – for example, new roles, people threatening to leave, exceptional results or balancing reward across similar roles.

> *The world over, appraisal processes are derided, if not fundamentally flawed.*

I am jaded, but before I go any further, I feel I must say that the world over, appraisal processes are derided, if not fundamentally flawed. While we had the potential for some emotional conversations in the bakery above, appraisals across an organisation ramp up the stress with deadlines, seemingly arbitrary decisions, and tens, even hundreds, of hours of work for people involved. If I lead a team of 20 people, and I meet with them for one hour each, write up my assessment, share it for review, make any modifications and submit it onward, that is already more than a week's work. More importantly, where a tacit link to reward exists, the exercise can quickly promote emotional and irrational responses: 'The boss doesn't like me, of course you've got a better result,' 'It's your fault I couldn't complete the project, you stopped the funding!' and so on. I had one person in a team years ago who printed over 500 pages of evidence – work that he had done in different systems, which was of course, already visible in those same systems – to demonstrate his contribution. What pushed him to this was a perceived unfairness in the process, and a feeling that what he deserved would be taken away with the smallest of excuses.

To be honest, I agreed with him, and because of an important word unspoken in this process: notoriety. Recall the idea of priming (Chapter 4), that with nudges, we can be steered into certain ways of thinking. In that case, it was a picture of some dirty hands, but what if engineer X was recently the hero of the hour? Or the one who dropped coffee on the CEO's laptop? Is the appraisal process going to be fair and include all the activities, good, bad or indifferent?

A telling example of this occurs at the point of 'calibration', after each of the teams have submitted their markings. It does not look good if Bill in marketing concludes that every single one of his team is well above expectations, when the never-satisfied Sophie in IT support marks every one of her team as under-performing. Therefore, those leaders or subsets of them come together to check that there is a good spread of results. When it comes around to discussing engineer X and their coffee-spilling incident, their leader must vigorously defend their honour and overturn biases to avoid a lower result.

A further confounding factor in traditional appraisals is that they are not well suited to matrix organisations and the flow of people around roles and projects. Imagine that I have ten software engineers to reward at appraisal time, five of whom have been working in the same place all year, and the other five of whom have each worked on three separate projects. Picking one from each set, how can I say that one has performed better than the other and should get a higher award? I must rely on testimony and recommendation, and notoriety applies once more.

Alternative ideas

There are alternatives to traditional appraisal-to-reward flows – for example, continuous assessment, peer-centred, team-based or the intentional detachment of reward from appraisals. There is too much to include here, so I provide only five perspectives. I encourage you to research further and be aware that you will never get it completely right!

1. Formula-based pay: Salary is defined based on factors such as role, qualifications, levels of experience and location. The UK civil service does this, aligning salary ranges with grades of roles. According to the Office for National Statistics, in 2022 a 'Grade 7' could earn between £51,055 and £60,189, or if in London, between £54,055 and £64,373.[84] There is still scope for some of the conversations above, since we can have two Grade 7s at either end of the scale, but it does at least make the reward transparent. When it comes to pay review time, formula-based pay often sets a single percentage across all employees, and for the civil service, reward rules are notified to all departments through the central cabinet office.

2. Market-based pay (or market pricing): Expanding on formula-based pay, salary is defined based on the market rate for a particular role or skills mix. Rates can be calculated by organisations themselves, or referenced from published surveys that aggregate data. Alongside data for basic salaries, these surveys can include information about complete reward and benefits packages for roles in different areas of the country. This data could be used as input to formula-based pay scales, or to be more granular, to inform us what we might pay a particular individual. Thinking back to bakery, we could source some data about average compensation for apprentice bakers and use that as input to our decision.

3. Value-based pay: It is through Laszlo Bock's book, *Work Rules!* that I really appreciated the issue of forcing performance distribution in teams into bell curves.[85] Bock was head of HR at Google and during that tenure, took this reality into policy. Instead of saying something arbitrary like 'left side of the bell curve: no pay rise, middle: x% and right: y%', he looked to recognise performance and pay appropriately. Referring to the power law graph, this could mean that two people tasked with the same work – one far left, one lower down the curve – could earn massively different amounts. In some respects, this idea is extremely fair. A person who generates ten times more value for the organisation – makes ten times the sales, gets ten times more customer praise, solves problems ten times more reliably, and so on – should receive ten times the salary of the person who is miles behind. This model exists comfortably in sales departments (through bonus schemes), and in the various sporting examples that I have shared in this chapter.

When I have discussed this idea with people in more traditionally minded, 'bell-curve' organisations, I meet resistance. How do we know that the person really is ten times more valuable? Are they always ten times more valuable? How could people tolerate being paid exponentially less than a colleague? One person was vehement that they could not stay at the company if they found out every minute of their own time was worth ten times less than their colleague. Of course, ten times is nothing when we look at pay ratios between CEOs and average workers. According to the Chartered Institute of Personnel and Development, in 2019 the mean average such ratio of pay was between 330:1 and 416:1, with the highest an astonishing 2,605:1.[86] Suddenly the idea of someone next to me earning much more because of the value they deliver is less radical.

4. Pay is only part of the story: An appropriate and self-recognised fair salary is an essential part of the reward structure. Intuitively, if I believe my wages are unsuitable for the work that I am doing – at least in the extremes – my sense of fairness will kick in. I have seen many people decide to leave an organisation, myself included, when the numbers are interpreted as a lack of respect, recognition or fairness.

However, once we get past that test of equity, what then keeps us engaged and in our roles? We have touched on a number of related points in this book so far. A person wanting to be part of something meaningful, like the NASA example, the chance to improve our skills and qualifications to make us more employable, or simply getting involved in something that piques our interest. Daniel Pink's popular book *Drive* goes deep into these motivations by citing work from a range of psychologists including Edward Deci and Richard Ryan, and it is well worth a read.[87] Pink concludes that, beyond pay, we need these other things and that intriguingly, in creative activities, pure monetary rewards reduce the results we achieve.

5. Do it yourself: From the various books and proponents of 'teal' thinking, more radical ideas for setting salary emerge, like the practices of complete transparency and self-set rewards. There are different methods out there, but one process goes something like this. In advance of salaries being awarded, information about everyone's current reward, sales pipelines, costs, market information and revenue are collated for everyone. With this input, each person then asks three other people to help them set their salary. The three people each suggest a range for the person's earnings, and then it is up to the individual to choose their final number from within those ranges. Another option can be to ask each person to propose a salary award, and then have that reviewed by a selected peer group. The group provides advice and recommendations which the person can choose to consider before setting their salary. This might be a nudge to go higher or a reminder about financial pressure to influence their decision.

In all of these cases, salaries cannot increase beyond revenue, and this prompts a general challenge for reward: What budget is available? If we take an industry number of a 39% payroll-to-revenue ratio (for professional, scientific, and technical services), that is a large chunk of our turnover.[88] If revenue has been static, or we have some other significant investments to make, logic demands a balance between the risk of alienating essential staff and a commitment to increased costs.

Chapter summary

Teams, being groups of people who come together to achieve something, can form in endless shapes and sizes. They can be regulated and hierarchical, can exist with no obvious structure, follow set patterns or forge their own. Ultimately, unless our goal is truly to copy another organisation, the litmus test for structure is whether our work inputs flow through to meaningful outcomes in good time and without too much waste.

- That members of a team know why the team exists is an easy assumption to make. Look out for signs of confusion and discuss the team's reason for being, when necessary. If it needs more definition, define it.
- Human alignment to in-groups has a significant impact on our actions and decisions. We will naturally behave 'groupishly' for *our* group, simultaneously – if not intentionally – disadvantaging others.
- Individual performance and skill across a team does not follow a bell curve. In practice, a small number will achieve (or be capable of) exponentially more than everyone else, in the shape of a power law distribution.
- Skills will erode if they are not used, and incidental training will not keep pace. Consider skill from the perspective of praxis, the meeting of theory and experience.
- Skill resilience in teams can be increased through combinations of 'shapes' – like T-shaped, pi-shaped, or comb-shaped – to adapt to changing situations.
- If it is not taboo in your organisation, discuss reward and how it is calculated. Conversations will give people a chance to evaluate whether they believe it is fair, and if it is not, you'll find out early that there's something to resolve.
- It is easy to confuse the words 'empowerment' and 'autonomy'. Take some extra time to check that there's a good level of shared understanding about boundaries, decision authority and freedom to act.

CHAPTER 8

Change and transformation

'Things do not change; we change.'
– Henry David Thoreau[89]

Changing, reshaping and transforming

Bob Dylan's song *The Times They Are A-Changin'* perfectly captures a common attitude to change – that the old is no longer good enough, whether we are talking about a self-generated move or a response to a market or customer.[90] We must, it seems, adopt the new and exit the past with all haste. If that future crowds out value that already exists or upsets some people, so be it. The future is where we need to be! You cannot make an omelette without breaking some eggs, no-pain-no-gain, that baby was hogging the bath anyway, and frankly, who would want to stay a caterpillar in a field full of butterflies?

Perhaps when we transform or otherwise compel our people to operate differently, the reality is not so extreme, and we are sensitive to context and current value. Perhaps. But the language of change frameworks and behaviours of leaders seem to stick to message. Consider a direction that I saw given to everyone in a 200-strong function to work with a new process, unimaginatively called the 'New Way'. Technically, there was no hard line to say that people could not do other things, but there was little choice for those wanting to have a simple life. It would have taken more energy to defend a successful alternative – especially the 'old way' – than a ~~failure~~ learning with the new process.

Meanwhile, for frameworks, they are all at it. McKinsey's 7-S Framework analyses current and future states to control alignment, Bridge's transition model achieves 'new beginnings' – a new world with a new identity – from 'endings', and Prosci's ADKAR moves us from a current state to a future one.

From what we have discussed so far, however, we know that the idea of change being a simple linear process to achieve the thing we want is flawed.

Take Lewin's Change Management Model as a perfect illustration. The model comprises three stages:

- Unfreeze: analysing, documenting, preparing for and compelling the change
- Change: to make the required moves and updates
- Refreeze: the locking down and stabilising of the new models, practices or otherwise.

Let us put that into an organisation. We would need to first generate an accurate, detailed picture of 'now', from which we can make decisions and create a plan of activity to execute. But can people, organisations and markets be studied, altered and mechanically reassembled into better results? Where would we even start? We can list the structures and the tools that we are using and make proclamations about where they will end up, but that leaves the intangibles. Our levels of knowledge and experience, relationships and degrees of trust, or awareness of what our competition and customers might be planning themselves. If we add the complication of time, that our picture will not remain static during the months of activity, we reach some Sisyphean ordeal. Faced with pushing a boulder up a hill for eternity, most rational change leaders thus restrict themselves to cursory analysis and modelling before getting on with the change anyway. So, we knuckle down and get changing. How close to our desired end point do you think we might end up?

A brief lesson in chaos and probability helps to answer that. Have you ever taken your headphones out of your pocket to discover the wires are tangled in ways that seem implausible? Actually, that mess is just one of many possibilities. If you consider all potential configurations for the headphone wires – how the wires *could* be – there are far fewer configurations where the cables are neatly organised, compared to the number where they would be disorganised.* Statistically, your wires are *more* likely to be tied up than not. Manufacturers tip the odds in our favour by imposing constraints, for example, the use of 'memory' materials that increase the chances of the wires returning to their desired configuration. We can improve our luck too by neatly winding up and putting away our headphones once we stop using

---

* Writing this section close to Christmas, I can also add a remarkably similar experience with my tree lights.

them, or by adding some Apple AirPods to our Christmas list. Apply this idea to our partially accurate model of the change we are making, and while we will certainly achieve something, our desired future state is one of an infinite number of other configurations.

Ah, but Stephen! You are talking about micro, not macro! Our change was to implement a major new way of working or start again with our structure. That is a binary thing, done or not done. Whether we end up using sticky notes, change some working relationships or start a tradition of guitars at retrospectives does not matter. Our change was a transformation, and we will or we will not have delivered it. I am afraid the statistics on the success rate of changes demonstrate something wrong with that idea. Some examples include: '84% Of Companies Fail At Digital Transformation' (Forbes),[91] 'The brutal fact is that about 70% of all change initiatives fail' (Harvard Business Review),[92] and '70 percent of change programs fail to achieve their goals' (McKinsey).[93] And putting to one side that the authors of such articles are often those who invoked the changes, what reasons are cited for these failures to achieve change? There are plenty, and all seem to express a lack of something, a lack of urgency, vision, communication, measures – even willpower. If you think these reasons do not have their feet firmly planted in the macro, by all means skip the rest of this chapter.

Systems and domains of change

Let us reflect on change from the perspective of the major domains within Cynefin. Knowing which domain we are changing should make it easier to decide on our approach as we make the journey, and I have provided an example of each below.

Clear: The introduction of an interactive voice response (IVR) system on the inbound phone line of a customer services team, to route calls more quickly to the correct department. By making limited changes to the phone system, and carrying out some short team training sessions, the system will be live. It will be easy to see whether the change has been implemented and to monitor any impact on routing as calls come in. Metaphorically, we could consider such a change as a train journey with a known start, fixed route and predictable end.

Complicated: The implementation of a new deployment pipeline for our software engineers, to limit the defects present in our releases. This is a more difficult change, but one where there are good practices and expertise available. Decisions will need to be made about tools, order of events and thresholds, like successful unit tests, but once we have those we can teach and monitor the practices. Continuing with the metaphor for travel, this would be more like a train journey across a country. The start and end points are clear, but the route has options and people might disagree about which to take. Once we pick our options, we can be confident of arriving at our destination.

Complex: The digitisation of our existing paper services, making them available online to save costs and make the experience easier for customers. As a quick reminder, a complex system is a dynamic network of interactions from multiple independent components. In such a system, we will be blind to the start and end points for whatever change we imagine. We do not have a straight line. Indeed, it is more appropriate to say that those independent components all start in separate places, and we only have a *sense* of where we might end up. This is a far more difficult proposition, and we have moving parts internally and externally to consider. Externally, how would we prepare our customers and how would they respond and work with the new approach? Internally, how do we handle the training, awareness, and shift of responsibilities (even redundancies in this case)? As we get started, the expertise that we have has never been applied in this particular set of circumstances, so we will need to try things out, observe and adapt along the way. Our metaphor now moves to a ship, rather than a train. We have a plotted course, but we must continue to monitor the weather and navigational charts to adjust our route each time it is necessary to do so.

Chaotic: Computer platforms down or other emergencies are not really the realm of planned organisational change. Indeed, chaotic elements are more likely to be caused by the change itself, like the switching off of a system that we thought was unused, or the routing of customers through a new process that does not have the capacity we thought. In such cases, urgent action must be taken – a change reversed, or a new change implemented – to attempt to move us to a different domain where we can take more considered steps. The ship metaphor does not work, and the image we should hold is more like falling out of a tree, attempting to grasp onto something solid before it is too late.

Excellent. If we work out which context our change is in, we can choose the most appropriate tools. Unfortunately, as you may have predicted, that is simplistic. When we are implementing a change, especially one involving people across an organisation, there will be elements that need attention across *every* domain. On a small scale, we might be able to get away with one approach, but even then, we can get bitten if we make assumptions about the approach. Indeed, even for the IVR example above, which seems simple on paper, we cannot guarantee the reaction. Here are some potential results, inspired by a similar change I was part of.

- The phone routing changes go smoothly, and you hear a customer saying their call was routed more quickly. Hooray!
- There is no impact on customer experience, good or bad.
- Inbound calls drop because 'It is harder to call you!'
- We hear team members apologising to customers for a new system that is out of their control.
- Customers get annoyed, saying, 'I didn't need you to do that. Why did you make that a focus?'
- Customers make more use of direct lines (which team members give them) to avoid the IVR system. Call statistics are inaccurate, and the change ineffective, but customers that understand who to call directly receive a great service.
- Because they no longer route calls, teams spend less time getting to know what other teams do. The change contributes to a slow reduction in cross-team collaboration.

These types of reaction occur regardless of context, and our ability to plan effectively for what might happen falls away sharply as we move away from clear elements of our change. In such cases, where we start with more moving parts, more stakeholders and people outside of our influence, the number of opportunities for unplanned events and perverse incentives goes one way.

A favourite illustration is the handling of a rat problem in Vietnam around the turn of the twentieth century. To control a burgeoning population, an incentive was publicised that rewarded people for each rat killed, evidenced by handing over rat tails. Within weeks, people realised that this could be exploited, and the scheme was dropped when officials started seeing rats without tails. Rat catchers were not killing their captures, merely removing their tails so they could breed more rats and claim more reward.

> *The common attitude to change and change frameworks is that we can apply a linear process and get to where we want to be.*

Briefly summarising, so far I have described that change occurs across domains with a vast number of possible end points, from a likely unknowable starting point. Despite this, the common attitude to change and change frameworks is that we can apply a linear process and get to where we want to be. So where do we go from here? To answer that, it would be useful to describe a better definition of change. At its most basic, change is about making something different to what it already is, and in our teams, organisations and societies, that change will always involve people. As such, I reach this description: change is something that causes or necessitates a shift in human behaviour.

Taken from this perspective, we perhaps look at change differently. No doubt, you will have experience of the difficulty of changing your own behaviour or influencing those closest to you. Whether you want to adhere to a diet or exercise regime, build routines around studying or writing, or stop yourself smoking, this stuff is not easy. There is an entire industry of therapy, coaching and a library of self-help books dedicated to changing some habit or another.*

Now take an extremely difficult change target presented to the British parliament in 2019: 'announcing a smoke-free 2030 ambition'.[94] Even if we target one current smoker, what does it take to change their behaviour? They might act autonomously on health advice or peer pressure and seek a method to quit, or they might only respond when cigarettes are banned by some governmental policy. Even if they are banned, does that mark the end of this person's smoking, or just a transition to vaping or their purchase of cigarettes from other, less legitimate sources? We can all quote examples of humans finding routes around or reasons to deny desired policy, from the 1920s underground alcohol industry during prohibition in the United States, to the

---

* Goodreads.com returned 90,135 results in a search for 'habits'.

more recent anti-vaccine proponents convinced that the government wanted to install location-tracking chips.[95] And of course, we are not talking about one smoker here, the target is some 6.4 million of them.[96]

The challenge has become Herculean, and we can see that no step-by-step change framework is going to cut it. There will be components from the tools that we can use, but much more important is approaching change in our organisation or society with humans placed foremost.

Understanding human behaviour

I had not thought that much about the cause of human behaviour before I started reading the work of Professor Robert Sapolsky.* I had the general idea of nature and nurture, the distinction between what we are born with and what we learn, and the opinion that behaviour could be adapted and changed. Those ideas certainly were not nuanced, and Sapolsky changed all of that for me. His Stanford lectures published on YouTube and his books have made me consider the layers of biology and experience that underpin everything that we do.[97] He is one of a limited set of authors to whom I can attribute a real movement in how I think.

The basic idea is as follows. Imagine I have just shouted at someone. A few milliseconds before that, a motor neuron fired in my brain and triggered the muscles in my body to shout. Milliseconds before that, a different neuron of my brain 'decided' that I was going to shout (which seems to happen before we are consciously aware of the intention, by the way). Seconds before that, a different mixture of hormones like adrenalin, dopamine and serotonin was flooding parts of my body and brain. Minutes before that, a situation I am in influences my thoughts, for example, I am at a railway station, and someone is getting close to the edge of the platform. Hours before that, the day that I am having and the food that I have eaten all affect my mood, alertness and energy. Days and months before that, the ups and downs of whatever I am doing affect my body, the state of repair of my muscles and my mental state. Years before that, I learn and absorb ideals and virtues that I respect from my

---

* Sapolsky, a neuroendocrinology researcher and author, holds his professorship at Stanford University, where he lectures on biology, neuroscience, and neurology.

parents, society and my own experiences, the things that I will later feel compelled to act upon and those that I will not. Before that, in the womb, my brain and body pick up cues about the world outside that affect my development. And then we have the genetics from my parents that produced the specific sequence for me, with the characteristics and potential tendencies laid out. And then we step back further into the evolution of the human species, the traits and compulsions that lie deep in my genes and mitochondrial DNA. Did I shout because I thought that person might be in danger? Perhaps. Maybe it was because I wanted to be home on time. Regardless, the cause of that behaviour is much deeper than we give credit for, and Sapolsky goes much further in his most recent and excellent book, *Determined*.[98]

Now think about some of the examples in the previous section – trying to get a society to quit smoking, digitising a currently paper-based service or even installing a basic IVR. We cannot begin to comprehend the background (from the milliseconds to the millennia) of the people involved. Given the subject of this chapter, that is going to put a stick in the spokes of most of our changes. More eloquently, I repeat Brenda Dervin's quote from my introduction to sense-making: 'Each person is a person who has past struggles, a body, mind, heart, and spirit moving through time and space, with a past history, a present reality and future dreams and ambitions.'[99] Boy, do we need to start listening and understanding each other better. In that quest, let us move onto culture.

Culture

No doubt you are familiar with the common tropes around culture, from the descriptive 'It's the way that things are done around here' to the more evocative 'Culture eats strategy for breakfast' often attributed to Peter Drucker. In both cases, we infer some invisible and non-traversable truth – a bedrock – that resides beneath a group or organisation and influences everything above.

Organisations definitely have habits, identities and acceptable levels of behaviour that grow organically in step with society at large. The difficulty with culture as a concept, however, is its breadth. When we use the term, we are wrapping immeasurable detail and nuance into a single word. Indeed, how easy is it to understand and embody the cultural realities of the Kazakhs in Kazakhstan, the gauchos in South America, Western European culture, British culture, Byzantine or Roman culture? More prosaically, how should we interpret it when an organisation says it has developed 'an innovative culture', 'a learning culture' or the paragon of our time, an 'agile culture'?

We could attempt to understand a culture by cataloguing the detail of how things are done. Say we observe that answering the phone quickly in a bright and smiling tone is rewarded, people tend to enjoy lunch together and that senior leadership is visible on the shop floor. Can we infer culture from that? As a single note is to a symphony, we are seeing such a small glimpse of the picture we cannot possibly be right. We need something in between this amorphous idea of culture and the individual actions that people might take.

Values

Values appear in several models as a core component of culture.* Enshrining ideals of an organisation into values provides some kind of reference point for that perceived or intended culture. For example, if we say that, as an organisation, we value candour, we would hope to see that played out somehow. Feedback should be prompt and direct, disagreements between peers should be openly shared and resolved, and so on.

Let us look at two real organisations and their values. I have added some narrative following each term based on my immediate interpretation of them.

Brighton & Hove District Council (UK): Values – collaboration, efficiency, respect, openness, creativity, customer focus[100]

- **Collaboration:** We should work with one another and our stakeholders. Collaboration is good, but it can also be inefficient.
- **Efficiency:** We should be looking for opportunities to save costs, limit waste and reduce repetitive work. Since the taxpayers are paying for all of this, that sounds sensible, but it might conflict with collaboration.
- **Respect:** Is it respectful to preserve the feelings of my colleagues, or is it better to tell them exactly what I think?
- **Openness:** Synonymous with truthfulness and being blunt, it is easier said than done when it will look bad on us and disappoint a customer. The source text also says that there should be openness 'whenever appropriate', so does that mean it is optional?

---

* For example, Schien's Culture Triangle or Hofstede's Cultural Dimensions Theory.

- **Creativity:** Creativity can be valuable, but where do we anticipate people will be creative, and at what cost? Assuming we are experimenting and attempting innovative ideas, we again risk our value of efficiency. Someone saying 'I've allocated all client accounts where the CEO's name starts with a C to Clifford' is certainly creative but simultaneously unhelpful and inefficient.
- **Customer focus:** The ubiquitous organisational aim, and interestingly the last of the values. It reads that just in case you thought everything up to now was inward looking, please also remember to focus on our customers. Probably we should respect them, be open and collaborate too.

IDS Medical Systems Group (USA): Values – balance, integrity, loyalty, care, agility, reliability, entrepreneurship[101]

- **Loyalty:** Referencing individuals and the company, I cannot help but think this arose because of a past problem. You certainly cannot force loyalty in either direction.
- **Integrity:** We hold ourselves to a higher, professional level regardless of who is watching or whether people want to hear something different.
- **Balance:** The contemporary idea of balance in our work and personal lives. A positive and well-meant idea, and notoriously difficult to achieve, especially under the typically demanding labour conditions of the US.
- **Care:** The site explanation is vague and unclear whether this is external or internal: 'When we make a big deal about things it is because we care.'
- **Entrepreneurship:** Good to see something in the list that speaks to commercial success rather than 'behave yourself'. However, I have never met an entrepreneur that says they have achieved balance, or even that they want to.
- **Reliability:** I wonder if the need to spell out that people should do what they say is rooted in another problem?
- **Agility:** Being responsive to change is understandable, and perhaps the clearest on this list.

You might accuse me of cherry-picking these examples, especially with a somewhat cynical analysis. However, look up lists of company values pasted across the internet, and you will find many similar, and many worse. Thinking back to the idea that 'culture eats strategy for breakfast', I am no wiser about what culture the organisations above have, apart from some basic rules of behaviour they seem to desire. The descriptions are more helpful than a general 'customer-centric culture' phrase, but there is still little to hang onto. What are the cues that tell us we are acting in accordance with each organisation's way of doing things?

Behaviours, vices and virtues

Let us instead try coming at this from the perspective of virtues and vices, the subject of Alasdair MacIntyre's enlightening book, *After Virtue*.[102] MacIntyre provides a broad and fascinating insight into moral theory and how, especially post-enlightenment, we have struggled to agree to shared moral principles. Central is a discussion about virtue. MacIntyre notes how what one society or group might find virtuous, another society may not. Pick up any newspaper and you will find examples of how attitudes vary – for example, towards women and girls in education across the globe, how refugees are treated, or a conversation about free speech.

A second observation from MacIntyre is that a virtue today can quickly transfer to a vice as time changes opinion. Consider ancient Greece, where the physical strength and military skill of a man were virtuous. A well-trained man, able to achieve martial feats, exemplified an ideal virtue in ancient Athens, but somehow that seems less fitting in modern-day Croydon. In Victorian England, many considered chastity a virtue, alongside deferential and overtly disciplined children. Even thievery is presented as a virtue in the story of Robin Hood. We know that Robin commits a crime when he robs carriages to give money to the poor, yet the moral position is accepted as virtue, especially in contrast to the vicious and uncaring Sheriff of Nottingham. This idea provides an advantage over values to describe culture by providing a second constraint: what we want, and what we do not. Indeed, regardless of the values that we plaster over our walls or distribute on rubber bracelets, the actions we take will be received by others on a scale from virtue to vice.

Some discovery of these expectations is made blind, or at least through experience: observing the congratulations someone receives for winning a client at a good margin; the stares from a manager when someone is not at their desk by 9 am; the cold response when a challenging question gets asked of a CEO; or the open disappointment when a manager 'has to intervene again'. More helpfully, organisations will often provide cues in the form of described behaviours or codes of practice that help keep us between the poles.

An example is the UK government's Service Standard, written to '[help] teams to create and run great public services'.[103] This includes 14 principles that government departments and the suppliers working with them are invited to use. Picking on one in the context of this book, teams should 'use agile ways of working – inspecting, learning and adapting as they go'. Read alongside the comprehensive government guide for agile delivery, I find this interesting against a higher civil service value of 'objectivity'.[104] Against that value, decisions should be made based on detailed evidence, so I cannot help but wonder if they risk neglecting more appropriate methods in a push for teams to use agile ways of working. Regardless, the implication of these codes and guides creates a norm for how things get done, and Government Digital Services (GDS, the digital arm of the Cabinet Office) went deeper to outline desired behaviours. A blog published in 2016 listed a set of unofficial expectations for working in GDS teams.[105] Following the words 'It's ok to…', are things like: 'put your headphones on', 'have a messy desk' and 'forget things'.

Multicultural emergence

Just as atoms of hydrogen and oxygen cannot be described as wet, and nor even single molecules of water, it is only when we have enough that the property of wetness emerges. Similarly, culture is not values or people, vices or virtues. It is not codes of practice, behavioural expectations or observed reactions to events. It is the combination of all these things that produces culture. Moreover, as our work, hierarchies and relationships change, these signposts, responses and therefore our culture will iterate.

> *Culture is not values or people, vices or virtues. It is not codes of practice, behavioural expectations or observed reactions to events. It is the combination of all these things.*

However, the GDS example also highlights that within an organisation it is likely that there are several identifiable cultures aligned to the functions and in-groups we are part of. We naturally accept that creative, non-process-following, free-radical culture has limited relevance in finance, much as we do not want conservatism and hard-line traditionalism in research and development. Take the example of GDS's messy desk. Within that team, it is easy to imagine that tolerance, but should a government minister, senior civil servant, auditor or champion of security walk past, would they ignore it and submit to the 'It's ok to…' poster? Or would their response and behaviour nudge and influence that cue? Much like the hierarchies in our in-groups, unless we rebel, we will ultimately be influenced by the dominant culture in our environment.

Safety

Safety is a practical reality of whatever a culture is, and to explain, I am going to take you back to ancient Greece and the parable of the Sword of Damocles. In the story, Damocles worked as a close servant of Dionysius I (406–367 BC), the ruler of Syracuse in Sicily. Damocles is said to have infuriated Dionysius by insisting that Dionysius' power meant that everything for him was simple; he had courtiers, cooks and concubines to fulfil his every need and he wanted for nothing. Frustrated by the accusation of an easy life and to prove just how precarious power was, Dionysius conceived of an idea. Damocles may experience that life for himself for one day, with all the finest foods, oils and luxuries, bounded by a single condition: that above Damocles would be suspended a sword, held by a single hair from a horse's tail. Dionysius' intent was to show Damocles that power, no matter what trappings come with it, is precarious and can leave as quickly as it arrives. Damocles, fearful for his life, requests to go back to servitude before the day is out, renewing an unquestioning respect for the ruler.

While Dionysius may have made his point, I would like you to focus on Damocles' behaviour when the sword was suspended above him. His fear of consequence meant that he chose to withdraw rather than persist with his chance to be the ruler for the day. He took the action that avoided the threat. Bringing us slowly up to date with some other examples, performance under threat also gets mentioned by Shakespeare. In *Cymbeline, King of Britain* (1609), we read:

> *Stand, stand, we have th'advantage of the ground.*
> *The lane is guarded. Nothing routs us but*
> *The villainy of our fears.*
> (Belarius, Act 5, Scene 2)

Then later, in *Measure for Measure* (1623) we have:

> *Our doubts are traitors,*
> *And make us lose the good we oft might win*
> *By fearing to attempt.*
> (Lucio, Act 1, Scene 5)

Two hundred years on, in Charles Dickens' *A Christmas Carol*, we find Scrooge's ex-fiancée, Belle, saying similar things too:

> *'You fear the world too much,' she answered gently. 'All your other hopes have merged into the hope of being beyond the chance of its sordid reproach.'*

Getting to within the last 50 years, and away from fiction, the fate of United Airlines Flight 173 serves as another, if incredibly sad, example. The flight from New York to Portland flew on 28 December 1978 with 189 people on board. In the cockpit was a highly experienced crew, including a pilot with over 27,500 hours of flight time, a first officer with over 5,000 hours and flight engineer with almost 4,000 hours. At 5.14 pm, the flight approached Portland airport, and the crew extended the flaps and lowered the landing gear. A loud thump was heard throughout the plane, and with no indicator to confirm whether the gear had dropped, the crew requested a holding pattern to investigate further. In the holding pattern for the next hour, the crew attempted to diagnose the problem and planned for an emergency landing at Portland without the landing gear. Tragically, at 6.14 pm, the engines ran out of fuel and the aircraft crashed into an area of suburban woodland seven miles from the airport, killing ten people. What had happened?

The landing gear was actually down, but the troubleshooting time meant their remaining fuel was burned and all engines finally flamed out. The transcript in the accident report is not easy to read, and while there are references to the fuel state, there also seems to be surprise when it runs out and the engines finally stop.[106] Apart from mechanical recommendations, the National Transportation Safety Board's (NTSB's) conclusion noted crew member failure to 'successfully communicate their [fuel state] concern to the captain'. More over, in their recommendations, they included 'participative management for captains and assertiveness training for other cockpit crewmembers'. That is, while the crew on the flight deck were aware of the severity of the situation, their attempts to engage the captain were vague and timid, sometimes only hinting at the problem. The observation from the NTSB was that the crew did not feel like they were safe to speak up to the more senior captain and this contributed to the accident.

'We installed them for motivation, but they sound really lovely when a breeze comes through'

Safety from what, exactly?

As the examples above illustrate, we have known for a very long time that people struggle to perform, think or create under threat. Thus, if we would like our teams unburdened to perform at their best, we should act to remove any threats that could exist. I categorise these into two areas:

- **Physical threat:** For Damocles, fear is clearly physical. He is under the jeopardy of the sword falling from its feeble support, and even if it did not kill him, severe injury would follow. Shakespeare's Cymbeline like-wise acknowledges physical fear preventing action, even with his strategic advantage, and Flight 173's perilous situation also counts as an obvious source of physical threat. In all these cases, we are at least distracted from our task, if not wholly focused on the threat itself.
- **Social threat:** Beyond the physical danger, the examples also highlight something of our behaviour in social situations. As we saw again in Chapter 7, there is no getting away from the fact that we are a social species, with an innate desire to belong. Social positioning, social acceptance, loss and a fear of rejection are key motivators for us, and we are compelled to act to secure and preserve better status. It truly is powerful stuff. Back in the cockpit of Flight 173, and in Belle's analysis of Scrooge, that is what is going on. The engineer and captain were unknowingly acting out a social norm: the captain knows best and should be respected. The flight engineer's language was cautious so as not to upset those expectations. Meanwhile, Scrooge's constant pursuit of gain secured his social position as a self-made success and kept him away from any reliance on others. *

Accordingly, the importance of helping teams to feel safe to act has made its way through experience, academia and consulting. Deming, who we met in Chapter 1, included a recommendation to 'drive out fear' as one of his

---

* If you would like to explore more examples, look up the Everest Expedition in 1996 or the Elaine Bromiley case from 2005, or pick up a copy of Matthew Syed's *Black Box Thinking: Marginal Gains and the Secrets of High Performance* (John Murray Press, 2016). All bear remarkably similar traits to Flight 173 and Syed's book goes into depth on these and others, discussing their ramifications.

14 points, and more recently, the term 'psychological safety' has been popularised by Professor Amy Edmondson. Edmondson's insight came through her work at Harvard Business School, investigating team performance in hospitals.[107] The research investigated the relationship between mistakes and the performance of those teams. What her own team had predicted before the research, that the hospitals reporting the highest number of mistakes would be the poorest performing, was shown to be false. Indeed, the opposite was found to be the case. Those hospitals reporting the highest number of mistakes performed the best. Moreover, despite reporting few mistakes, those hospitals performing poorly were actually found to be making a high number. The mistakes were there, but they were not being reported.

What was going on? Why would people be making mistakes and then not reporting them? Back to Damocles, the story ends with him stepping back from opportunity because of a threat. While there was no mortal threat hanging over the medical teams, the culture in these hospitals remained threatening. People did not feel comfortable reporting mistakes, whether due to management pressure, fear of career impact, reputational loss or otherwise.

The ramifications of this are wide. Not only did the poor-performing hospitals not report the statistical information, but they also lost the opportunity to learn and to adapt practices that could have improved their performance. By contrast, the high-performing hospitals were performing better, at least in part, because they were open about their mistakes. There are many other articles with similar findings. The not so snappily titled 'Investigating factors associated with not reporting medical errors from the medical team's point of view in Jahrom, Iran' looked at the same problem.[108] Educational hospitals in Iran were not reporting medical errors and several of the causes were fear-based: 'fear of legal pursuit', 'fear of inadequacy', 'fear of position', 'managers worry about defamation' and 'focus on wrongdoer, not reason for occurrence'. This is not restricted to healthcare – there are comparable stories of poor psychological safety across business, academia, aviation, sport, aerospace and more. In 2012, and supported by Edmondson, Google launched its 'Project Aristotle' research into what makes a successful team. After two years it concluded that, for Google, the most important aspect of team effectiveness was – you guessed it – psychological safety.[109] As Google's study suggests, it is not just errors that are missing from reports, omissions extend to the sharing of ideas and information, voicing of critical opinions, and adopting new working practices.

Around 2020, I was part of a consulting team delivering IT service management expertise to a large corporate client. We were engaged in improving major incident management practices, since the client's record for recovery time and identifying the root cause of problems was both poor and under pressure. Even if you have limited IT experience, you will appreciate the impact of a platform going offline. Think back to the last Facebook, Google, Instagram or other system failure that affected you; it is clearly imperative for the provider to get things back as quickly as possible.

Two examples of gaps in psychological safety then turned up within a week of each other. The first related to the 15 full-time major incident managers. As we collaborated and developed new processes, many of the team tried this with some good results, but one of the most experienced managers was hesitant. After some conversations, he acknowledged his concern: 'What will people think about our team if, with the new process, we're less effective?' That sounds familiar, and like the educational hospitals, rooted in a concern about reputation. This was sufficient to outweigh both the potential upside and the current, intensifying criticism about performance. Knowing this position, we were able to engage with the sponsors to publicly support the changes. By acknowledging a risk of short-term worsening, but a commitment to improvement, the team was given some space to breathe. To offer a military analogy, the sponsor had provided air cover for the ground troops.

A few days later, in another team, one monitoring engineer was making great progress with some newly trained concepts. By way of recognition, and an opportunity to nudge everyone else, I prepared a certificate and bought a bottle of champagne on my way through the airport. Conveniently, I was booked in with the responsible director that morning. The director was three or four steps above the engineer in the hierarchy, and as it happened, three or four floors higher in the building. As our meeting concluded, I invited them to hand over the gift and congratulate the engineer. I was prepared to receive a response like 'I don't have time, *you* do it' or a simple agreement. What I did not anticipate was this: 'Really? How do I do that? Won't they be embarrassed by me doing it? What do I say when I give it to him?'

After some discussion and assurance that the team would respond well, they did deliver the gift with some words of encouragement. As it played out, after the initial surprise at seeing the director, the engineer was pleased with the attention and a few others engaged more in the changes. Moreover, the director came back several more times during the time I was working there to check in with the team, and some bridges developed as a result. For a director many levels above the engineer, the reticence does not appear career-related (the interaction would not impact a pay review, for example), but there was clearly social awkwardness. Perhaps it was a similar concern about judgement or perception from others. Perhaps it was embarrassment at not having been more connected with the team already. Whatever the cause, please do not presume that gaps in psychological safety are only ever experienced by 'employees' and caused by 'superiors.' Feeling safe to take risks and be vulnerable in front of others is a social matter, not just a hierarchical one.

Finally, considering the physical and psychological safety of your teams is important, but I want to offer a few words of nuance before closing this section. First, you cannot be responsible for it all. In answering the question of whether I feel safe to act or speak up, there is much more at play than what my boss or organisational culture dictates. For example, imagine that due to job loss, I am in a perilous financial situation. In such a case, my threshold for what feels safe would fall and I would be less inclined to rock the boat. Would I choose this moment to challenge the CEO on the ethics of their recent decisions? Second, feeling safe does not automatically equate to speaking up or acting. Just because I could, does not mean that I will, and I may choose to keep the peace, defer a comment to a more appropriate time, or let it go completely.

'Do say what you feel, Jeremy. This is a safe space.'

Practical concepts for change

Given the context of change involving a shift in human behaviour, we must engage and allow the time to discuss current states and future possibilities with the people involved. There is no linear process to do this, so the following are some ideas and actions that you might attempt to support changes that you make.

Beneficence and non-maleficence

First published in 1979, *Principles of Biomedical Ethics* provides an analysis of the moral standards that should apply in medicine.[110] Known as the four pillars of medical (or biomedical) ethics, practitioners and researchers are encouraged to adhere to beneficence, non-maleficence, justice and autonomy. All four can bring value and thoughtful conversation in relation to change, but I will describe only the first two.

Non-maleficence is derived from the Latin phrase *primum non nocere*, meaning 'first, do no harm'. Essentially, this guides the surgeon or other medical practitioner to make decisions that do not worsen a patient's health or prognosis. That could mean choosing not to carry out a risky operation, being careful to accurately prescribe medication, or more simply, responding to the medical emergency of a person collapsing in the street. Google's 'Do no evil' principle is a contemporary example of this intention. Beneficence, by contrast, seeks to consider options, so that treatment is in the best interest of the patient *and* the human being. Consider a patient with a decaying tooth at the back of their mouth. Observing that the decay is significant, a dental surgeon could – in true Victorian style – remove *all* the patient's teeth to eliminate the problem and the risk of future decay.* This is in the interest of the patient as it will solve the problem, and they will have no further issues with their teeth! For the human being, however, the change in life that this would entail should encourage different treatment options.

Transferring these two ideas to a change in a business context, we can use their framing to consider our actions. Will we cause no unnecessary harm to the organisation, customers or people within it, by intention or neglect? Are our actions in the best interests of the organisation, customers and people within it?

The reality and complexity of an organisation will mean we cannot be certain, just like a doctor cannot guarantee their assessment or treatment, but discussing a change in these terms can save some pain. Think back to the example of a paper-based system moving online to save costs and improve customer experience. Examining this from the perspective of non-maleficence could reveal a risk of harm, like a limited level of customer readiness. Indeed, we have a real example of this in the move online for vehicle tax in the UK. The change initially caused a surge in car tax evasion, in part due to forgetfulness, and a substantial loss of government revenue.[111] Through beneficence, alternative strategies to achieve the desired outcomes may be found. Practically, we could conduct a two-axis sense-making exercise and plot our intended strategies and actions to compare them relatively.

---

* The practice of removing all teeth, sometimes as a birthday or wedding present, was a way to prevent future discomfort and dental bills. Against a background of increasing sugar consumption and poor hygiene, dentures provided an alternative and people continued to do this as late as the 1940s.

Cognitive closure

Regarding a sense of safety for a person, consider what happens when we tear up an organisation chart, or tell everyone that there is a new way of doing things. For a person that is experienced and skilled in one way of working, being expected to operate differently creates vulnerability. Questions like: 'Where do I fit in?' or 'What's my role in the new organisation?' or 'What skills do I need for the new role?' all come from a place of uncertainty, and that state will dominate the thinking and priorities for many people. The urge to find stability in uncertainty has been studied, and the individual differences in need were discussed by Kruglanski and Webster in their 1994 paper.[112] Their study, building on work by the psychologist Jerome Kagan in the 1970s, asserts that a resolution of uncertainties – a need for cognitive closure (NFCC) is a core driver of human behaviour. There are many potential reasons for this, from pressure of time and work demand, to levels of interest and social and cultural acceptability. Similarly to other motivations, individuals possess different levels of need for finding closure. As you might imagine, our character traits correlate. People intolerant of ambiguity have higher NFCC, and those comfortable with cognitive complexity lower. A further study by Calogero, Bardi and Sutton looked at possible links between NFCC and core values drawn from Schwartz's Theory of Basic Values – ten ideas recognised by people in all cultures.[113] As anticipated, more traditional values connected with high NFCC and vice versa. As we drive change in a team or organisation, we can use NFCC as another sense-making frame to discuss and develop deeper shared understanding of peoples' motivations and actions.

Playing chess without a board

If you are constrained, are you free? On first examination that question might seem like a contradiction, but a thought experiment from Jean-Jacques Rousseau, a Genevan political philosopher and author of *The Social Contract* helps us dig a bit deeper.[114] Imagine that you live on your own island, with no government oversight, no policies, no rules. All your days are your own, with no boss, banks or outside intervention. In such a situation, would you be free? Perhaps the idea is tempting, and indeed you could consider the many ways that you are free. However, to Rousseau, you have merely replaced the restrictions and binds of government with new constraints. The urgent need for health, shelter, food and safety would be oppressive, and you would not truly be free at all. On your island, you would never find the time and resources to write a book, compose an opera or paint a masterpiece. Would you find the time to ponder the stars, the origins of the universe or your reason for existence? Rousseau's assertion was thus that the state, by providing a fixed level of control, resources and constraint on the people actually made them, in context, *more* free.

I have always found this an interesting idea. When we think about constraints, there is a tendency to assume that they – by definition of the word – hold us back. The lean-thinking theory of constraints prioritises the removal of constraints to increase flow.[115] In practice, we identify a process, a tool, or a skill that limits flow, and we target that to improve the overall system. In this interpretation, constraints removed are seen as bad, but Rousseau's experiment opens that up. Much like the farmer in the Taoist parable from Chapter 2, with his consistent response of 'maybe' to the events befalling him, we should perceive constraints as neither good nor bad in themselves, and only make that evaluation with context.

Here are three examples of constraints, to illustrate:

1. **A chessboard:** Playing chess with the constraint of squares on a chessboard makes the game rules and moves repeatable, allowing players to concentrate on strategy rather than the relative positions of pieces. We could also consider that the number and direction of potential moves is artificially restricted and prevents wider creativity that a board-free game would allow.

2. **The 2023 introduction of a 20 mph speed limit in Wales:** Roads are safer because accidents at the new speed limit have been proven to have better outcomes. In turn, this change will save money for health and emergency services. However, imposition of speed limits on roads is perceived as an erosion of rights and, as one spokesperson stated, 'You are in fact going to damage the economy, thrashing people's livelihoods and hampering emergency services response times.'[116]

3. **Reduction in the tax-free personal allowance as income increases:** Those that have the means and earn the money pay more into the nation's treasury for the benefit of everyone. Or a more conservative

view would hold that the money I have worked hard to earn is disproportionately taken away and distributed to others who do not necessarily deserve it.

Alongside these visible and policy-based constraints we are also subject to the effects of, as David Snowden terms them, 'dark' constraints.[117] These are the non-explicit, unspoken constraints that govern what we do. They are the assumed or absent rules, the operating culture and presumed parameters in relationships that influence how we think and how we act. An organisation's use of OKRs, introduced experimentally into a leadership team, demonstrates further. After a few months, without any instruction, several teams had also adopted OKR practices, but in quite different ways. Some were fully aligned to the leadership team, some used them to capture operational work, and others simply renamed existing practice. When asked why they were using them, I received responses including 'I didn't want to be the one team not doing OKRs' and 'I heard that OKRs are needed for appraisals.' None of these were imposed constraints, they were personal interpretations of what was acceptable behaviour made manifest.

For any given behaviour that we would like, whether a speed limit or the regular update of meeting data into a corporate CRM, how might we benefit from these ideas? In line with the theory of constraints, constraints that are preventing us performing can be removed, and others can be used as drivers, filters and nudges towards that goal. Imagine that we are attempting to get our users to adopt a new online support platform. Discussing and researching the situation, we create a view that includes the constraints we can identify that could influence behaviour. We might produce a summary like this:

Target behaviour: Users adopt the new online support platform
Constraints that could prevent adoption:

- Users must contact us to create an account on the new platform.
- All users need to be trained on the new platform.
- Some staff are not trained and cannot help users.
- Users' computers need to have the latest version of Chrome to use the site properly.

Constraints that could promote adoption:

- Limit the performance of the existing platform once the new platform is available.
- At date X, redirect all support traffic to the new platform.

Constraints that are known to be absent:

- There is no policy about what happens if a user calls in.
- Apart from a few test users, we do not know the willingness of our users to transfer to a new system.

Thinking about the constraints in play, we can choose to strengthen or remove them as we see fit. Ideally, if the constraints likely to promote the change outweigh the others, we should be in a good starting position for things to happen. This same exercise can be applied to teams, functions and even individuals if needed.*

Ants and the travelling salesman problem

The travelling salesman problem is a well-known optimisation puzzle, as follows: Given a set of cities and known distance between every pair of cities, find the shortest possible route that visits every city exactly once and returns to the starting point.

Starting with a simple example, where our salesman must visit four cities (A, B, C and D, starting at A), the salesman can visit those cities in six configurations: ABCDA, ABDCA, ACDBA, ACBDA, ADBCA or ADCBA. Ignoring complications of traffic or other travel restrictions, we can use these options to calculate an optimal route. Mathematically, this problem is known as a Hamiltonian cycle. For n nodes (or cities to visit), starting in a fixed place, the number of distinct options is $(n-1)!$ Hamilton cycles. With four cities that

---

* At the risk of stating the obvious, be careful with this. Assessing the reasons why an individual is doing or not doing something from an outside perspective is a) just a perspective and probably biased, b) exclusionary to the person involved, and c) patronising and upsetting, especially if the person 'finds out' how analytically you're thinking about them. Speaking and taking time to listen to them is a much, much better place to start.

is easy to work out by hand, but finding an optimal solution quickly gets more difficult as the number of stops increases.

4 cities = (4-1)! = 6 possible cycles
8 cities = (8-1)! = 5,040 possible cycles
16 cities = (16-1)! = 1.31 x 10^{12} possible cycles
100 cities = (100-1)! = 9.33 x 10^{155} possible cycles

The good news is that since these are cycles, we have the option of going clockwise or anticlockwise around each. In other words, the number of different cycles we want to choose from is 50% of the numbers above, and our equation is:

$$\frac{(n-1)!}{2}$$

In our organisations, there are many millions of possible configurations, even if we limit ourselves to the elements we can control. Making a change in an organisation is much like this salesman problem. There will be some kind of ideal configuration, or at least a set of configurations that are within an acceptable range, but based on everything we have discussed, how do we go about finding them out? To answer that, let us learn something from ants.

Ant colonies often relocate to new areas.[118] To choose a new nest location, they follow a similar pheromonal process to mark and communicate food sources. Scouts are sent out from the nest, depositing a pheromone trail as they explore. As ants find locations of interest, they return and share with the colony, encouraging further exploration.[119] As more ants go out and follow those initial paths, they also leave a pheromone trail such that, as the cycle repeats, a few routes begin to amplify above all others. These popular paths culminate in a final location for the new colony being decided, and the transfer of larvae and resources begins.

Intriguingly, this same concept of exploration, communication and reinforcement of good or shorter paths can be successfully applied to the travelling salesman problem. In computer simulations, ant colonies were able to efficiently generate solutions to 50-city problems.[120] Shorter paths, and therefore more efficient options, are discovered and amplified over those that are less effective.

In the case of an organisation, these are useful ideas. With many possible configurations and even assuming a high tolerance for variability, finding an effective layout and combination of practices will be challenging. Learning from the ants, we might consider running multiple, simultaneous experiments to test the suitability of ideas. As we generate data, successful patterns will emerge alongside poor-performing ones, giving us clarity on where to continue our investment. More, since we are familiar with the idea that the answer to a problem may not be the obvious one, simultaneous experiments also make it easier to include more radical and oblique ideas.[121] That is, if we can only carry out one experiment at a time, what are the chances that we choose something new – even bonkers – instead of an established practice?

Here is an example making use of agile techniques: An IT organisation has 30 delivery teams, currently aligned to PRINCE2, and a desire to consider agile practices. Funding is made available for an initial three-month trial and five teams commit to attempting agile ways of working, using Scrum, Kanban, DSDM or blends of these frameworks, coupled with a variety of other tools. After a month, one group has abandoned the experiment altogether, one team is particularly successful, and another – using only sticky notes – has reported well above average collaboration. With practices emerging as valuable, investment continues for the next quarter with an evolved configuration of teams and approaches used. Experiences and insights from the work continue to be absorbed into developing good practices that begin to spread more widely.

Purpose, narratives and heuristics

All the change frameworks, like Kotter and ADKAR, talk about the need for a change purpose. In other words, a description of the change that encompasses the *why* of the work: the big reason or the prize being sought. In Chapter 5, I described how these ideas help significantly in aligning people to a cause, especially when combined with information about strategy and the *what*. I also discussed some ideas and techniques for communicating strategy and purpose, ideally getting people to hear and absorb that information.

In relation to the topic of change, however, I will call out three specific thoughts.

1. Assume that both your change purpose and strategy will evolve: The extremely challenging goal of stopping smoking in the UK by 2030 serves as an example. Imagining any strategy to achieve this outcome, it is likely that, over time, some options will close and others will open up as we see the response to our efforts. Experiments will succeed and fail, national sentiment will shift, and technological changes – like the current proliferation of vaping devices – may render our original ideas invalid. Moreover, with enough contextual change, even our original purpose may become incorrect. Sticking fast to both our original purpose and strategy when it is obvious to everyone that circumstances have changed is both foolish and frustrating for all involved.

2. Prioritise narrative difference: Being able to share examples and tell stories that encapsulate goals and their relevance to groups of stakeholders is an invaluable skill. To increase our effectiveness, we can lean on a powerful ability that we all have to observe differences. For example, if one computer works, while an identical one does not, we have a strong lead to investigate. If a fellow athlete is generating superior results with new training, we can compare our own schedule and see what we can learn. If you put a large bowl of sweets in front of one child, and an apple in front of another, both will immediately tune in to the disparity.

In change, we are intrinsically shifting from an A to a B, thus highlighting the distinction can be incredibly helpful in describing expectations. Consider a shift to ways of working, where we are seeking more active collaboration between functions. Finding examples, like: 'In situation A, we accelerated a project by teams working alongside each other' and 'In situation B, delays were created because we relied on systems for all communication', we can invite people to think about how they can generate more of A and less of B.

3. Iterate habits and heuristics: Heuristics are the reliable shortcuts that humans rely on to reach a solution quickly – our 'System 1 thinking' as Daniel Kahneman describes it.[122] These rules of thumb (or, with a more negative perspective, biases) simplify and speed up our decision-making and problem-solving. In the organisational state prior to invoking any change, people from all corners of the organisation will have developed their own heuristics, and these may no longer have relevance.

Examples of habits could include:

- A sales team always start price negotiation with an artificially high anchor, correlating it to better revenue.
- An engineer who automatically restarts a machine before any further troubleshooting (or a senior manager that insists as much).
- Approaching all projects from a predictive point of view before understanding what it is that is needed.
- Rejecting candidates without university degrees before assessing suitability for roles.
- Automatically celebrating and valuing the commencement of projects over their completion.
- Not working with someone, a team or supplier because of a previous incident where they made a mistake.

Where we discover such habits, we can discuss, demonstrate or use narrative difference to help iterate the heuristic to a conscious new behaviour, and ultimately a new habit.

Chapter summary

Change is something that causes or necessitates a shift in human behaviour and it is always going to land in the middle of established patterns and culture. Thus, no matter which process or framework we use, we are going to be tripped up by the complexity of the countless relationships, perceptions and experiences that exist. That does not mean we cannot make change happen, rather that we must be sensitive to those nuances and invest in our engagement with them.

- Change exists across contexts. There will be clear and simple activities that can be achieved without fuss alongside deeply complex problems that you will need to feel your way through.
- Constraints can amplify or reduce the effects of changes that you are making. Those constraints can be intentional, legislative or simply exist because of unspoken habits or beliefs.
- Humans are sensitive to differences, so vices and virtues present a more complete view of an organisation's existing (or intended) habits and beliefs than a flat list of values.
- For problems or changes that have multiple options or no clear conclusions, take inspiration from a re-homing ant colony and try things! Experiment widely and curiously, narrow the field through the results you get back.
- Ideas from medicine, such as beneficence and non-maleficence, provide interesting sense-making exercises that explore the impact of the change you are trying to make.
- Viewed as a whole, an organisation will tend towards complexity due to the independent moving parts. Thus, any purpose or strategy for change may quickly go out of date and dogmatism for a lost cause is unlikely to yield useful results. To give yourself a fighting chance, actively check for things shifting around you and refine your approach.

CHAPTER 9

A final word

'Science, my lad, has been built upon many errors; but they are errors which it was good to fall into, for they led to the truth.'

— JULES VERNE (1864)

As has been shown throughout this book, the importance of context is profound, and our ability to interpret and respond to it crucial. Your customers' needs, your markets, regulations and locations, systems and resources, your people, their skills and their countless connections all add up to an unknowable and intricate tapestry of relationships. To imagine that in such a world, we can apply a packaged style of leadership or practice and perform at our best is false, and those that sell such promises are attempting to deceive. Sure, results will be achieved if you can go ahead and copy the operating model of Spotify, follow Facebook's approach to software deployment, or teach all your leaders to be authentic, but they will not guarantee to unlock hitherto unseen success.

Unless like Spotify, you produce a high-scale and ever-changing application, have attracted communicative, self-starting, and technically brilliant engineers, and choose to give them an environment to flourish, then a structure of tribes, guilds and squads is more likely to confuse and impair progress while people work out what is happening. Likewise, Facebook's approaches are based on high numbers of exceptional people developing methods that work for them, and after years of praxis. Installing their tools and reading their blogs is not a miracle drug. Authentic leadership too – even if we can agree on what that means – is inevitably going to be out of context, and the shape of what we end up with will be crude, like a child's first attempts at drawing a face.

There is, however, hope. While I listed many cynical reasons for our desire to pick up recipes and copy other people at the start of this book, many are driven by a genuine belief that things could be better, or that the world is shifting in such a way that they cannot keep up. The adage that what worked today may not work tomorrow continues to be true in organisations across the planet.

Thus, instead of picking formula after formula and waiting to see if they do anything, I encourage you to begin in a different place: *start with sense*. Experiment, learn, and experience what it is like to have meaningful and open-ended conversations about what is going on. Discover with your teams the various perceptions and realities of the contexts you are in, and then use that insight to decide on your strategies. That decision could be to try something radical, or it could even be a recipe, but it is now embarked upon from a firmer foundation. In effect, you are testing a hypothesis, or parallel testing many, with a far better understanding of which indicators to monitor, and results to check. From there, the next time you face a decision, test an assumption or the world around you moves, your knowledge, library of tools, and responses will be deeper, and will continue to expand.

I warmly wish you every success and thank you again for picking up a copy of this book.

Acknowledgements

There are many people that have helped me to write this book. If I have worked with you, have read your books, papers and articles, or I have discussed leadership, delivery and organisations with you, you are part of the fabric of this book. Thank you.

I extend specific recognition and appreciation to Caroline Seidel, Elise Foster, David Harding, James Sperring and Fiona Harrild. As my earliest readers, critics, advocates and motivators to get this thing done, I will be forever grateful.

There have also been many other people who have applied their brilliance to shape this book into something much better. The team at the Choir Press, and notably Rachel Woodman for her patience, encouragement and guidance from our first conversation to the very end. The invaluable editing and insightful recommendations from Mary Davis, the epitome of excellent service. The incredible attention to detail and deeply considered suggestions from Helena Nowak-Smith that refined this book well beyond a final proof-read. And the inimitable talents of Nick Gowman, the artist behind the wonderful illustrations in this book, and someone able to read my mind and then improve on what he found. All your input has been immeasurable.

Finally, it is for my wife, Juliet, that I reserve my greatest thanks. You have been with me for every single moment of this rollercoaster ride, and I simply could not have done it without you.

Copyright acknowledgements

PART II – A credible alternative

About the author

Stephen is an accomplished and award-winning IT leader with over 20 years of experience in complex, uncertain and high-scale technical organisations. During that time, he has led customer, infrastructure, product and software functions in rapid-growth and highly regulated environments.

Today, Stephen provides consultancy and support to C-suite and other senior leaders in companies ranging from start-ups through to established global organisations in the science, technology, education and mathematics (STEM) space. He provides expertise in sense-making, context-driven leadership, complexity, agility and organisational transformation. He is well respected by his clients and speaking audiences for his insightful observations and rich combination of theory and real-world experience.

Stephen lives near the New Forest in the UK with his wife, son and implausibly loud cat. He would say sorry for the cringeworthy jokes presented in this book, but that just wouldn't be authentic.

Endnotes

PART I

Chapter 1 – All hail the right way!
[1] Friedrich Nietzsche, *Thus Spake Zarathustra: A Book for All and None*, translated by Alexander Tille (Macmillan & Co Ltd, 1896), 284.
[2] Hamid Hassan, Sarosh Asad, and Yasuo Hoshino, 'Determinants of Leadership Style in Big Five Personality Dimensions', *Universal Journal of Management* 4, no. 4 (Apr. 2016): 161–179, https://doi.org/10.13189/ujm.2016.040402.
[3] This opinion apparently has 'excessive citations' – a rare occurrence on Wikipedia. 'Erwin Rommel', Wikipedia, https://en.wikipedia.org/wiki/Erwin_Rommel (accessed 26 Jan. 24).
[4] Robin Lane Fox, *The Search for Alexander*, 1st ed (Boston: Little, Brown, 1980), 34-36.
[5] Peter Green, *Alexander of Macedon, 356-323 B.C: A Historical Biography* (Oxford, England: University of California Press, 1991).
[6] Plutarch, *Lives, Volume VII: Demosthenes and Cicero. Alexander and Caesar*, translated by Bernadotte Perrin, Loeb Classical Library 46 (Cambridge, MA: Harvard University Press, 1919).
[7] Sarah B Pomeroy et al., *A Brief History of Ancient Greece: Politics, Society, and Culture* (New York London: Oxford University Press, 2004).
[8] John Maxwell O'Brien, 'Alexander the Great', *Alcohol and Alcoholism* 16, no. 1 (Mar. 1981): 39–40, https://doi.org/10.1093/oxfordjournals.alcalc.a044252.
[9] W. H. Weston, *Plutarch's Lives for Boys and Girls* (New York: Frederick A. Stokes, 1900), https://archive.org/details/plutarchslivesfo00westrich/mode/2up, 135.
[10] Peter Turchin, Jonathan M. Adams, and Thomas D. Hall, 'East-West Orientation of Historical Empires and Modern States', *Journal of World-Systems Research* 12, no. 2 (2006): 219–29, https://doi.org/10.5195/jwsr.2006.369.
[11] Rein Taagepera, 'Expansion and Contraction Patterns of Large Polities: Context for Russia', *International Studies Quarterly* 41, no. 3 (Sep. 1997): 475–504, https://doi.org/10.1111/0020-8833.00053.
[12] Johannes Giessauf, 'A Programme of Terror and Cruelty. Aspects of Mongol Strategy in the Light of Western Sources', *Chronica*, no. 7–8 (2007-2008), https://acta.bibl.u-szeged.hu/5837/1/chronica_007_008_085-096.pdf.

13 Neometrics, 'Twentieth Century Atlas – Historical Body Count', https://necro-metrics.com/pre1700a.htm#Mongol (accessed 26 Jan. 24).

14 Julia Pongratz et al., 'Coupled Climate–Carbon Simulations Indicate Minor Global Effects of Wars and Epidemics on Atmospheric CO2 between AD 800 and 1850', *The Holocene* 21, no. 5 (2011): 843–51, https://doi.org/10.1177/0959683610386981.

15 Altangherel Tserendorjiin, 'Genghis Khan's Impact on Human History', *Otoch Manramba University* (2021).

16 W. H. Weston, *Plutarch's Lives for Boys and Girls* (New York: Frederick A. Stokes, 1900), https://archive.org/details/plutarchslivesfo00westrich/mode/2up, 36.

17 'Millennium Top Ten', *Time* magazine, 15 Oct. 1992, https://time.com/archive/6721422/millennium-top-ten and Joel Achenbach, 'The Era of his ways', *The Washington Post*, 30 Dec. 1995, https://www.washingtonpost.com/archive/lifestyle/1995/12/31/the-era-of-his-ways (accessed 26 Jan. 24).

18 Ernle Bradford, *Nelson, the Essential Hero* (New York: Jovanovich, 1977), 209.

19 David Davies, *A Brief History of Fighting Ships: Ships of the Line 1793–1815* (London: Robinson, 1996), 102.

20 'Lord Admiral Horatio Nelson: A Rebel with a Cause', HistoryExtra, https://www.historyextra.com/period/georgian/horatio-nelson-lord-admiral-life-facts-wives-battles-death (accessed 26 Jan. 24).

21 Kate Williams, 'Nelson and Lady Hamilton: A Very Public Affair', BBC History, https://www.bbc.co.uk/history/british/empire_seapower/nelson_emma_01.shtml (accessed 26 Jan. 24).

22 'Slave Trade. Copy of a Letter from Lord Nelson to Mr Simon Taylor of Jamaica, dated, Victory off Martinico, June 10, 1805', *Cobbett's Weekly Political Register*, https://archive.org/details/cobbettsweeklyp01goog/page/n162/mode/2up, (accessed 26 Jan. 24). Amendments were made, according to 'The Nelson Dispatch', *Journal of the Nelson Society* 3, no. 12 (Autumn 2020): 724–743, https://nelson-society.com/the-nelson-dispatch.

23 Juan José Sánchez Arreseigor, 'Vlad the Impaler's thirst for blood was an inspiration for Count Dracula', *National Geographic*, 28 Oct. 2021, https://www.nationalgeographic.com/history/history-magazine/article/vlad-the-impalers-thirst-for-blood-was-one-inspiration-behind-count-dracula (accessed 26 Jan. 24).

24 Dominic Rushe et al., 'Twitter Slashes Nearly Half Its Workforce as Musk Admits "Massive Drop" in Revenue', *The Guardian*, 5 Nov. 2022, sec. Technology, https://www.theguardian.com/technology/2022/nov/04/twitter-layoffs-elon-musk-revenue-drop and Alex Veiga, 'Musk Restores Trump's Twitter Account after Online

Poll', *AP News*, https://apnews.com/article/elon-musk-biden-twitter-inc-technology-congress-d88e3de4b3cc095926dc133f53dc3320 (accessed 26 Jan. 24).

[25] Aisha Counts and Tom Maloney, 'Twitter Now Worth Just One-Third of What Musk Paid for It', *Time* magazine, 31 May 23, https://time.com/6283658/twitter-worth-third-musk-price-fidelity (accessed 27 Jan. 24).

[26] Koh Ewe, 'Elections Around the World in 2024', *Time* magazine, 28 Dec. 2023, https://time.com/6550920/world-elections-2024 (accessed 28 Jan. 24).

[27] Stefan Sveningsson and Mats Alvesson, *Managerial Lives: Leadership and Identity in an Imperfect World* (Cambridge: Cambridge University Press, 2016).

[28] Stefan Sveningsson and Mats Alvesson, *Managerial Lives*, 4.

[29] Stefan Sveningsson and Mats Alvesson, *Managerial Lives*, 122.

[30] Stefan Sveningsson and Mats Alvesson, *Managerial Lives*, 196.

[31] Thomas Carlyle, *On Heroes, Hero-Worship, and the Heroic in History*, 1840, https://www.gutenberg.org/files/1091/1091-h/1091-h.htm (accessed 28 Jan. 24).

[32] Charles Bird, *Social Psychology*, (Appleton-Century, 1940), 379.

[33] 'The Nuclear Attack on the UK That Never Happened', *BBC News*, 30 Oct. 2014, https://www.bbc.com/news/magazine-29804446 (accessed 28 Jan. 24).

[34] '[Re:Work] Manager Feedback Survey', *Google Re:Work*, https://docs.google.com/forms/d/e/1FAIpQLSdTeBHKoI3784y7xsT_-Mh2jhlbW1NXR5McNuhUiCzhGSCWMw/viewform (accessed 5 Feb. 24).

[35] John C. Maxwell, *The 21 Irrefutable Laws of Leadership: Follow Them and People Will Follow You* (Nashville, Tenn: Thomas Nelson, 1998).

[36] Robert K. Greenleaf, *The Servant as Leader* (Newton Center, Massachusetts: Robert K Greenleaf Center, 1973), 7.

[37] James W. Sipe, Don M. Frick, *Seven Pillars of Servant Leadership: Practicing the wisdom of leading by serving* (Paulist Press, 2009).

[38] Ken Blanchard and Renee Broadwell, *Servant Leadership In Action: How you can achieve great relationships and results* (Berrett-Koehler, 2018), 145.

[39] Shann Ray Ferch, Larry C. Spears, *The Spirit of Servant-Leadership* (Paulist Press, 2011).

[40] Patrick Lencioni in Ken Blanchard and Renee Broadwell, *Servant Leadership In Action*, 95.

[41] Farida Saleem et al., 'Impact of Servant Leadership on Performance: The Mediating Role of Affective and Cognitive Trust', *Sage Open* 10, no. 1 (2020), https://doi.org/doi: 10.1177/2158244019900562.

[42] William L. Gardner et al., 'Authentic Leadership Theory: The Case for and Against', *The Leadership Quarterly* 32, no. 6 (2021), https://doi.org/10.1016/j.leaqua.2021.101495.

[43] Lucilla Crosta and David McConnell, 'Challenging the Traditional Theorisation

on Group Development: An International Online Perspective', in Lone Dirckinck-Holmfeld et al., *Proceedings of the Seventh International Conference on Networked Learning* (2010).

[44] Sigmund Freud, *Group Psychology and the Analysis of the Ego,* translated by James Strachey (Hogarth Press, 1949), 92.

[45] Stanley Lieberson and James F. O'Connor, 'Leadership and Organizational Performance: A Study of Large Corporations.', *American Sociological Review* 37, no. 2 (1972): 117–130, https://doi.org/10.2307/2094020.

[46] Markus A. Fitza, 'The Use of Variance Decomposition in the Investigation of CEO Effects: How Large Must the CEO Effect Be to Rule out Chance?', *Strategic Management Journal* 35, no. 12 (2014): 1839–52, https://doi.org/10.1002/smj.2192.

[47] Sigmund Freud, *Group Psychology and the Analysis of the Ego*, 89.

[48] Nicolas Bastardoz and Mark Van Vugt, 'The Nature of Followership: Evolutionary Analysis and Review', *The Leadership Quarterly* 30, no. 1 (Feb. 2019): 81–95, https://doi.org/10.1016/j.leaqua.2018.09.004.

[49] William Shakespeare, *Henry IV, Part 2,* Act 3, Scene 1.

[50] Nicolas Bastardoz and Mark Van Vugt, 'The Nature of Followership', 85.

[51] Nicolas Bastardoz and Mark Van Vugt, 'The Nature of Followership', 88.

[52] Karen A Jehn, 'A Qualitative Analysis of Conflict Types and Dimensions in Organizational Groups', *Administrative Science Quarterly* 42, no. 3 (1997): 530–557, https://doi.org/10.2307/2393737.

[53] Noelle Baird and Alex J. Benson, 'Getting Ahead While Getting Along: Followership as a Key Ingredient for Shared Leadership and Reducing Team Conflict', *Frontiers in Psychology* 13 (27 Jun. 2022): 923150, https://doi.org/10.3389/fpsyg.2022.923150.

[54] Nicolas Bastardoz and Mark Van Vugt, 'The Nature of Followership', 90.

[55] Nicolas Bastardoz and Mark Van Vugt, 'The Nature of Followership', 90.

[56] David A. Garvin, Alison Berkley Wagonfeld and Liz Kind, 'Google's Project Oxygen: Do Managers Matter?' *Harvard Business School* Case 313-110, 2013 (revised Oct. 2013).

[57] S. Alexander Haslam, Mats Alvesson, and Stephen D. Reicher, 'Zombie Leadership: Dead Ideas That Still Walk among Us', *The Leadership Quarterly* 35, no. 3 (2024): 101770, https://doi.org/10.1016/j.leaqua.2023.101770.

[58] In my research, guilds in Europe have been more studied and recorded, but they were not unique. See Tirthankar Roy, 'The Guild in Modern South Asia', *International Review of Social History* 53, no. S16 (2008): 95–120, https://doi.org/10.1017/S0020859008003623.

[59] James R. Farr, *Artisans in Europe, 1300–1914* (Cambridge: Cambridge University Press), 56.

[60] Johann Joachim Becher, 'Complete Dictionary of Scientific Biography' *Encyclopedia.com.* (15 Aug. 2024).
https://www.encyclopedia.com/science/dictionaries-thesauruses-pictures-and-press-releases/becher-johann-joachim-0.

[61] James R. Farr, *Artisans in Europe*, 20.

[62] 'Alfred P. Sloan interview on Running a Successful Business (1954)', *Manufacturing Intellect* YouTube channel, 6 Jul. 2018,
https://www.youtube.com/watch?v=w52SYCtG94o (accessed 20 Jun. 24).

[63] John Seddon, *In Pursuit of Quality: The Case Against ISO 9000* (Oak Tree Press, 2000).

[64] D. J. Pratt, 'British Standard (BS) 5750—Quality Assurance?', *Prosthetics and Orthotics International* 19, no. 1 (Apr. 1995): 31–36,
https://doi.org/10.3109/03093649509078229.

[65] William Edwards Deming, *Out of the Crisis* (MIT Press: 1982, revised 2018).

[66] William Edwards Deming, *Out of the Crisis*, 227.

[67] 'Capacity and Performance Management: Practice Guide', *Axelos*,
https://www.axelos.com/resource-hub/practice/capacity-and-performance-management-itil-4-practice-guide.

[68] 'SAFe 4.5 Introduction: Overview of the Scaled Agile Framework for Lean Enterprises, *Scaled Agile*, Aug. 2017,
https://scaledagileframework.com/wp-content/uploads/delightful-downloads/2017/10/White_Paper_SAFe-4.5.pdf (accessed 28 Jul. 24).

Chapter 2 – Systems and context

[69] 'Great Storm 1987', *BBC Suffolk* (2008),
https://www.bbc.co.uk/suffolk/content/articles/2007/10/13/great_storm_1987_michael_fish_feature.shtml (accessed 28 Jul. 24).

[70] Alex Spiro, Quinn Emanuel Trial Lawyers, Legal letter to Mark Zuckerberg, Meta, 5 Jul. 2023,
https://cdn.sanity.io/files/ifn0l6bs/production/27109f01431939c8177d408d3c9848c3b46632cd.pdf (accessed 28 Jul. 24).

[71] 'Geiriadur', Welsh–English/English–Welsh On-line Dictionary, *University of Wales*, https://geiriadur.uwtsd.ac.uk (accessed 8 Feb. 24).

[72] David Snowden, 'The Cynefin Framework as at February 2021', *Cynefin.io*,
https://cynefin.io/wiki/Cynefin (accessed 28 Jul. 24).

73 'Who first originated the term VUCA (Volatility, Uncertainty, Complexity and Ambiguity)?', *US Army Heritage and Education Center*, https://usawc.libanswers.com/faq/84869 (accessed 20 Aug. 24).

74 Robin I. M. Dunbar, 'Neocortex Size as a Constraint on Group Size in Primates', *Journal of Human Evolution* 22, no. 6 (1992): 469–93, https://doi.org/10.1016/0047-2484(92)90081-J.

75 Shai Danziger, Jonathan Levav, and Liora Avnaim-Pesso, 'Extraneous Factors in Judicial Decisions', *Proceedings of the National Academy of Sciences* 108, no. 17 (2011): 6889–92, https://doi.org/10.1073/pnas.1018033108.

76 'In Conversation E6 Brenda Dervin', *Project Oneness World* YouTube channel, https://www.youtube.com/watch?v=VneXr3rzMyU (accessed 14 Apr. 24).

Chapter 3 – Our compulsion to follow

77 'Charles Kuralt Commencement Address 1996', *UNCA Ramsey Library Video Production* YouTube channel, https://www.youtube.com/watch?v=Jy8Z_nqn_Q0 (accessed 14 Apr. 24).

78 John Doerr, *Measure What Matters: How Google, Bono, and the Gates Foundation Rock the World with OKRs* (New York: Penguin, 2018).

79 Marsh describes this evocatively in this BBC interview. Private Passions: Henry Marsh, *BBC Radio 3*, 17 Jan. 2016, https://www.bbc.co.uk/programmes/b061fmcf (accessed 14 Aug. 24).

80 Mats Alvesson, 'Upbeat Leadership: A Recipe for – or against – "Successful" Leadership Studies', *The Leadership Quarterly* 31, no. 6 (Dec. 2020): 101439, https://doi.org/10.1016/j.leaqua.2020.101439.

81 Everett Rogers, *Diffusion of Innovations* 5th edition (Simon & Schuster, 2003).

82 David A. Pizarro et al., 'Ripple Effects in Memory: Judgments of Moral Blame Can Distort Memory for Events', *Memory & Cognition* 34, no. 3 (1 Apr. 2006): 550–555, https://doi.org/10.3758/BF03193578.

83 John Doerr, *Measure What Matters*.

84 Tyler Vigen, 'Spurious correlation 1522: The distance between Saturn and the Sun', *Tylervigen.com*, https://www.tylervigen.com/spurious/correlation/1522_the-distance-between-saturn-and-the-sun_correlates-with_google-searches-for-how-to-make-baby (accessed 6 Feb. 24).

85 'Rumsfeld / Knowns', *CNN* YouTube channel, https://www.youtube.com/watch?v=REWeBzGuzCc (accessed 21 Aug. 24).

86 'Employer Skills Survey, Calendar Year 2022', *GOV.UK*, https://explore-education-statistics.service.gov.uk/find-statistics/employer-skills-survey (accessed 21 Aug. 24).

87 'Industries in the UK', *Parliament House of Commons Library*, https://commonslibrary.parliament.uk/research-briefings/cbp-8353 (accessed 21 Aug. 24).

88 Like ex-Prime Minister, Liz Truss's fierce defence of her economic policy that caused the Bank of England to implement emergency measures. Ben Riley-Smith, 'Liz Truss to Argue UK Economic Growth Would Be Stronger in 2030 If Her Policies Were Still in Place', *The Telegraph*, 17 Sept. 2023, https://www.telegraph.co.uk/politics/2023/09/17/liz-truss-defends-mini-budget-higher-economic-growth (accessed 21 Aug. 24).

89 'Concorde fallacy', *Cambridge Dictionary*, https://dictionary.cambridge.org/us/dictionary/english/concorde-fallacy (accessed 8 Feb. 24).

90 Michael I. Norton, Daniel Mochon, and Dan Ariely, 'The IKEA Effect: When Labor Leads to Love', *Journal of Consumer Psychology* 22, no. 3 (2012): 453–460, https://doi.org/10.1016/j.jcps.2011.08.002.

PART II

Chapter 4 – The sense making leader

1 Quote by Fritz Perls, source unavailable. Quoted at 'Fritz Perls', *Anil Thomas: The Gestalt Experience, Principles on Gestalt Concepts*, https://www.anilthomasgestalt.com/about-fritz (accessed 15 Apr. 24).

2 Ken Schwaber and Jeff Sutherland, 'The Scrum Guide', *Scrum.org*, 2020, https://scrumguides.org/docs/scrumguide/v2020/2020-Scrum-Guide-US.pdf (accessed 25 Mar. 24).

3 'Context', *Cambridge English Dictionary* online, https://dictionary.cambridge.org/dictionary/english/context (accessed 25 Mar. 24).

4 Naresh Kumar Agarwal, *Exploring Context in Information Behavior: Seeker, Situation, Surroundings, and Shared Identities* (Springer, 2017).

5 'Stanford Prison Experiment – Spotlight at Stanford', *Stanford University*, https://exhibits.stanford.edu/spe (accessed 23 Mar. 24).

6 Alex Haslam and Steve Reicher, 'The BBC Prison Study', http://bbcprisonstudy.org (accessed 24 Mar. 24).

7 Martin G. Moore, 'You're a Leader Now. Not Everyone is Going to Like You', *Harvard Business Review*, Sept. 2021, https://hbr.org/2021/09/youre-a-leader-now-not-everyone-is-going-to-like-you and Martin G. Moore, '5 Things That Change When You Become a Leader', *Harvard Business Review*, Jan. 2022, https://hbr.org/2022/01/5-things-that-change-when-you-become-a-leader (accessed 10 May 24).

[8] Karl E. Weick, *The Social Psychology of Organizing* (New York: McGraw-Hill, 1979).

[9] Matteo Cristofaro, 'Organizational Sensemaking: A Systematic Review and a Co-Evolutionary Model', *European Management Journal* 40, no. 3 (Jun. 2022): 393–405, https://doi.org/10.1016/j.emj.2021.07.003.

[10] Zone, 'The Timely Benefits of Finding The Last Responsible Moment', *Medium*, https://thisiszone.medium.com/the-timely-benefits-of-finding-the-last-responsible-moment-2b81970dc975 (accessed 17 May 24).

[11] Amazon Staff, 'Jeff Bezos' 2016 Letter to Amazon Shareholders', 17 Apr. 2017, https://www.aboutamazon.com/news/company-news/2016-letter-to-shareholders (accessed 21 Aug. 24).

Chapter 5 – Direction and strategy

[12] 'Address at Rice University on the Nation's Space Effort, September 12, 1962', *John F. Kennedy Presidential Library and Museum*, https://www.jfklibrary.org/archives/other-resources/john-f-kennedy-speeches/rice-university-19620912 (accessed 21 Feb. 2024).

[13] Friedrich Nietzsche, *The Twilight of the Idols, Or, How to Philosophise with the Hammer*, translated by Anthony M. Ludovici (1911), 2.

[14] 'Purpose Statement Disconnect Prompts Staff to Quit', *Institute of Chartered Accountants in England and Wales*, Nov. 2022, https://www.icaew.com/insights/viewpoints-on-the-news/2022/nov-2022/purpose-statement-disconnect-prompts-staff-to-quit (accessed 21 Feb. 24).

[15] 'John F. Kennedy: Speeches' (filtered, 1962), *John F. Kennedy Presidential Library and Museum*, https://www.jfklibrary.org/archives/other-resources/john-f-kennedy-speeches (accessed 21 Feb. 2024).

[16] Justin McCarthy, '50 Years After Moon Landing, Support for Space Program High', *Gallup*, 11 Jul. 2019, https://news.gallup.com/poll/260309/years-moon-landing-support-space-program-high.aspx (accessed 21 Feb. 2024).

[17] See much more about Simon Wardley and his strategic tools by searching for 'Wardley Maps.'

[18] Simon Wardley, *Wardley Maps* (Amazon KDP, 2022),13. Also available free online, *Simon Wardley, The Book*, https://learnwardleymapping.com/book.

[19] Brian Barrett, 'McDonald's Doubles Down on Tech With Voice AI Acquisition', *Wired* magazine, 18 Sep. 2019, https://www.wired.com/story/mcdonalds-acquires-apprente-voice-ai (accessed 21 Aug. 24).

[20] 'Our Approach & Progress', *McDonalds*, https://www.mcdonalds.com/corpmcd/our-purpose-and-impact/impact-strategy-and-reporting.html (accessed 27 Feb. 24).

[21] Stephen R. Covey, *The 7 Habits of Highly Effective People* (London: Simon & Schuster UK, 2004), 98.

[22] George T. Doran, 'There's a S.M.A.R.T. way to write management's goals and objectives', *Management Review* 70, no. 11 (1981): 35–36.

[23] Peter Drucker, *The Practice of Management: A Study of the Most Important Function in American Society* (Harper & Brothers, 1954).

[24] Robert Bordley, Marco Licalzi, and Luisa Tibiletti, 'A Target-Based Foundation for the "Hard-Easy Effect" Bias', in *Country Experiences in Economic Development, Management and Entrepreneurship*, ed. Mehmet Huseyin Bilgin et al. (Cham: Springer International Publishing, 2017), 659–671.

[25] Tom Gilb, a pioneer in software development, author of *Competitive Engineering* and staunch advocate of value, talks often on this theme: Meeting customer requirements does *not* always mean writing software, and existing tools may well do the job for a fraction of the cost. Tom Gilb, *Competitive Engineering: A Handbook For Systems Engineering, Requirements Engineering, and Software Engineering Using Planguage* (Butterworth-Heinemann, 2005).

[26] 'Andy Grove's Last Stand', *Forbes*, https://www.forbes.com/forbes/2008/0128/070.html (accessed 17 May 24).

[27] 'Ford Focus Hatchback (1998–2004) 1.4 CL 5d (01) Specs & Dimensions', *Parkers Guide*, https://www.parkers.co.uk/ford/focus/hatchback-1998/14-cl-5d-(01)/specs (accessed 27 Feb. 24).

[28] 'Electoral statistics, UK: December 2020', *Office for National Statistics*, https://www.ons.gov.uk/peoplepopulationandcommunity/elections/electoralregistration/bulletins/electoralstatisticsforuk/december2020 (accessed 21 Aug. 24).

[29] Dale Carnegie, *How to Win Friends and Influence People* (first edition: Simon & Schuster, 1936); and Dwight Garner, 'Classic Advice: Please, Leave Well Enough Alone', *The New York Times*, 5 Oct. 2011, https://www.nytimes.com/2011/10/05/books/books-of-the-times-classic-advice-please-leave-well-enough-alone.html (accessed 21 Aug. 24).

[30] 'I have two employees that usually leave work at 6 pm. They are good, but I don't like that their commitment lasts for work hours only. What should I do as a CEO?', *Quora*, https://www.quora.com/I-have-two-employees-that-usually-leave-work-at-6-pm-They-are-good-but-I-don-t-like-that-their-commitment-lasts-for-work-hours-only-What-should-I-do-as-a-CEO (accessed 29 Feb. 24).

[31] Stephen R. Covey, *The 7 Habits of Highly Effective People*, 235.

[32] Hermann Ebbinghaus, *Memory: a contribution to experimental psychology* (Teachers College, Columbia University, 1913).

[33] Tara Swart, *The Source: Open your mind, Change your life* (Vermillion, 2020).

[34] Daniel Kahneman, *Thinking, Fast and Slow* (Farrar, Straus, and Giroux, 2011).

[35] The Rule of Seven has been around for decades and continues to be recommended. Mike Neumeier, 'Why Marketers Should Follow The Rule Of Seven', *Forbes*, 21 Sept. 2023, https://www.forbes.com/sites/forbescommunicationscouncil/2023/09/21/why-marketers-should-follow-the-rule-of-seven (accessed 21 Aug. 24).

[36] Several papers challenged Maslow's hierarchy of needs after publication, e.g., Douglas T. Hall and Khalil E. Nougaim, 'An Examination of Maslow's Need Hierarchy in an Organizational Setting', *Organizational Behavior and Human Performance* 3, no. 1 (1968): 12–35, https://doi.org/10.1016/0030-5073(68)90024-X.

[37] At least a modern translation! Sun Tzu et al., *The Art of War: Including the Translated The Sayings of Wu Tzu* (West Sussex, United Kingdom: Capstone, 2010).

Chapter 6 – Delivery, delivery, delivery

[38] 'Mike Tyson on his iconic saying "Everyone got a plan until they're punched in the face", *ESNEWS* YouTube channel, 3 Oct. 2021, https://www.youtube.com/watch?v=MEtFk9KaglA (accessed 20 Aug. 24).

[39] Eric Ries, *The Lean Startup* (Penguin, 2011).

[40] Frank Turley, 'Plans', *PRINCE2* wiki, https://prince2.wiki/theme/plans (accessed 29 Feb. 24).

[41] Hannah Kane, 'Scrum your wedding: how to plan your wedding like a software developer', *offbeat wed* (Apr. 2015), https://offbeatwed.com/scrum-your-wedding, (accessed 21 Aug. 24).

[42] Roger Bacon, *Opus Majus* (Oxford: Clarendon Press, 1897), 168.

[43] Roger Bacon, *Opus Majus,* 153.

[44] Fyodor Dostoyevsky, *Crime and Punishment* (Journalled in The Russian Messenger, 1866).

[45] Colonel John Boyd, 'Patterns of Conflict', 1986, *Oodaloop.com*, https://www.oodaloop.com/wp-content/uploads/2022/02/patterns-of-conflict.pdf (accessed 21 Aug. 24).

[46] Colonel John Boyd, 'Patterns of Conflict', 5.

[47] 'The OODA Loop Explained: The Real Story about the Ultimate Model for Decision-Making in Competitive Environments', *OODA Loop*, https://www.oodaloop.com/the-ooda-loop-explained-the-real-story-about-the-ultimate-model-for-decision-making-in-competitive-environments (accessed 15 May 24).

[48] Kent Beck et al, 'Manifesto for Agile Software Development', 2001, https://agilemanifesto.org (accessed 21 Jan 24).

[49] Ian Roper, Rea Prouska, and Uracha Chatrakul Na Ayudhya, 'The Rhetorics of

"Agile" and the Practices of "Agile Working": Consequences for the Worker Experience and Uncertain Implications for HR Practice', *The International Journal of Human Resource Management* 33, no. 22 (2022): 4440–4467, https://doi.org/10.1080/09585192.2022.2099751.

50 'What Is ITIL?', *Axelos*, https://www.axelos.com/certifications/itil-service-management/what-is-itil (accessed 19 May 24).

51 'World Rowing – 2017 World Rowing Cup II', *World Rowing*, https://worldrowing.com/event/2017-world-rowing-cup-ii (accessed 21 Aug. 24).

52 'Sex ban doesn't apply to Sven', *The Mirror* newspaper, 28 Nov. 2005.

53 Kevin Garside, 'Ashes 2023: What Bazball got wrong – and right – in the 1st Test defeat', *Independent*, 20 Jun. 2023. Stephan Shemilt, 'Ashes 2023: Why England's Bazball style is starting to lose its shine', *BBC News*, 30 Jun. 2023. Gautam Sodhi, 'Explained: How Bazball-led England messed up golden chance to win home Ashes against ageing Aussie side', *WIO News*, 24 Jul. 2023. Nick Hoult, 'Bazball vindicated despite England drawing Ashes series', *The Telegraph* newspaper, 31 Jul. 2023.

54 Rachel Schraer, 'Covid: Misleading Stat Claims More Vaccinated People Die', *BBC News*, 1 Jul. 2021, https://www.bbc.com/news/health-57610998 (accessed 21 Aug. 24).

55 Isabelle Gerretsen, 'The Adverts Banned for Misleading Climate Claims', *BBC Future*, https://www.bbc.com/future/article/20220302-the-adverts-that-were-banned-for-misleading-climate-claims (accessed 21 Aug. 24).

56 'The £350m Line on the Brexit Bus Was Wrong. The Real Figure Is Higher', *The Spectator*, https://www.spectator.co.uk/article/the-350m-line-on-the-brexit-bus-was-wrong-the-real-figure-is-higher (accessed 21 Aug. 24).

57 Jussi Mäkelä, 'Episode 1: Succeeding in product development with Kai Gilb', *Scraping Toasts* podcast, Sept. 22, https://www.scrapingtoasts.com/podcast/episode-1-succeeding-in-product-development-with-kai-gilb (accessed 18 Feb. 24).

Chapter 7 – Teams, identity and organisational structure
58 Margaret Atwood, *The Testaments*, (London: Chatto & Windus, 2019) ,148.

59 Roy F. Baumeister and Mark R. Leary, 'The Need to Belong: Desire for Interpersonal Attachments as a Fundamental Human Motivation.', *Psychological Bulletin* 117, no. 3 (1995): 497–529, https://doi.org/10.1037/0033-2909.117.3.497.

60 Henri Tajfel and John C. Turner, 'The Social Identity Theory of Intergroup Behavior', in *Political Psychology* (Psychology Press, 2004), 276–93, https://doi.org/10.4324/9780203505984-16.

61 Jonathan Haidt, *The Righteous Mind: Why Good People are Divided by Politics and Religion* (Penguin, 2013).

62 'How Working Together on Patrols Benefits Chimps', *ScienceBlog.com*, 28 Jun.

2017, https://scienceblog.com/494917/working-together-patrols-benefits-chimps (accessed 21 Aug. 24).

[63] For example, Patrick Lencioni's famous analysis cites trust as a foundation stone of effective teams. Patrick Lencioni, *The Five Dysfunctions of a Team, A Leadership Fable* (Wiley, 2002).

[64] Henri Tajfel, 'Experiments in Intergroup Discrimination', *Scientific American* 223, no. 5 (1970): 96–103. http://www.jstor.org/stable/24927662.

[65] 'Sarbanes–Oxley Act of 2002', 107th Congress Public Law 204, *US Government Printing Office*, https://www.govinfo.gov/content/pkg/PLAW-107publ204/html/PLAW-107publ204.htm (accessed 21 Aug. 24).

[66] 'Every Angle of Peter Crouch's STUNNING Volley against Man City!' *Stoke City FC* YouTube channel, 24 Mar. 2023, https://www.youtube.com/watch?v=f5E64pG0M-Q (accessed 21 Aug. 24).

[67] Frédéric Laloux, *Reinventing Organizations: A Guide to Creating Organizations Inspired by the Next Stage of Human Consciousness* (Nelson Parker, 2014).

[68] Christopher C. Cowan and Natasha Todorovic, *The Never Ending Quest: Clare W. Graves Explores Human Nature* (Santa Barbara: ECLET Publishing, 2005).

[69] Don E. Beck and Christopher C. Cowan, *Spiral Dynamics, Mastering Values, Leadership, and Change: Exploring the New Science of Memetics* (Blackwell Business, 1996).

[70] Noelle Baird and Alex J. Benson, 'Getting Ahead While Getting Along', 4.

[71] Saeed Khanagha et al., 'Mitigating the Dark Side of Agile Teams: Peer Pressure, Leaders' Control, and the Innovative Output of Agile Teams', *Journal of Product Innovation Management* 39, no. 3 (May 2022): 334–350, https://doi.org/10.1111/jpim.12589.

[72] Karen Julie Mickle et al., 'Foot Shape of Older People: Implications for Shoe Design', *Footwear Science* 2, no. 3 (Sept. 2010): 131–39, https://doi.org/10.1080/19424280.2010.487053.

[73] Ernest O'Boyle Jr and Herman Aguinis, 'The Best And The Rest: Revisiting the norm of normality of individual performance', *Personnel Psychology* 65, no. 1 (2012): 79–119, https://doi.org/10.1111/j.1744-6570.2011.01239.x.

[74] 'Richest 1% Grab Nearly Twice as Much New Wealth as Rest of the World Put Together', *Oxfam GB*, 16 Jan. 2023, https://www.oxfam.org.uk/media/press-releases/richest-1-grab-nearly-twice-as-much-new-wealth-as-rest-of-the-world-put-together (accessed 21 Aug. 24).

[75] 'The Scale of Economic Inequality in the UK', Equality Trust (blog), 14 Aug. 2024, https://equalitytrust.org.uk/scale-economic-inequality-uk (accessed 21 Aug. 24).

[76] '2023–2024 Premier League Salaries and Contracts', *Capology*,

https://capology.com/uk/premier-league/salaries/2023-2024 (accessed 21 Aug. 24).

[77] 'Pole Vault – Men – Senior – All – 2014', *World athletics*, https://worldathletics.org/records/toplists/jumps/pole-vault/all/men/senior/2014 and 'Pole Vault – Men – Senior – All – 2023', *World athletics*, https://worldathletics.org/records/toplists/jumps/pole-vault/all/men/senior/2024 (accessed 20 Aug. 24).

78 '100 Metres – Men – Senior – All', *World athletics*, https://worldathletics.org/records/all-time-toplists/sprints/100-metres/outdoor/men/senior?regionType=world (accessed 20 Mar. 24).

[79] 'Marathon – Women – Senior – All', *World athletics*, https://worldathletics.org/records/all-time-toplists/road-running/marathon/outdoor/women/senior?regionType=world (accessed 20 Mar. 24).

80 'Most Subscribed 500 Youtube Channels', *YouTubers.me*, https://us.youtubers.me/global/all/top-500-most-subscribed-youtube-channels (accessed 28 Jun. 24).

81 Laurence J. Peter and Raymond Hull, *The Peter Principle: Why Things Always Go Wrong* (London: Souvenir Press, 1994).

82 David Snowden, 'Three Basic Rules for Knowledge Managers', *KMWorld Conference* YouTube channel, https://www.youtube.com/watch?v=mDENsTqY-Rg (accessed 21 Aug. 24).

83 'IDEO CEO Tim Brown: T-Shaped Stars: The Backbone of IDEO's Collaborative Culture', https://chiefexecutive.net/ideo-ceo-tim-brown-t-shaped-stars-the-backbone-of-ideoaes-collaborative-culture__trashed (accessed 25 May 24).

84 'ONS Civil Servant Grades and Salary Bands', *Office for National Statistics*, https://www.ons.gov.uk/aboutus/transparencyandgovernance/freedomofinformation-foi/onscivilservantgradesandsalarybands (accessed 21 Aug 24).

85 Laszlo Bock, *Work Rules!: Insights from Inside Google That Will Transform How You Live and Lead* (London: John Murray, 2015).

86 'Executive Pay in the FTSE 100: 2020 Review', *Chartered Institute for Personnel and Development*, https://www.cipd.org/uk/knowledge/reports/Executive-pay-in-the-FTSE-100-2020-review (accessed 21 Aug. 24).

87 Daniel H. Pink, *Drive: The Surprising Truth About What Motivates Us* (New York: Penguin Group US, 2011).

88 Mark Holliday, 'How to Calculate Small Business Payroll Percentage', *Oracle Netsuite* 2021, https://www.netsuite.co.uk/portal/uk/resource/articles/financial-management/small-business-payroll-percentage.shtml (accessed 21 Aug 24).

Chapter 8 – Change and transformation

[89] Henry David Thoreau, *Walden* (New York: Thomas Y. Cromwell & Co, 1910), 433.

[90] Bob Dylan, *The Times They Are A-Changin'*, Warner Bros, 1963.

[91] Bruce Rogers, 'Why 84% Of Companies Fail At Digital Transformation', Jan 2016, *Forbes*, https://www.forbes.com/sites/brucerogers/2016/01/07/why-84-of-companies-fail-at-digital-transformation (accessed 21 Aug. 24).

[92] 'Cracking the Code of Change', *Harvard Business Review* (2000), https://hbr.org/2000/05/cracking-the-code-of-change (accessed 21 Aug. 24).

[93] 'Changing Change Management', *McKinsey*, https://www.mckinsey.com/featured-insights/leadership/changing-change-management (accessed 21 Aug. 24).

[94] 'Advancing Our Health: Prevention in the 2020s – Consultation Document', *GOV.UK*, https://www.gov.uk/government/consultations/advancing-our-health-prevention-in-the-2020s/advancing-our-health-prevention-in-the-2020s-consultation-document (accessed 21 Aug. 24).

[95] Saranac Hale Spencer, 'COVID-19 Vaccines Don't Have Patient-Tracking Devices', *FactCheck.Org* (2020), https://www.factcheck.org/2020/12/covid-19-vaccines-dont-have-patient-tracking-devices (accessed 21 Aug. 24).

[96] 'Adult Smoking Habits in the UK', *Office for National Statistics* (2022), https://www.ons.gov.uk/peoplepopulationandcommunity/healthandsocialcare/healthandlifeexpectancies/bulletins/adultsmokinghabitsingreatbritain/2022 (accessed 21 Aug. 24).

[97] For example, '1. Introduction to Human Behavioral Biology', *Stanford University* YouTube channel, https://www.youtube.com/watch?v=NNnIGh9g6fA (accessed 21 Aug. 24).

[98] Robert M. Sapolsky, *Determined: A Science of Life without Free Will* (Penguin Random House, 2023).

[99] 'In Conversation E6 Brenda Dervin', *Project Oneness World* YouTube channel, https://www.youtube.com/watch?v=VneXr3rzMyU (accessed 14 Apr. 24).

[100] 'Values', *Brighton, and Hove Council*, https://www.brighton-hove.gov.uk/council-and-democracy/brighton-hove-city-council-plan-2020-2023/values (accessed 21 Aug. 24).

[101] 'IDS Medical Systems | Vision, Values and Manifesto', *idsMED*, https://www.idsmed.com/visi.html (accessed 18 Jun. 24).

[102] Alasdair MacIntyre, *After Virtue* (University of Notre Dame Press, 1982).

[103] 'Service Standard – Service Manual', *GOV.UK*, https://www.gov.uk/service-manual/service-standard (accessed 18 Mar. 24).

[104] 'Agile Delivery – Service Manual', *GOV.UK*, https://www.gov.uk/service-manual/agile-delivery (accessed 18 Mar. 24).

[105] Giles Turnbull, 'It's Ok to Say What's Ok', *Government Digital Service* (2016), https://gds.blog.gov.uk/2016/05/25/its-ok-to-say-whats-ok (accessed 18 Mar. 24).

[106] Aircraft Accident Report, *National Transportation Safety Board Report*, 28 Dec. 1978, https://libraryonline.erau.edu/online-full-text/ntsb/aircraft-accident-reports/AAR79-07.pdf (accessed 21 Aug.24).

[107] Amy C. Edmondson, *The Fearless Organization: Creating Psychological Safety in the Workplace for Learning, Innovation, and Growth* (Wiley, 2018).

[108] Zohreh Badiyepeymaie Jahromi, Nehleh Parandavar, and Saeedeh Rahmanian, 'Investigating Factors Associated with Not Reporting Medical Errors From the Medical Team's Point of View in Jahrom, Iran', *Global Journal of Health Science* 6, no. 6 (15 Jul. 2014): p96, https://doi.org/10.5539/gjhs.v6n6p96.

[109] Charles Duhigg, 'What Google Learned From Its Quest to Build the Perfect Team', *The New York Times*, 25 Feb. 2016, https://www.nytimes.com/2016/02/28/magazine/what-google-learned-from-its-quest-to-build-the-perfect-team.html (accessed 21 Aug.24).

[110] Tom L. Beauchamp and James F. Childress, *Principles of Biomedical Ethics* (Oxford University Press, 1979).

[111] Kat Hall, 'Car Tax Evasion Has Soared since Paper Discs Scrapped', *The Register* (2017), https://www.theregister.com/2017/11/17/car_tax_evasion_continues_to_soar_after_abolition_of_paper_tax_discs (accessed 21 Aug.24).

[112] Donna M. Webster and Arie W. Kruglanski, 'Individual Differences in Need for Cognitive Closure.', *Journal of Personality and Social Psychology* 67, no. 6 (1994): 1049–62, https://doi.org/10.1037/0022-3514.67.6.1049.

[113] This study: Meera Komarraju et al., 'The Big Five Personality Traits, Learning Styles, and Academic Achievement', *Personality and Individual Differences* 51, no. 4 (2011): 472–477, https://doi.org/10.1016/j.paid.2011.04.019 making use of this theory: Shalom H. Schwartz, 'An Overview of the Schwartz Theory of Basic Values', *Online Readings in Psychology and Culture* 2, no. 1 (2012), https://doi.org/10.9707/2307-0919.1116.

[114] Jean-Jacques Rousseau, *The Social Contract; or Principles of Political Right* (1762).

[115] Eliyahu M. Goldratt and Jeff Cox, *The Goal: A Process of Ongoing Improvement* (Great Barrington, MA: North River Press, 1992).

[116] Adrian Browne, 'Tories Accused of False Claims on New 20mph Limit by Minister', *BBC News*, 12 Sept. 2023, https://www.bbc.com/news/uk-wales-politics-66739588 (accessed 21 Aug. 24).

[117] David Snowden, 'Habits', *Cynefin.io* (2023), https://cynefin.io/wiki/Habits (accessed 21 Aug. 24).

[119] Nick Stockton, 'Ants Regularly Pack Up and Dig New Nests, and Nobody Knows

Why', *Wired* magazine, https://www.wired.com/2014/11/harvester-ants-randomly-move-their-nests (accessed 21 Aug. 24).

[119] Elizabeth Evesham, 'When Ants "Move House"', *Royal Society of Biology* (2021), https://www.rsb.org.uk//biologist-features/why-do-ants-move-house-2 (accessed 21 Aug. 24).

[120] Marco Dorigo and Luca Maria Gambardella, 'Ant Colonies for the Travelling Salesman Problem', *Biosystems* 43, no. 2 (Jul. 1997): 73–81, https://doi.org/10.1016/S0303-2647(97)01708-5.

[121] John Kay, *Obliquity: Why Our Goals Are Best Achieved Indirectly* (Penguin, 2011).

[122] Daniel Kahneman, *Thinking, Fast and Slow*.

www.ingramcontent.com/pod-product-compliance
Lightning Source LLC
Chambersburg PA
CBHW041733200326

41518CB00020B/2582